BAPTIST CONFESSIONS, COVENANTS, AND CATECHISMS

John A. Broadus

TIMOTHY AND DENISE GEORGE, EDITORS

PUBLISHING GROUP
Nashville, Tennessee

978-0-8054-2076-0

Dewey Decimal Classification: 286
Subject Heading: BAPTISTS—DOCTRINES/CHURCH COVENANTS
Library of Congress Card Catalog Number: 96-16491

Unless otherwise stated all Scripture is from the King James Version.

Acquisitions and Development Editor: John Landers
Interior design by Leslie Joslin
Cover Design by Steve Diggs & Friends

Library of Congress Cataloging-in-Publication Data
Baptist confession, covenants, and catechisms / Timothy & Denise
George, general editors.
    p. cm. — (Library of Baptist classics ; vol. 11)
    Includes bibliographical references and index.
    ISBN 0-8054-2076-2
    1. Baptist—Creeds. 2. Covenants—Religious aspects—Baptists—
History of doctrines—Sources. 3. Baptists—Catechisms—English.
4. Baptists—Doctrines—History—Sources.
I. George, Timothy. II. George, Denise. III. Series.
BX6335.B29 1996
238'.6—dc20   96-16491
                                                   CIP

ISBN 978-0-8054-2076-0 (pb)

02 03 04 05 06 11 10 09 08

Contents

Contents

Part II: Covenants

Part III: Catechisms

General Editors' Introduction

The Baptist movement as we know it today began as a small persecuted sect in pre-Revolutionary England. One critic labeled them as "miscreants begat in rebellion, born in sedition, and nursed in faction." Excluded by law from the English universities, Baptists developed their own structures for pastoral training. They also wrote hymns, preached sermons, published confessions, and defended their beliefs against skeptics, detractors, and rival religious groups of all kinds. From the popular works of John Bunyan and Benjamin Keach to the learned theology of John Gill and Andrew Fuller, Baptists wrote with a passion and with a purpose. In time, a large body of Baptist literature was developed, writings that both reflected and contributed to the emerging sense of Baptist identity.

The Southern Baptist Convention (SBC) was organized in 1845 for the purpose of "eliciting, combining, and directing the energies of the whole denomination in one sacred effort, for the propagation of the gospel." This was an ambitious undertaking for the 293 "delegates," as they were then called, who gathered in Augusta, Georgia, and embraced this far-reaching vision at the founding meeting of the Convention. Through the years the SBC has suffered numerous setbacks and distractions—the Civil War, Reconstruction, the Great Depression, social unrest, denominational strife, and much more. But through it all God has graciously blessed Southern Baptists in ways that future historians will surely record as remarkable. By the end of the twentieth century, Southern Baptists had grown into America's largest Protestant denomination, a fellowship of some fifteen million members in nearly forty thousand congregations supporting more than nine thousand missionaries.

Drawing on this rich heritage, the Library of Baptist Classics presents a series of books reflecting the faith and vision of Southern Baptists over the past 150 years. We are republishing in fresh editions and with new introductions a collection of seminal writings. These works have proven their worth as classics among Southern Baptists in the past and still speak powerfully to Baptists and other evangelical Christians today.

The Library of Baptist Classics includes writings of pastors, theologians, missionary statesmen, and denominational leaders from the past. Some of them are popular, others scholarly in form. They include sermons, doctrinal treatises, missionary biographies, and an anthology of Baptist confessions, covenants, and catechisms. Most of these writings have long been out of print. We present them now in the fervent hope that the Lord will see fit to use them again, as He has in the past, not only to remind us of the great legacy we have received, but also to inspire us to be faithful shapers of the future under the lordship of Jesus Christ.

Timothy George and Denise George,
General Editors

Introduction

TIMOTHY GEORGE

John H. Leith has written that "the primary source of the malaise of the church is the loss of a distinctive Christian message and of the Biblical and theological competence that made its preaching effective." Across the past four centuries, Baptist Christians have set forth their most cherished convictions about God, salvation, the church, and the life of faith in the kinds of documents which are included in this volume: confessions, covenants, and catechisms. In recent years these classic texts have been forgotten and discarded by many Baptists. The malign neglect of these important primary sources has certainly contributed to the theological amnesia and spiritual myopia which afflict all too many Baptists today. Real revival and true reformation will not be built on flimsy foundations. We have assembled this unique collection of historic texts from the Baptist tradition because we believe that it is vitally important for Bap-

1

tists today to know who we are and where we have come from. Such knowledge can both save us from "the imperialism of the present" and also help us to become faithful shapers of the future under the Lordship of Jesus Christ.

Historically Baptists have been staunch advocates of religious liberty, the priesthood of all believers, and the inviolability of the individual conscience before God. These principles, sacred to Baptists across the centuries, are all enshrined in the documents contained in this volume. However, in recent years, these tenets have been wrenched from their original confessional context and have been made to serve a new mythology of Baptist identity which runs something like this: "Baptists are not essentially a doctrinal people. We have no creed but the Bible, which everyone should be left to interpret according to his or her personal predilection. The basic criterion of theology is individual experience. The right of private judgment in matters religious supremely overrules specific norms of belief. Baptist means freedom, freedom to think, believe, and teach without constraints."

Perhaps it was this kind of stereotype that Martin Marty had in mind when he referred to the "Baptistification" of religious life in America, that is, the prevalence of pragmatism and individualism in all sectors of contemporary American Christianity. While not for a moment denying the validity of this analysis, there is good reason to question whether this characterization can legitimately fly under the banner of historic Baptist values. No doubt, many of the framers of the confessions, covenants, and catechisms published in this volume would be hard pressed to recognize as their spiritual heirs certain present-day Baptists who advance an ideology of indifference to the great doctrines of the faith for which their forebearers suffered and sometimes died. Before introducing the specific documents reprinted in this volume, let us consider the frequently-asked question, "Are Baptists a creedal people?"

Are Baptists a Creedal People?

Many contemporary Baptists are surprised to learn that such venerable shapers of the Baptist tradition as Andrew Fuller,

James P. Boyce, B. H. Carroll, and E. Y. Mullins used the word "creed" in a positive sense and often spoke in an affirming way of "the Baptist creed." It is nonetheless true that Baptists have never advocated *creedalism*. In two very important senses Baptists are not, and never have been, a creedal people. First, Baptists of all theological persuasions have been ardent supporters of religious liberty, opposing state-imposed religious conformity and the attendant civil sanctions associated therewith. In this vein, Roger Williams opposed the Congregationalist ecclesiocracy in New England, and John Leland went to prison in Virginia rather than acquiesce to the Anglican state church. Believing that God alone is the Lord of the conscience, Baptists deny that civil magistrates have any legitimate authority to regulate or coerce the internal religious life of voluntary associations.

Second, Baptists are not creedal in that they have never elevated any man-made doctrinal construct above Holy Scripture. As Baptist confessions themselves invariably declare, the Bible alone remains the *norma normans* for all teaching and instruction, "the supreme standard by which all human conduct, creeds, and religious opinion should be tried." Because of this unswerving commitment to the priority of Scripture, Baptists have never "canonized" any of their confessions, but rather have held them all to be revisable in the light of the Bible, God's infallible, unchanging revelation.

Despite this aversion to creedalism, however, the idea that voluntary, conscientious adherence to an explicit doctrinal standard is somehow foreign to the Baptist tradition is a peculiar notion not borne out by careful examination of our heritage. During his lifetime and indeed for many years after his death in 1815, Andrew Fuller was doubtless the most influential theologian among Baptists in both England and America. In an essay on "Creeds and Subscriptions," he declared:

> It has been very common among a certain class of writers, to exclaim against creeds or systems in religion as inconsistent with Christian liberty and the rights of conscience; but every well-informed and consistent believer must have a creed, a system which he supposes to contain the leading principles of divine revelation. . . . If the arti-

cles of faith be opposed to the authority of Scripture, or substituted in the place of such authority, they become objectionable and injurious; but if they simply express the united judgment of those who voluntarily subscribe them, they are incapable of any such imputation.

In this tradition James P. Boyce, the founder of Southern Seminary, set forth a rationale for strict subscription to that institution's Abstract of Principles:

> You will infringe the rights of no man, and you will secure the rights of those who have established here an instrumentality for the production of a sound ministry. It is no hardship to those who teach here to be called upon to sign the declaration of their principles, for there are fields of usefulness open elsewhere to every man, and none need accept your call who can not conscientiously sign your formulary.

Similarly, E. Y. Mullins, the champion of soul liberty, outlined various basic Christian beliefs (e.g. biblical inspiration, the miracles of Christ, His vicarious atonement, bodily resurrection, literal ascension, and actual return) and declared before the SBC in 1923: "We believe that adherence to the above truths and facts is a necessary condition of service for teachers in our Baptist schools." This statement served as an impetus for the formulation of *The Baptist Faith and Message* of 1925 of which Mullins was a principal architect.

The documents included in this volume not only span four centuries of Baptist historical development; they also reflect a great deal of theological and ecclesiological diversity within the Baptist heritage itself. While certain confessions have been more influential than others, the sheer proliferation of these standards shows that Baptists have been, in the past no less than today, a fissiparous folk. Although these documents generally embody a set of common themes, they demonstrate variety of form and scope as well as substance. Each of the confessions, covenants, and catechisms reprinted here was first set forth by a specific body of Baptists in a particular historical context. We shall now briefly describe the original setting of these documents.

Baptist Confessions

The Reformation of the sixteenth century has sometimes been called the Age of Confessions because of the numerous statements of faith written and adopted by many Christian churches in that time. However, the word "confession" can be traced back to the New Testament itself, to Paul's exhortation to Timothy to "take hold of the eternal life to which you were called when you made the good confession in the presence of many witnesses" (I Timothy 6:13). In the early church a *confessor* was one whose loyalty to the Christian faith had been tested by persecution to the point of a willingness to undergo martyrdom. In time it became a title of great honor as applied, for example, to Maximus the Confessor, a leading Greek theologian of the seventh century. During the Reformation era confessions of faith were set forth by Lutheran, Reformed, and Anglican Christians in order to declare publicly and formally their adherence to the great doctrinal truths rediscovered by the reformers. Of the many confessional statements written during the Reformation, the three most widely accepted are the Augsburg Confession (1530) of the Lutherans, the Thirty-Nine Articles (1563) of the Church of England, and the Westminster Confession (1646) of the English and Scottish Presbyterians.

The first confession included in this volume antedates the emergence of the seventeenth-century Baptist tradition. We have included this document because it demonstrates certain affinities between Baptists and earlier dissenting groups. *The Brotherly Union of a Number of Children of God Concerning Seven Articles*, better known as the *Schleitheim Confession*, was written by Michael Sattler, a leader of the Anabaptist group known as the Swiss Brethren. Sattler composed this statement on February 24, 1527, three months before he was burned alive at the stake for his religious convictions.

Each of the seven articles presents Anabaptism as a countercultural movement radically at odds with the prevailing patterns of religious life in that day. For example, true believers were to abstain from taking an oath or wielding "the sword," a prohibition which included the holding of public office. Infant baptism is called "the highest and chief abomination of the pope." True Christian baptism presupposes repentance and faith, as does the Lord's Supper, a fellowship meal to be shared only among those who "walk of the obedience of faith."

Some historians have exercised great ingenuity in arguing for a genetic connection between the continental Anabaptists and the English Baptists of a later day. The most charitable judgment which can be rendered on this effort is the Scottish verdict of "not proved." At the same time, we should recognize that many of the motifs first articulated by the Anabaptists were indeed later picked up and owned afresh by the Baptists. These include the principles of religious liberty, believers' baptism, congregational autonomy, and a zeal for missions and evangelism. More Anabaptists were killed for their faith in the sixteenth century than all of the martyrs of the early church combined. The *Schleitheim Confession* is an important document for contemporary Baptists because it recalls the legacy of the "church under the cross."

The English Baptist movement took its rise from John Smyth who in the winter of 1609 took water from a basin and poured it over his head in the name of the Father, the Son, and the Holy Ghost, rebaptizing himself and then his entire Separatist congregation at Amsterdam. Because of his self-baptism, Smyth soon became known among his contemporaries as John the Se-Baptist! Through his study of the Scriptures, Smyth had come to differ from the earlier Separatist tradition over the validity of infant baptism. He also rejected the classic Reformation doctrines of original sin, election, and justification. Article Ten of his *Short Confession* is a clear denial of the doctrine of justification by faith alone. Indeed, one would be hard pressed to find anything in this article which could not have satisfied the Roman Catholic theologians at the Council of Trent!

Although he was a well-trained scholar, Smyth was known for his inconstancy—"a variable chameleon," whose "course is as changeable as the moon," his old friend Richard Bernard said. Near the end of his life, Smyth came to regret his act of self-baptism and sought membership in a Dutch Anabaptist congregation of Waterlander Mennonites. (They eventually acted on his petition for membership posthumously!) While the larger part of his congregation was thus absorbed into the Anabaptist tradition, a smaller contingent, led by Thomas Helwys, returned to England in 1612 and founded at Spitalfields near London what has rightly been called the first Baptist church on English soil. The General Baptists, so called because of their advocacy of general redemption, arose out of this single congregation.

The Particular Baptists began somewhat later from a church established at London in 1616 by Henry Jacob, a Puritan minister who remained on friendly terms both with Separatists like John Robinson and godly ministers within the Church of England. By the 1630's several members of this congregation had begun to question the validity of infant baptism. Under the leadership of Richard Blount, Thomas Killcop, Hanserd Knollys, and William Kiffin, they formed separate underground congregations gathered on the principle of believers' baptism by immersion. In 1644 seven Particular Baptist congregations near London published their first confession of faith in fifty-three articles. They affirmed the doctrinal essentials of the Reformation, congregational church order, believers' baptism by immersion, and their loyalty to the duly constituted authority of the king.

The framers of the 1644 Confession said that their desire to vindicate the truth was "the main wheel at this time that sets us awork." The seven congregations they represented had been pilloried and maligned both in pulpit and print and they wanted to set the record straight. They had been falsely charged, they said, with "holding free will, falling away from grace, denying original sin, disclaiming of magistracy, and . . . doing acts unseemly in the dispensing the ordinance of baptism, not to be named amongst Christians." Just as believers in the early church were accused of cannibalism because they met secretly to observe the Lord's Supper, so too the Baptists of the 1640's were accused of practicing immersion in the nude and even of impregnating certain female converts in this way. Article Forty included an explanatory note which denied this outrageous claim: "The word *baptizo*, signifying to dip under water, yet so as with convenient garments both upon the administrator and subject, with all modesty."

The *London Confession of 1644* affirmed the classic doctrines of grace as set forth in the teachings of John Calvin and promulgated in the canons of the Synod of Dort (1618–19). At the same time, there were important nuances of difference in the way the Baptists described these doctrines. For example, Article Three of the Separatist Manifesto, *A True Confession* (1596) declared that God "to His just purpose ordained . . . both angels and men to eternal condemnation," whereas the 1644 London Confession ascribed the just condemnation of sinners to God's "leaving [them] in their sin." The Baptists of 1644 clearly affirmed a high predestinarian theology including the doctrines of unconditional election and particular redemption. But their belief in God's sovereignty in salvation in no way mitigated their affirmation of human responsibility. The evangelical Calvinism of this confession became one of the hallmarks of the mainstream Particular Baptist tradition from John Bunyan to Charles Haddon Spurgeon.

The *London Confession of 1644* was published at a time when the English nation was in the grips of civil war. The first Particular Baptist congregations were seeking a measure of respect and acceptability in revolutionary times. The confession was reprinted several times and became a rallying cry for Calvinistic Baptists throughout the land. Its clear articulation of Reformed doctrine also helped the Particulars to distinguish their brand of Baptist church life from that of the more Arminianized General Baptists. At the same time, this confession also propelled the Baptists into the limelight of controversy when its frank espousal of immersion was answered by the Anglican apologist Daniel Featley who published in 1645 a treatise entitled *The Dippers Dipt or, The Anabaptists Duck't and Plunged Over Head and Ears*.

Between 1644 and 1677 England underwent the convulsions of the Puritan Revolution, the execution of King Charles I, the Protectorate of Oliver Cromwell, the restoration of the Stuart monarchy, the imposition of a new Act of Uniformity, and the wholesale persecution of religious dissenters of all stripes. This was a period of testing for the Baptists who, along with many others, suffered great hardship because of their refusal to conform to the rigid policies of the civil authorities. In this context the Particular Baptists set forth what was to become the most influential confession of faith in the history of the Baptist movement. In this volume we have included this document under the title it was given by Baptists in America, *The Philadelphia Confession*. However, because of its earlier publication in England (1677, 1689), it is frequently referred to as the *Second London Confession*. A cursory examination of this document will show it to be a Baptist adaptation of the famous *Westminster Confession of Faith* (1646), the official standard of the Church of Scotland and the authoritative confession of English Presbyterians.

In 1658 the Congregationalists had adopted the *Savoy Declaration*, a replication of the *Westminster Confession* with only slight alterations. The Particular Baptists followed suit in 1677 with their *Second London Confession*. They acknowledged their indebtedness to the excellent work of the Westminster divines and declared "our hearty agreement with them in that wholesome Protestant doctrine which, with so clear evidence of scriptures, they have asserted." Leon McBeth has correctly observed that Baptists have "often used confessions not to proclaim 'Baptist distinctives' but instead to show how similar Baptists were to other orthodox Christians." In the tense atmosphere of the 1670's, it was important for Baptists and other Reformed nonconformists to present a united front in order to thwart, as much as possible, the overt hostility of the powers that be. Eleven years later a great assembly of "ministers and messengers" representing some one hundred Particular Baptist churches throughout England and Wales gathered in London and reissued a definitive edition of the Second London Confession (1689). Hanserd Knollys, pastor of the Broken Wharf congregation in London and one of the venerable statesmen of this assembly, had also been among the signatories of the (1646 edition) *First London Confession*.

In 1707 the first Baptist association in America was organized at Philadelphia. As theological disputes arose among the Baptists of the New World, they appealed to "the Confession of Faith, set forth by the elders and brethren met in London in 1689, and owned by us," as their standard of doctrine. When the association gathered at Philadelphia on September 25, 1742, they ordered a new printing of this by then classic statement of faith which became known on this side of the Atlantic as the *Philadelphia Confession of Faith*. The 1742 edition of the *Philadelphia Confession* was printed by Benjamin Franklin, whose deistic views were at great odds with those of his Baptist neighbors in Philadelphia!

While taking over wholesale the English Baptist emendations of Westminster, the *Philadelphia Confession* added two new articles, "Of Singing Psalms" and "Laying on of Hands," reflecting issues of great controversy among Baptists on both sides of the Atlantic. Many Baptists, along with other Reformed dissenters of that day, believed that only the Psalms should be sung in the public worship of the church. Hymns, they felt, while perhaps edifying, were not on an equal par with the divinely inspired text of Holy Scripture and should thus be relegated to personal devotional use.

The *Philadelphia Confession of Faith*, however, rejects this line of thought citing the example of Christ and encouraging congregations to sing "psalms, hymns, and spiritual songs . . . in their public assemblies, as well as private Christians." Significantly, the 1742 edition of the *Philadelphia Confession* was published in the midst of the First Great Awakening when the hymns of Isaac Watts and Charles and John Wesley were gaining wide acceptance with the growing success of the revival movement. The laying on of hands had nothing to do with ordination to a special church office, but was a rite imposed on all baptized believers as a confirmation of their faith and "a further reception of the Holy Spirit of promise." In time, the laying on of hands disappeared almost completely among Baptists in America while the singing of hymns (regrettably, to the exclusion of Psalms!) became the norm.

The *Philadelphia Confession of Faith* was transplanted to the Charleston Baptist Association in South Carolina. It soon became the most widely accepted, definitive confession among Baptists in America both North and South. Each of the 293 "delegates," as they were then called, who gathered in Augusta to organize the Southern Baptist Convention in 1845, belonged to congregations and associations which had adopted the *Philadelphia/Charleston Confession of Faith* as their own. When James P. Boyce was considering a suitable confessional standard for Southern Baptists' first seminary, he originally planned to use the Philadelphia/Charleston Confession of Faith as the doctrinal basis for this new institution. When he became convinced that a briefer, more succinct summary of doctrine would be more useful for this purpose, he commissioned Basil Manly, Jr., to draft an Abstract of Principles based on the Philadelphia/ Charleston standard.

Returning to England, we recall that two distinct streams of the Baptist tradition had emerged by the mid-seventeenth century: General Baptists were influenced by Arminian views of salvation, while Particular Baptists emphasized a Calvinistic understanding of the doctrines of grace. The Particulars tended to be better educated, better organized and more successful than the Generals. The Generals, on the other hand, were more sectarian and more susceptible to subversion by radical groups such as the Ranters, Seekers, Quakers, and Unitarians. Nonetheless, there was a steady stream of evangelical Arminian Baptists who maintained a high view of Scripture and resisted the inroads of rationalism and deism which decimated the General Baptist denomination as a whole in the eighteenth century.

In 1679 a group of General Baptists from the Midlands counties of Buckinghamshire, Hertfordshire, Bedfordshire, and Oxford published *An Orthodox Creed, or A Protestant Confession of Faith, Being an Essay to Unite and Confirm All True Protestants in the Fundamental Articles of the Christian Religion.* As the title suggests, this confession of faith sought to emphasize those doctrines held by all true Christians including the attributes of God, the Holy Trinity, the person and work of Jesus Christ, creation, providence, etc. Article Nine, "Of Predestination and Election," is a carefully crafted statement which attempts to steer a straight course between the Arminian-Calvinistic debate. Article Twenty-Nine affirms the "one, holy, Catholic church," which is said to consist of "the whole number of the elect that have been, are, or shall be gathered in one body under Christ." Article Thirty-Eight incorporates the Apostles,' Nicene, and Athanasian creeds and declares that all three "ought thoroughly to be received, and believed. For we believe, that they may be proved, by most undoubted authority of Holy Scripture and are necessary to be understood of all Christians."

While Philadelphia was the nerve center for Baptist development in the American colonies, New England had also produced outstanding Baptist leaders such as Roger Williams, John Clarke, Obadiah Holmes, and Isaac Backus. In 1833, the Baptist Convention of New Hampshire published a "Declaration of Faith" which was to have a far-reaching influence among Baptists in the late nineteenth and early twentieth centuries. In 1853 J. Newton Brown, one of the original drafters of the New Hampshire Confession, revised this statement of faith and published it in *The Baptist Church Manual*. In 1867 J. M. Pendleton included Brown's revised edition of the New Hampshire Confession in his own *Church Manual*.

Pendleton was a leader among the Landmark Baptists of the day and greatly appreciated the New Hampshire Confession's ecclesiology which excluded any reference to the universal church. Through Brown and Pendleton's manuals, the New Hampshire Confession became widely accepted, especially among Baptists in the South, eventually displacing the Philadelphia Confession as the doctrinal standard of choice. On issues of soteriology, the New Hampshire Confession follows the Reformed orientation of the Philadelphia Confession, but its treatment of the doctrines of grace is briefer, less specific, and more susceptible to theological ambiguity.

In 1925 the Southern Baptist Convention adopted its first denomination-wide confession, The *Baptist Faith and Message*. Based on the New Hampshire Confession, this statement of faith became a rallying cry for conservative theology combined with missionary and evangelistic fervor. The SBC also adopted the Cooperative Program in 1925 thus providing both a confessional and financial basis of cooperation. During the Fundamentalist-Modernist Controversy, Southern Baptists became more intentional about their confessional identity while Northern Baptists consistently refused to adopt any confession of faith. During this same era Northern Baptists were fragmenting into several competing denominational bodies, while the SBC remained united in its commitment to conservative evangelical theology and a streamlined program of denominational growth.

In 1963 the SBC, under the leadership of Herschel H. Hobbs, adopted a revised edition of *The Baptist Faith and Message*. A storm over biblical authority had been brewing in the SBC for several years resulting in a crisis over Ralph Elliott's 1961 book, *The Message of Genesis*. The 1963 edition of *The Baptist Faith And Message* was a response to this crisis. While duly noting the dangers of creedalism in a prefatory statement, the framers of the 1963 *Baptist Faith and Message* pointed out that "this emphasis should not be interpreted to mean that there is an absence of certain definite doctrines that Baptists believe, cherish, and with which they have been and are now closely identified." The 1963 revision made several substantive changes over the original 1925 edition including a reference in Article Six to the church universal: "The New Testament speaks also of the church as the body of Christ which includes all of the redeemed of all the ages."

While many leaders of the SBC hoped that the near unanimous adoption of *The Baptist Faith and Message* in 1963 would result in an era of theological tranquility and denominational unity, it was really the first round of a prolonged controversy which would convulse the convention over the next three decades. In 1993 SBC President H. Edwin Young appointed a theological study committee to review theological concerns in light of the 1963 confession. While reaffirming *The Baptist Faith and Message*, this committee also set forth five articles dealing with recent challenges to the Christian faith such as a compromised view of biblical truthfulness, process theology, feminist language for God, and universalist and pluralist views of salvation. The committee also commended the *Chicago Statement of Biblical Inerrancy* (1978) and the *Chicago Statement on Biblical Hermeneutics* (1982) as "biblically grounded and sound guides worthy of respect in setting forth a high view of Scripture." In 1994 the SBC unanimously adopted a resolution accepting the report of the Presidential Theological Study Committee and commending it to all agencies and boards of the Convention.

Covenants and Catechisms

Part Two of this volume reproduces seventeen church covenants from diverse congregational and historical contexts. English Baptists took over from their Separatist forbears the concept of a church covenant as a solemn agreement voluntarily entered into by a particular congregation of believers. In 1581, Robert Browne and Robert Harrison having decided to "remove themselves" from the parish churches of England, gathered with their followers at Norwich. On this occasion they "gave their consent to joined themselves to the Lord, in one covenant and fellowship, and to keep and seek agreement under His law and government."   William Bradford, one of the Pilgrim Fathers, recalled a similar covenant-taking ceremony in his congregation: "The Lord's free people joined themselves (by a covenant of the Lord) into a church estate, in the fellowship of the Gospel, to walk in all His ways made known or to be made known unto them, according to their best endeavors, whatever it should cost them." When Baptist churches began to organize congregations in the seventeenth century, they too adopted church covenants along with confessions of faith. Indeed, church covenants were the ethical counterparts to confessions of faith. Confessions dealt with what one believed; church covenants spoke about how one should live. Frequently, Baptist churches asked new members to sign the church covenant as a public pledge of their commitment to live according to the standards and expectations of the congregation.

Baptist church covenants vary greatly in length from statements of just a few lines to veritable treatises on the Christian life. Among early Baptists the 1697 covenant of Benjamin and Elias Keach was one of the most frequently reprinted and influential documents of its kind. The Keaches' relate the church covenant to "the everlasting covenant" of God's free grace, thus directly connecting the life of the church to God's eternal purpose and plan of salvation. In this covenant, church members are asked to make eight specific promises all of which relate to their responsibility to one another in the fellowship of the congregation.

Common themes which resound through the various church covenants reprinted in this volume include a commitment to doctrinal fidelity, the maintenance of family worship, mutual prayer and watchfulness over one another, financial support for the church, the faithful administration of the ordinances and discipline of the congregation together with the public worship of God, and an openness to receive further light from God's revealed Word. In 1806 Peter Philanthropos Roots published a covenant in both prose and poetic editions. Roots (d. 1828) was a Baptist missionary and evangelist who had a great influence among Baptists in Canada and several American states.

Doubtless, the church covenant printed in J. Newton Brown's Baptist *Church Manual* in 1853 has had a more lasting influence on Southern Baptist churches than any other similar document. However, churches organized in recent years have sometimes preferred to draft their own covenants rather than duplicate the model made popular by Brown. For example, one inner-city congregation committed to an interracial membership includes in its covenant the pledge to be both "warmly evangelical and socially concerned."

Charles W. Deweese has defined a church covenant as "a series of written pledges based on the Bible which church members voluntarily make to God and to one another regarding their basic moral and spiritual commitments and the practice of their faith." Deweese notes a decline in covenanting among Southern Baptists in recent years, a loss which he attributes to various causes including the failure to take seriously the doctrine of the church as expressed in historic Baptist confessions as well as a lack of discipleship and spiritual formation within many congregations. For all this, church covenants are deeply rooted in the Baptist heritage and can still be used with great effect as an instrument for good in cultivating responsible church membership and promoting a clearer Christian witness to a culture which has lost its moral footing.

Part Three of this volume contains three classic catechisms from the Baptist heritage. In the introduction to his anthology of Baptist catechisms, Thomas J. Nettles notes that "many contemporary Baptists would consider the juxtaposition of the words 'Baptist Catechism' an oxymoron." Yet from their earliest days, Baptists have published catechisms and used them as a means of imparting basic Christian instruction to new believers and passing on the faith intact to the rising generations.

The Purtian Hugh Peters spoke for many Baptists when he admonished parents to catechize their children, warning them that "if ever your poor infants be driven to wildernesses, to hollow caves, to faggot and fire, or to sorrows of any kind, they will thank God and you, they were well catechized." Although this remark was originally made in 1630, it is still relevant in the late 1990's when the allure of the world and the strategems of Satan are ever more menacing to Christian families. The three catechisms reprinted in this volume are classic texts which have served earlier Baptist generations well. They may still be used with great profit although every pastor and every parent should adapt or write a catechism which is useful in their own context.

Henry Jessey (d. 1663) was an outstanding scholar and leading pastor among the Particular Baptists of seventeenth-century England. Educated at St. John's College, Cambridge, Jessey had spent several years as a tutor in the household of a wealthy family. No doubt his experience as a teacher of young children made him sensitive to the kind of instruction required for "little ones." *A Catechism for Babes* contains an initial set of questions and answers dealing with basic theological themes. This is followed by a poetic summary of the principal points of the catechism and a summary of the Ten Commandments. Then the drama of human sin and redemption is presented in terms of "the four conditions of every man," namely, what was, what is, what may be, and what must be to all eternity. The catechism concludes with several brief prayers and graces at mealtime.

Benjamin Keach (d. 1704) was an outstanding leader among the Particular Baptists of seventeenth-century England. Baptized at age fifteen in a General Baptist church, Keach later came to reject the Arminianism of this tradition in favor of a full-orbed evangelical Calvinism. For many years, Keach was pastor of the large Horsleydown Church in the Southwark area of London. He was a signatory to the Second London Confession and an able advocate of the corporate singing of hymns. His son Elias Keach played a significant role in transplanting the Particular Baptist tradition from England to the New World.

One of Keach's first publications, now no longer extant, was *The Child's Instructor*, published in 1664. The catechism presented under Keach's name in this volume was drafted in the early 1690's with the assistance of Williams Collins. It soon became the most widely used catechism among Baptists in both England and America. In the nineteenth century, Charles Haddon Spurgeon published a shortened version of this catechism for use among the children of his congregation. In commending the use of the catechism, Spurgeon declared: "In matters of doctrine you will find orthodox congregations frequently change to heterodoxy in the course of thirty or forty years, and it is because too often there has been no catechizing of the children in the essential doctrines of the Gospel. For my part, I am more and more persuaded that the study of a good Scriptural catechism is of infinite value to our children. Even if the youngsters do not understand all the questions and answers . . . yet, abiding in their memories, it will be infinite service when the time of understanding comes, to have known these very excellent, wise and judicious definitions of the things of God."

Through the early twentieth century, Southern Baptists followed Spurgeon's wise counsel and regularly used catechisms in the religious education of their children. In fact, when the Baptist Sunday School Board was organized in 1891, the very first publication projected was *A Catechism of Bible Teaching* by John

A. Broadus. Several years ago while I was serving as the interim pastor of a Southern Baptist congregation, one of the elderly members presented me with a first-edition copy of Broadus' catechism. It was worn with age and torn along the edges from many years of storage in her attic trunk. Her grandmother, she said, had used this catechism to acquaint her with the rudiments of the Christian faith many years before. More than one hundred years after Broadus' catechism first appeared in 1892, we present it again with the fervent prayer that it, and other worthy instruments of sound teaching, may be used by a new generation of Southern Baptists to bring up their own children in the nurture and admonition of the Lord.

Sources

Since this book is intended to present these classic documents in a popular, reader-friendly format, we have not included references to historical and critical issues which a more scholarly presentation of this material would require. In this same vein, we have taken the liberty to modernize spelling, capitalization, and punctuation except where such alterations would change the original intent of the document. Readers who desire a more comprehensive collection and critical edition of these historic documents should consult the following works: Charles W. Deweese, *Baptist Church Covenants* (Nashville: Broadman Press, 1990); W. L. Lumpkin, *Baptist Confessions of Faith* (Valley Forge: Judson Press, 1959); W. J. McGlothlin, *Baptist Confessions of Faith* (Philadelphia: American Baptist Publication Society, 1911); Tom J. Nettles, *Baptist Catechisms* (privately published, 1983); G. Keith Parker, *Baptists in Europe: History and Confessions of Faith* (Nashville: Broadman Press, 1982).

PART I
Confessions

CHAPTER ONE

The Schleitheim Confession: *Brotherly Union of a Number of Children of God Concerning Seven Articles* (1527)

May joy, peace, and mercy from our Father through the atonement of the blood of Christ Jesus, together with the gifts of the Spirit—who is sent from the Father to all believers for their strength and comfort and their perseverance in all tribulation until the end, Amen—be to all those who love God, who are the children of light, and who are scattered everywhere as it has been ordained of God our Father, where they are with one mind assembled together in one God and Father of us all: Grace and peace of heart be with you all, Amen.

Beloved brethren and sisters in the Lord: First and supremely we are always concerned for your consolation and the assurance of your conscience (which was previously misled) so that you may not always remain foreigners to us and by right almost completely excluded, but that you may turn again to the true implanted members of Christ, who have been armed through patience and knowledge of themselves, and have therefore again been united with us in the strength of a godly Christian spirit and zeal for God.

It is also apparent with what cunning the devil has turned us aside, so that he might destroy and bring to an end the work of God which in mercy and grace has been partly begun in us. But Christ, the true Shepherd of our souls, who has begun this in us, will certainly direct the same and teach [us] to His honor and our salvation. Amen.

Dear brethren and sisters, we who have been assembled in the Lord at Schleitheim on the Border, make known in points and articles to all who love God that as concerns us we are of one mind to abide in the Lord as God's obedient children, [His] sons and daughters, we who have been and shall be separated from the world in everything, [and] completely at peace. To God alone be praise and glory without the contradiction of any brethren. In this we have perceived the oneness of the Spirit of our Father and of our common Christ with us. For the Lord is the Lord of peace and not of quarreling, as Paul points out. That you may understand in what articles this has been formulated you should observe and note [the following].

A very great offense has been introduced by certain false brethren among us, so that some have turned aside from the faith, in the way they intend to practice and observe the freedom of the Spirit and of Christ. But such have missed the truth and to their condemnation are given over to the lasciviousness and self-indulgence of the flesh. They think faith and love may do and permit everything, and nothing will harm them nor condemn them, since they are believers.

Observe, you who are God's members in Christ Jesus, that faith in the heavenly Father through Jesus Christ does not take such form. It does not produce and result in such things as these false brethren and sisters do teach. Guard yourselves and be warned of such people, for they do not serve our Father, but their father, the devil.

But you are not that way. For they that are Christ's have crucified the flesh with its passions and lusts. You understand me well and know the brethren whom we mean. Separate yourselves from them for they are perverted. Petition the Lord that they may have the knowledge which leads to repentance, and pray for us that we may have constancy to persevere in the way which we have espoused, for the honor of God and of Christ, His Son, Amen.

The articles which we discussed and on which we were of one mind are these:

1. Baptism
2. The Ban [Excommunication]
3. Breaking of Bread
4. Separation from the Abomination
5. Pastors in the Church
6. The Sword
7. The Oath

First: Baptism

Observe concerning baptism: Baptism shall be given to all those who have learned repentance and amendment of life, and who believe truly that their sins are taken away by Christ, and to all those who walk in the resurrection of Jesus Christ, and wish to be buried with Him in death, so that they may be resurrected with Him, and to all those who with this significance request it baptism of us and demand it for themselves. This excludes all infant baptism, the highest and chief abomination of the pope. In this you have the foundation and testimony of the apostles (Matt. 28; Mark 16; Acts 2, 8, 16, 19). This we wish to hold simply, yet firmly and with assurance.

Second: The Ban

We are agreed as follows on the ban: The ban shall be employed with all those who have given themselves to the Lord, to walk in His commandments, and with all those who are baptized into the one body of Christ and who are called brethren or sisters, and yet who slip sometimes and fall into error and sin, being inadvertently overtaken. The same shall be admonished twice in secret and the third time openly disciplined or banned according to the command of Christ (Matt. 18). But this shall be done according to the regulation of the Spirit (Matt. 5) before the breaking of bread, so that we may break and eat one bread, with one mind and in one love, and may drink of one cup.

Third: Breaking of Bread

In the breaking of bread we are of one mind and are agreed as follows: All those who wish to break of one bread in remembrance of the broken body of Christ, and all who wish to drink of one drink as a remembrance of the shed blood of Christ, shall be united beforehand by baptism in one body of Christ which is the church of God and whose head is Christ. For as Paul points out we cannot at the same time be partakers of the Lord's table and the table of devils; we cannot at the same time drink the cup of the Lord and the cup of the devil. That is, all those who have fellowship with the dead works of darkness have no part in the light. Therefore all who follow the devil and the world have no part with those who are called unto God out of the world. All who lie in evil have no part in the good.

Therefore it is and must be thus: Whoever has not been called by one God to one faith, to one baptism, to one Spirit, to one body, with all the children of God's church, cannot be made into one bread with them, as indeed must be done if one is truly to break bread according to the command of Christ.

Fourth: Separation from the Abomination

We are agreed as follows on separation: A separation shall be made from the evil and from the wickedness which the devil planted in the world; in this manner, simply that we shall not have fellowship with them the wicked and not run with them in the multitude of their abominations. This is the way it is: Since all who do not walk in the obedience of faith, and have not united themselves with God so that they wish to do His will, are a great abomination before God, it is not possible for anything to grow or issue from them except abominable things. For truly all creatures are in but two classes, good and bad, believing and unbelieving, darkness and light, the world and those who have come out of the world, God's temple and idols. Christ and Belial; and none can have part with the other.

To us then the command of the Lord is clear when He calls upon us to be separate from the evil and thus He will be our God and we shall be His sons and daughters.

He further admonishes us to withdraw from Babylon and the earthly Egypt that we may not be partakers of the pain and suffering which the Lord will bring upon them.

From this we should learn that everything that is not united with our God and Christ cannot be other than an abomination which we should shun and flee from. By this is meant all popish and antipopish works and church services, meetings and church attendance, drinking houses, civic affairs, the commitments made in unbelief and other things of that kind, which are highly regarded by the world and yet are carried on with all the unrighteousness which is in the world. From all these things we shall be separated and have no part with them for they are nothing but an abomination, and they are the cause of our being hated before our Christ Jesus, who has set us free from the slavery of the flesh and fitted us for the service of God through the Spirit whom He has given us.

Therefore there will also unquestionably fall from us the unchristian, devilish weapons of force—such as sword, armor, and the like, and all their use either for friends or against one's enemies—by virtue of the word of Christ, resist not him that is evil.

Fifth: Pastors in the Church

We are agreed as follows on pastors in the church of God: The pastor in the church of God shall, as Paul has prescribed, be one who out-and-out has a good report of those who are outside the faith. This office shall be to read, to admonish and teach, to warn, to discipline, to ban in the church, to lead out in prayer for the advancement of all the brethren and sisters, to lift up the bread when it is to be broken, and in all things to see to the care of the body of Christ, in order that it may be built up and developed, and the mouth of the slanderer be stopped.

This one moreover shall be supported of the church which has chosen him, wherein he may be in need, so that he who serves the gospel may live of the gospel as the Lord has ordained. But if a pastor should do something requiring discipline, he shall not be dealt with except on the testimony of two or three witnesses. And when they sin they shall be disciplined before all in order that the others may fear.

But should it happen that through the cross this pastor should be banished or led to the Lord through martyrdom another shall be ordained in his place in the same hour so that God's little flock and people may not be destroyed.

Sixth: The Sword

We are agreed as follows concerning the sword: The sword is ordained of God outside the perfection of Christ. It punishes and puts to death the wicked, and guards and protects the good. In the Law the sword was ordained for the punishment of the wicked and for their death, and the same sword is now ordained to be used by the worldly magistrates.

In the perfection of Christ, however, only the ban is used for a warning and for the excommunication of the one who has sinned, without putting the flesh to death—simply the warning and the command to sin no more.

Now it will be asked by many who do not recognize this as the will of Christ for us, whether a Christian may or should employ the sword against the wicked for the defense and protection of the good, or for the sake of love.

Our reply is unanimously as follows: Christ teaches and commands us to learn of Him, for He is meek and lowly in heart and so shall we find rest to our souls. Also Christ says to the heathenish woman who was taken in adultery, not that one should stone her according to the Law of his Father (and yet He says, As the Father has commanded Me, thus I do), but in mercy and forgiveness and warning, to sin no more. Such an attitude we also ought to take completely according to the rule of the ban.

Second, it will be asked concerning the sword, whether a Christian shall pass sentence in worldly disputes and strife such as unbelievers have with one another. This is our united answer: Christ did not wish to decide or pass judgment between brother and brother in the case of the inheritance, but refused to do so. Therefore we should do likewise.

Third, it will be asked concerning the sword, Shall one be a magistrate if one should be chosen as such? The answer is as follows: They wished to make Christ king, but He fled and did not view it as the arrangement of His Father. Thus shall we do as He did, and follow Him, and so shall we not walk in darkness. For He Himself says, He who wishes to come after Me, let him deny himself and take up his cross and follow Me. Also, He Himself forbids employment of the force of the sword, saying, The worldly princes lord it over them . . . but not so shall it be with you. Further, Paul says, Whom God did foreknow He also did predestinate to be conformed to the image of His Son. Also Peter says, Christ has suffered (not ruled) and left us an example, that you should follow His steps.

Finally it will be observed that it is not appropriate for a Christian to serve as a magistrate because of these points: The government magistracy is according to the flesh, but the Christian's is according to the Spirit; their houses and dwelling remain in this world, but the Christian's are in heaven; their citizenship is in this world, but the Christian's citizenship is in heaven; the weapons of their conflict and war are carnal and against the flesh only, but the Christian's weapons are spiritual, against the fortification of the devil. The worldlings are armed with steel and iron, but the Christian is armed with the armor of God, with truth, righteousness, peace, faith, salvation, and the Word of God. In brief, as is the mind of Christ toward us, so shall the mind of the members of the body of Christ be through Him in all things, that there may be no schism in the body through which it would be destroyed.

For every kingdom divided against itself will be destroyed. Now since Christ is as it is written of Him, His members must also be the same, that His body may remain complete and united to its own advancement and upbuilding.

Seventh: The Oath

We are agreed as follows concerning the oath: The oath is a confirmation among those who are quarreling or making promises. In the Law it is commanded to be performed in God's name, but only in truth, not falsely. Christ, who teaches the perfection of the Law, prohibits all swearing to His followers, whether true or false—neither by heaven, nor by the earth, nor by Jerusalem, nor by our head—and that for the reason which He shortly thereafter gives, For you are not able to make one hair white or black. So you see it is for this reason that all swearing is forbidden: we cannot fulfill that which we promise when we swear, for we cannot change even the very least thing on us.

Now there are some who did not give credence to the simple command of God, but object with this question: Well now, did not God swear to Abraham by Himself (since He was God), when He promised him that He would be with him and that He would be his God if he would keep His commandments—why then should I not also swear when I promise to someone? Answer: Hear what the Scripture says: God, since He wished more abundantly to show unto the heirs the immutability of His counsel, inserted an oath, that by two immutable things (in which it is impossible for God to lie) we might have a strong consolation. Observe the meaning of this Scripture: What God forbids you to do, He has power to do, for everything is possible for Him. God swore an oath to Abraham, says the Scripture, so that He might show that His counsel is immutable. That is, no one can withstand or thwart His will; therefore He can keep His oath. But we can do nothing, as is said above by Christ, to keep or perform [our oaths]: therefore we shall not swear at all.

Then others further say as follows: It is not forbidden of God to swear in the New Testament, when it is actually commanded in the Old, but it is forbidden only to swear by heaven, earth,

Jerusalem, and our head. Answer: Hear the Scripture, he who swears by heaven swears by God's throne and by Him who sitteth thereon. Observe: it is forbidden to swear by heaven, which is only the throne of God. How much more is it forbidden to swear by God Himself! Ye fools and blind, which is greater, the throne or Him that sitteth thereon?

Further some say, because evil is now in the world, and because man needs God for the establishment of the truth, so did the apostles Peter and Paul also swear. Answer: Peter and Paul only testify of that which God promised to Abraham with the oath. They themselves promise nothing, as the example indicates clearly. Testifying and swearing are two different things. For when a person swears he is in the first place promising future things, as Christ was promised to Abraham whom we a long time afterwards received. But when a person bears testimony he is testifying about the present, whether it is good or evil, as Simeon spoke to Mark about Christ and testified. Behold this child is set for the fall and rising of many in Israel, and for a sign which shall be spoken against.

Christ also taught us along the same line when He said, Let your communication be Yea, yea; Nay, nay; for whatsoever is more than these cometh of evil. He says, Your speech or word shall be yea and nay. However, when one does not wish to understand, he remains closed to the meaning. Christ is simply Yea and Nay, and all those who seek Him will understand His Word. Amen.

Dear brethren and sisters in the Lord: These are the articles of certain brethren who had heretofore been in error and who had failed to agree in the true understanding, so that many weaker consciences were perplexed, causing the name of God to be greatly slandered. Therefore there has been a great need for us to become of one mind in the Lord, which has come to pass. To God be praise and glory!

Now since you have so well understood the will of God which has been made known by us, it will be necessary for you to achieve perseveringly, without interruption, the known will of

God. For you know well what the servant who sinned knowingly heard as his recompense.

Everything which you have unwittingly done and confessed as evildoing is forgiven you through the believing prayer which is offered by us in our meeting for all our shortcomings and guilt. This state is yours through the gracious forgiveness of God and through the blood of Jesus Christ. Amen.

Keep watch on all who do not walk according to the simplicity of the divine truth which is stated in this letter from [the decisions of] our meeting, so that everyone among us will be governed by the rule of the ban and henceforth the entry of false brethren and sisters among us may be prevented.

Eliminate from you that which is evil and the Lord will be your God and you will be His sons and daughters.

Dear brethren, keep in mind what Paul admonishes Timothy when he says, the grace of God that bringeth salvation hath appeared to all men, teaching us that, denying ungodliness and worldly lusts, we should live soberly, righteously, and godly, in this present world; looking for that blessed hope, and the glorious appearing of the great God and our Savior Jesus Christ; who gave Himself for us, that He might redeem us from all iniquity, and purify unto Himself a people of His own, zealous of good works. Think on this and exercise yourselves therein and the God of peace will be with you.

May the name of God be hallowed eternally and highly praised, Amen. May the Lord give you His peace, Amen.

The Acts of Schleitheim on the Border [Canton Schaffhausen, Switzerland], on Matthias' [Day], Anno MDXXVII.

CHAPTER TWO

Short Confession of Faith in Twenty Articles by John Smyth (1609)

We Believe with the Heart and with the Mouth Confess:

1. That there is one God, the best, the highest, and most glorious Creator and Preserver of all; who is Father, Son, and Holy Spirit.

2. That God has created and redeemed the human race to His own image, and has ordained all men (no one being reprobated) to life.

3. That God imposes no necessity of sinning on any one; but man freely, by Satanic instigation, departs from God.

4. That the law of life was originally placed by God in the keeping of the law; then, by reason of the weakness of the flesh, was, by the good pleasure of God, through the redemption of Christ, changed into justification of faith; on which account, no one ought justly to blame God, but rather, with his inmost heart, to revere, adore, and praise His mercy, that God should have rendered that possible to man, by His grace, which before, since man had fallen, was impossible by nature.

5. That there is no original sin (lit., *no sin of origin or descent*), but all sin is actual and voluntary, viz., a word, a deed, or a design against the law of God; and therefore, infants are without sin.

6. That Jesus Christ is true God and true man; viz., the Son of God taking to Himself, in addition, the true and pure nature of a man, out of a true rational soul, and existing in a true human body.

7. That Jesus Christ, as pertaining to the flesh, was conceived by the Holy Spirit in the womb of the Virgin Mary, afterwards was born, circumcised, baptized, tempted; also that He hungered, thirsted, ate, drank, increased both in stature and in knowledge; He was wearied, He slept, at last was crucified, dead, buried, He rose again, ascended into heaven; and that to Himself as only King, Priest, and Prophet of the church, all power both in heaven and earth is given.

8. That the grace of God, through the finished redemption of Christ, was to be prepared and offered to all without distinction, and that not feignedly but in good faith, partly by things made, which declare the invisible things of God, and partly by the preaching of the Gospel.

9. That men, of the grace of God through the redemption of Christ, are able (the Holy Spirit, by grace, being before unto them) to repent, to believe, to turn to God, and to attain to eternal life; so on the other hand, they are able themselves to resist the Holy Spirit, to depart from God, and to perish for ever.

10. That the justification of man before the Divine tribunal (which is both the throne of justice and of mercy), consists partly of the imputation of the righteousness of Christ apprehended by

faith, and partly of inherent righteousness, in the holy themselves, by the operation of the Holy Spirit, which is called regeneration or sanctification; since any one is righteous, who doeth righteousness.

11. That faith, destitute of good works, is vain; but true and living faith is distinguished by good works.

12. That the church of Christ is a company of the faithful; baptized after confession of sin and of faith, endowed with the power of Christ.

13. That the church of Christ has power delegated to themselves of announcing the Word, administering the sacraments, appointing ministers, disclaiming them, and also excommunicating; but the last appeal is to the brethren or body of the church.

14. That baptism is the external sign of the remission of sins, of dying and of being made alive, and therefore does not belong to infants.

15. That the Lord's Supper is the external sign of the communion of Christ, and of the faithful amongst themselves by faith and love.

16. That the ministers of the church are, not only bishops ("Episcopos"), to whom the power is given of dispensing both the Word and the sacraments, but also deacons, men and widows, who attend to the affairs of the poor and sick brethren.

17. That brethren who persevere in sins known to themselves, after the third admonition, are to be excluded from the fellowship of the saints by excommunication.

18. That those who are excommunicated are not to be avoided in what pertains to worldly business ("civile commercium").

19. That the dead (the living being instantly changed) will rise again with the same bodies; not the substance but the qualities being changed.

20. That after the resurrection, all will be borne to the tribunal of Christ, the Judge, to be judged according to their works; the pious, after sentence of absolution, will enjoy eternal life with Christ in heaven; the wicked, condemned, will be punished with eternal torments in hell with the devil and his angels.

CHAPTER THREE

The London Confession (1644)

The Confession of Faith, of those churches which are commonly (though falsely) called Anabaptists: presented to the view of all that fear God, to examine by the touchstone of the Word of Truth: As likewise for the taking off those aspersions which are frequently both in pulpit and print, (although unjustly) cast upon them.

Acts 4:20:
"We cannot but speak the things which we have seen and heard."

Isaiah 8:20:
"To the Law and to the testimony, if they speak not according to this rule, it is because there is no light in them."

2 Corinthians 1:9–10:
"But we had the sentence of death in ourselves,
that we should not trust in ourselves , but in the living God,
which raiseth the dead; who delivered us from so great a death,
and doth deliver, in whom we trust that He will yet deliver."

LONDON: Printed by Matthew Simmons in Aldersgate-street, 1644.

To All That Desire . . .

The lifting up of the name of the Lord Jesus in sincerity, the poor despised churches of God in London send greeting, with prayers for their further increase in the knowledge of Christ Jesus.

We question not but that it will seem strange to many men, that such as we are frequently termed to be, lying under that calumny and black brand of heretics, and powers of division as we do, should presume to appear so publicly as now we have done: but yet notwithstanding we may well say, to give answer to such, what David said to his brother, when the Lord's battle was a fighting, (1 Sam. 29:30). "Is there not a cause?" Surely, if ever people had cause to speak for the vindication of the truth of Christ in their hands, we have, that being indeed the main wheel at this time that sets us awork; for had anything by men been transacted against our persons only, we could quietly have sat still, and committed our cause to Him who is a righteous Judge, who will in the great day judge the secrets of all men's hearts by Jesus Christ: But being it is not only us, but the truth professed by us, we cannot, we dare not speak; it is no strange thing to any observing man, what sad charges are laid, not only by the world, that know not God, but also by those that think themselves much wronged, if they be not looked upon as the chief worthies of the church of God, and watchmen of the city: But it hath fared with us from them, as from the poor spouse seeking her beloved, Cant. 5:6, 7. They finding us out of that common roadway themselves walk, have smote us and taken away our veil, that so we may by them be recommended odious in the eyes of all that behold us, and in the hearts of all that think upon us, which they have done both in pulpit and print, charging us with holding free-will, falling away from grace, denying original sin, disclaiming of Magistracy, denying to assist them either in persons or purse in any of their lawful commands, doing acts unseemly in the dispensing the ordinance of baptism, not to be named amongst Christians: All which charges we disclaim as notoriously untrue, though by reason of these calumnies cast upon us, many that fear God are discouraged and forestalled in harboring a good thought, either of us or what we profess; and many that know not God encouraged, if they can find the place of our meeting, to get together in clusters to stone us, as looking upon us as a people holding such things, as that we are not worthy to live: We have therefore for the clearing of the truth we profess, that it may be at liberty, though we be in bonds, briefly published a confession of our faith, as desiring all that fear God, seriously to consider whether (if they compare what we here say and confess in the presence of the Lord Jesus and His saints) men have not with their tongues in pulpit, and pens in print, both spoken and written things that are contrary to truth; but we know our God in His own time will clear our cause, and lift up His Son to make Him the chief cornerstone, though He has been (or now should be) rejected of master builders. And because it may be conceived, that what is here published, may be but the judgment of some one particular congregation, more refined than the rest; we do therefore here subscribe it, some of each body in the name, and by the appointment of seven congregations, who though we be distinct in respect of our particular bodies, for convenience sake, being as many as can well meet together in one place, yet are all one in communion, holding Jesus Christ to be our head and Lord; under whose government we desire alone to walk, in following the Lamb wheresoever He goeth; and we believe the Lord will daily cause truth more to appear in the hearts of His saints, and make them ashamed of their folly in the land of their nativity, that so they may with one shoulder, more sturdy to lift up the name of the Lord Jesus, and stand for His appointments and laws; which is the desires and prayers of the condemned churches of Christ in London for all saints. Subscribed in the names of seven churches in London:

William Kiffin	*John Mabbatt*
Thomas Patience	*John Webb*
John Spilsbery	*Thomas Killcop*
George Tipping	*Paul Hobson*
Samuel Richardson	*Thomas Goare*
Thomas Skippard	*Joseph Phelpes*
Thomas Munday	*Edward Heath*
Thomas Gunne	

The Confession of Faith of Those Churches Which Are Commonly (Though Falsely) Called Anabaptists.

1. That God as He is in Himself, cannot be comprehended of any but Himself, dwelling in that inaccessible light, that no eye can attain unto, whom never man saw, nor can see; that there is but one God, one Christ, one Spirit, one faith, one baptism, one rule of holiness and obedience for all saints, at all times, in all places to be observed.

2. That God is of Himself, that is, neither from another, nor of another, nor by another, nor for another: but is a Spirit, who as His being is of Himself, so He gives being, moving, and preservation to all other things, being in Himself eternal, most holy, every way infinite in greatness, wisdom, power, justice, goodness, truth, etc. In this God-head, there is the Father, the Son, and the Spirit; being every one of them one and the same God; and therefore not divided, but distinguished one from another by their several properties; the Father being from Himself, the

Son of the Father from everlasting, the Holy Spirit proceeding from the Father and the Son.

3. That God hath decreed in Himself from everlasting touching all things, effectually to work and dispose them according to the counsel of His own will, to the glory of His name; in which decree appeareth His wisdom, constancy, truth, and faithfulness; wisdom is that whereby He contrives all things; constancy is where by the decree of God remains always immutable; truth is that whereby He declares that alone which He hath decreed, and though His sayings may seem to sound sometimes another thing, yet the sense of them doth always agree with the decree; faithfulness is that whereby He effects that He hath decreed, as He hath decreed. And touching His creature man, God had in Christ before the foundation of the world, according to the good pleasure of His will, foreordained some men to eternal life through Jesus Christ, to the praise and glory of His grace, leaving the rest in their sin to their just condemnation, to the praise of His justice.

4. In the beginning God made all things very good, created man after His own image and likeness, filling him with all perfection of all natural excellency and uprightness, free from all sin. But long he abode not in this honor, but by the subtilty of the serpent, which Satan used as his instrument, himself with his angels having sinned before, and not kept their first estate, but left their own habitation; first Eve then Adam being seduced did wittingly and willingly fall into disobedience and transgression of the commandment of their great Creator, for the which death came upon all, and reigned over all, so that all since the fall are conceived in sin, and brought forth in iniquities, and so by nature children of wrath, and servants of sin, subjects of death, and all other calamities due to sin in this world and for ever, being considered in the state of nature, without relation to Christ.

5. All mankind being thus fallen, and become altogether dead in sin and trespasses, and subject to the eternal wrath of the great God by transgression; yet the elect, which God hath loved with an everlasting love, as redeemed, quickened, and saved, not

by themselves, neither by their own works, lest any man should boast himself, but wholly and only by God of His free grace and mercy through Jesus Christ, who of God is made unto us wisdom, righteousness, sanctification, and redemption, that as it is written, "He that rejoices, let him rejoice in the Lord."

6. This therefore is life eternal, to know the only true God, and whom He hath sent Jesus Christ. And on the contrary, the Lord will render vengeance in flaming fire to them that know not God, and obey not the Gospel of our Lord Jesus Christ.

7. The rule of this knowledge, faith, and obedience, concerning the worship and service of God, and all other Christian duties, is not man's inventions, opinions, devices, laws, constitutions, or traditions unwritten whatsoever, but only the Word of God contained in the canonical Scriptures.

8. In this written Word God hath plainly revealed whatsoever He hath thought needful for us to know, believe, and acknowledge, touching the nature and office of Christ, in whom all the promises are Yea and Amen to the praise of God.

9. Touching the Lord Jesus, of whom Moses and the prophets wrote, and whom the apostles preached, is the Son of God the Father, the brightness of His glory, the engraven form of His being, God with Him and with His Holy Spirit, by whom He made the world, by whom He upholds and governs all the works He hath made, who also when the fullness of time was come, was made man of a woman, of the tribe of Judah, of the seed of Abraham and David, to wit, of Mary that blessed virgin, by the Holy Spirit coming upon her, and the power of the most High overshadowing her, and was also in all things like unto us, sin only excepted.

10. Touching His office, Jesus Christ only is made the Mediator of the new covenant, even the everlasting covenant of grace between God and man to be perfectly and fully the Prophet, Priest, and King of the Church of God for evermore.

11. Unto this office He was foreordained from everlasting, by the authority of the Father, and in respect of His manhood, from the womb called and separated, and anointed also most

fully and abundantly with all gifts necessary, God having without measure poured the Spirit upon Him.

12. In this call the Scripture holds forth two special things considerable; first, the call to the office; secondly, the office itself. First, that none takes this honor but He that is called of God, as was Aaron, so also Christ, it being an action especially of God the Father, whereby a special covenant being made, He ordains His Son to this office; which covenant is, that Christ should be made a sacrifice for sin, that He shall see His seed, and prolong His days, and the pleasure of the Lord shall prosper in His hand; which calling therefore contains in itself choosing, foreordaining, sending. Choosing respects the end, foreordaining the means, sending the execution itself, all of mere grace, without any condition foreseen either in men, or in Christ Himself.

13. So that this office to be mediator, that is, to be Prophet, Priest, and King of the Church of God, is so proper to Christ, as neither in the whole, nor in any part thereof, it can be transferred from Him to any other.

14. This office itself of which Christ was called is threefold, of a Prophet, of Priest, and of a King: this number and order of offices is showed; first, by men's necessities grievously laboring under ignorance, by reason whereof they stand in infinite necessity of the prophetical office of Christ to relieve them. Secondly, alienation from God, wherein they stand in need of the priestly office to reconcile them: thirdly, our utter disability to return to Him, by which they stand in need of the power of Christ in His kingly office to assist and govern them.

15. Touching the prophesy of Christ, it is that whereby He hath perfectly revealed the whole will of God out of the bosom of the Father, that is needful for His servants to know, believe and obey; and therefore is called not only a Prophet and a Doctor, and the Apostle of our profession, and the Angel of the Covenant; but also the very wisdom of God, and the treasures of wisdom and understanding.

16. That He might be such a Prophet as thereby to be every way complete, it was necessary that He should be God, and

withall also that He should be man; for unless He had been God, He could never have perfectly understood the will of God, neither had He been able to reveal it throughout all ages; and unless He had been man, He could not fitly have unfolded it in His own person to man.

17. Touching His Priesthood, Christ being consecrated, hath appeared once to put away sin by the offering and sacrifice of Himself, and to this end hath fully performed and suffered all those things by which God, through the blood of that His Cross in an acceptable sacrifice, might reconcile His elect only; and having broken down the partition wall, and therewith finished and removed all those rites, shadows, and ceremonies, is now entered within the Vail, into the Holy of Holiest, that is, to the very heavens, and presence of God, where He forever liveth and sitteth at the right hand of Majesty, appearing before the face of His Father to make intercession for such as come to the throne of grace by that new and living way; and not that only, but makes His people a spiritual house, a holy priesthood, to offer up spiritual sacrifice acceptable to God through Him; neither doth the Father accept, or Christ offer to the Father, any other worship or worshippers.

18. This Priesthood was not legal, or temporary, but according to the order of Melchizedek; not by a carnal commandment, but by the power of an endless life; not by an order that is weak and lame, but stable and perfect, not for a time, but forever, admitting no successor, but perpetual and proper to Christ, and of Him that ever liveth. Christ Himself was the Priest, Sacrifice, and Altar: He was Priest, according to both natures, He was a sacrifice most properly according to His human nature: when in the Scripture it is wont to be attributed to His body, to His blood; yet the chief force whereby this sacrifice was made effectual, did depend upon His divine nature, namely, that the Son of God did offer Himself for us: He was the Altar properly according to His divine nature, it belonging to the Altar to sanctify that which is offered upon it, and so it ought to be of greater dignity than the sacrifice itself.

19. Touching His kingdom, Christ being risen from the dead, ascended into heaven, sat on the right hand of God the Father, having all power in heaven and earth, given unto Him, He doth spiritually govern His Church, exercising His power over all angels and men, good and bad, to the preservation and salvation of the elect, to the overruling and destruction of His enemies, which are reprobates, communicating and applying the benefits, virtue, and fruit of His prophecy and Priesthood to His elect, namely, to the subduing and taking away of their sins, to their justification and adoption of sons, regeneration, sanctification, preservation and strengthening in all their conflicts against Satan, the world, the flesh, and the temptations of them, continually dwelling in, governing and keeping their hearts in faith and filial fear by His Spirit, which having given it, He never takes away from them, but by it still begets and nourisheth in them faith, repentance, love, joy, hope, and all heavenly light in the soul unto immortality, notwithstanding through our own unbelief, and the temptations of Satan, the sensible sight of this light and love be clouded and overwhelmed for the time. And on the contrary, ruling in the world over his enemies, Satan, and all the vessels of wrath, limiting, using, restraining them by His mighty power, as seems good in His divine wisdom and justice to the execution of His determinate counsel, delivering them up to a reprobate mind, to be kept through their own deserts, in darkness and sensuality unto judgment.

20. The kingdom shall be then fully perfect when He shall the second time come in glory to reign amongst His saints, and to be admired of all them which do believe, when He shall put down all rule and authority under His feet, that the glory of the Father may be full and perfectly manifested in His Son, and the glory of the Father and the Son in all His members.

21. That Christ Jesus by His death did bring forth salvation and reconciliation only for the elect, which were those which God the Father gave Him; and that the Gospel which is to be preached to all men as the ground of faith is that Jesus is the Christ, the Son of the ever blessed God, filled with the perfec-

tion of all heavenly and spiritual excellencies, and that salvation is only and alone to be had through the believing in His name.

22. That faith is the gift of God wrought in the hearts of the elect by the Spirit of God, whereby they come to see, know, and believe the truth of the Scriptures, and not only so, but the excellency of them above all other writings and things in the world as they hold forth the glory of God in His attributes, the excellency of Christ in His nature and offices, and the power of the fullness of the Spirit in its workings and operations; and thereupon are enabled to cast the weight of their souls upon this truth thus believed.

23. Those that have this precious faith wrought in them by the Spirit, can never finally nor totally fall away; and though many storms and floods do arise and beat against them, yet they shall never be able to take them off that foundation and rock which by faith they are fastened upon, but shall be kept by the power of God to salvation, where they shall enjoy their purchased possession, they being formerly engraven upon the palms of God's hands.

24. That faith is ordinarily begot by the preaching of the Gospel, or Word of Christ, without respect to any power or capacity in the creature, but it is wholly passive, being dead in sin and trespasses, doth believe, and is converted by no less power than that which raised Christ from the dead.

25. That the tenders of the Gospel to the conversion of sinners is absolutely free, no way requiring, as absolutely necessary, any qualifications, preparations, terrors of the law, or preceding ministry of the law, but only and alone the naked soul, as a sinner and ungodly to receive Christ as crucified, dead, and buried, and risen again, being made a Prince and a Savior for such sinners.

26. That the same power that converts to faith in Christ, the same power carries on the soul still through all duties, temptations, conflicts, sufferings, and continually whatever a Christian is, he is by grace, and by a constant renewed operation from God, without which he cannot perform any duty to God, or undergo any temptations from Satan, the world, or men.

27. That God the Father and Son and Spirit is one with all believers in their fullness, in relations as head and members, as house and inhabitants, as husband and wife, one with Him, as light and love, and one with Him in His inheritance, and in all His glory; and that all believers by virtue of this union and oneness with God, are the adopted sons of God and heirs with Christ, co-heirs and joint heirs with Him of the inheritance of all the promises of this life, and that which is to come.

28. That those which have union with Christ are justified from all their sins, past, present, and to come, by the blood of Christ; which justification we conceive to be a gracious and free acquittance of a guilty, sinful creature, from all sin by God, through the satisfaction that Christ hath made by His death; and this applied in the manifestation of it through faith.

29. That all believers are a holy and sanctified people, and that sanctification is a spiritual grace of the new covenant and effect of the love of God, manifested to the soul, whereby the believer is in truth and reality separated, both in soul and body, from all sin and dead works, through the blood of the everlasting covenant, whereby he also presseth after a heavenly and evangelical perfection in obedience to all the commands which Christ as Head and King in this new Covenant has prescribed to him.

30. All believers through the knowledge of that justification of life given by the Father and brought forth by the blood of Christ, have this as their privilege of that new Covenant, peace with God and reconciliation whereby they that were afar off were brought nigh by that blood and have (as the Scripture speaks) peace passing all understanding, yea, joy in God through our Lord Jesus Christ by whom we have received the atonement.

31. That all believers in the time of this life are in continual warfare, combat, and opposition against sin, self, the world, and the devil, and liable to all manner of afflictions, tribulations and persecutions, and so shall continue until Christ comes in His kingdom, being predestinated and appointed thereunto and whatsoever the saints, any of them do possess or enjoy of God in this life, is only by faith.

32. That the only strength by which the saints are enabled to encounter with all opposition and to overcome all afflictions, temptations, persecutions, and trials, is only by Jesus Christ, who is the captain of their salvation, being made perfect through sufferings, who hath engaged His strength to assist them in all their afflictions and to uphold them under all their temptations, and to preserve them by His power to His everlasting kingdom.

33. That Christ hath here on earth a spiritual kingdom which is the Church, which He hath purchased and redeemed to Himself as a peculiar inheritance: which Church, as it is visible to us, is a company of visible saints, called and separated from the world, by the Word and Spirit of God, to the visible profession of the faith of the Gospel, being baptized into that faith and joined to the Lord and each other by mutual agreement, in the practical enjoyment of the ordinances, commanded by Christ their head and King.

34. To this Church He hath made His promises and given the signs of His covenant, presence, love, blessing, and protection: here are the fountains and springs of His heavenly grace continually flowing forth; thither ought all men to come, of all estates, that acknowledge Him to be their Prophet, Priest, and King, to be enrolled amongst His household servants, to be under His heavenly conduct and government, to lead their lives in His walled sheepfold and watered garden, to have communion here with the saints, that they may be made to be partakers of their inheritance in the kingdom of God.

35. And all His servants are called thither, to present their bodies and souls, and to bring their gifts God hath given them; so being come, they are here by Himself bestowed in their several order, peculiar place, due use, being fitly compact and knit together, according to the effectual working of every part, to the edification of itself in love.

36. That being thus joined, every Church has power given them from Christ for their better well-being, to choose to themselves meet persons into the office of pastors, teachers, elders, deacons, being qualified according to the Word, as those which Christ has appointed in His Testament, for the feeding, govern-

ing, serving, and building up of His Church, and that none other have power to impose them, either these or any other.

37. That the ministers aforesaid, lawfully called by the Church, where they are to administer, ought to continue in their calling, according to God's ordinance, and carefully to feed the flock of Christ committed to them, not for filthy lucre, but of a ready mind.

38. That the due maintenance of the officers aforesaid, should be the free and voluntary communication of the Church, that according to Christ's ordinance, they that preach the Gospel, should live on the Gospel and not by constraint to be compelled from the people by a forced law.

39. That baptism is an ordinance of the New Testament, given by Christ, to be dispensed only upon persons professing faith, or that are disciples, or taught, who upon profession of faith, ought to be baptized.

40. The way and manner of the dispensing of this ordinance the Scripture holds out to be dipping or plunging the whole body under water: it being a sign, must answer the thing signified, which are these: first, the washing the whole soul in the blood of Christ. Secondly, that interest the saints have in the death, burial, and resurrection. Thirdly, together with a confirmation of our faith, that as certainly as the body is buried under water, and riseth again, so certainly shall the bodies of the saints be raised by the power of Christ, in the day of the resurrection to reign with Christ. [The word *Baptizo*, signifying to dip under water, yet so as with convenient garments both upon the administrator and subject, with all modesty.]

41. The persons designed by Christ to dispense this ordinance, the Scriptures hold forth to be a preaching disciple, it being no where tied to a particular Church, officer, or person extraordinarily sent, the commission enjoining the administration, being given to them under no other consideration, but as considered disciples.

42. Christ has likewise given power to His whole Church to receive in and cast out, by way of excommunication, any member; and this power is given to every particular congregation,

and not one particular person, either member or officer, but the whole.

43. And every particular member of each Church, how excellent, great, or learned soever, ought to be subject to this censure and judgment of Christ; and the Church ought with great care and tenderness, with due advice to proceed against her members.

44. And as Christ for the keeping of this Church in holy and orderly communion, placeth some special men over the Church, who by their office are to govern, oversee, visit, watch; so likewise for the better keeping thereof in all places, by the members, He hath given authority, and laid duty upon all, to watch over one another.

45. That also such to whom God hath given gifts, being tied in the Church, may and ought by the appointment of the congregation, to prophecy, according to the proportion of faith, and so teach publicly the Word of God, for the edification, exhortation, and comfort of the Church.

46. Thus being rightly gathered, established, and still proceeding in Christian communion and obedience of the Gospel of Christ, none ought to separate for faults and corruptions, which may, and as long as the Church consists of men subject to failings, will fall out and arise amongst them, even in true constituted Churches, until they have in due order sought redress thereof.

47. And although the particular congregations be distinct and several bodies, every one a compact and knit city in itself; yet are they all to walk by one and the same rule, and by all means convenient to have the counsel and help one of another in all needful affairs of the Church, as members of one body in the common faith under Christ their only Head.

48. That a civil magistracy is an ordinance of God set up by God for the punishment of evil doers, and for the praise of them that do well; and that in all lawful things commanded by them, subjection ought to be given by us in the Lord; and that we are to make supplication and prayer for kings, and all that are in authority, that under them we may live a peaceable and quiet life in all godliness and honesty.

49. The supreme magistracy of this kingdom we believe to be the King and Parliament freely chosen by the kingdom, and that in all those civil laws which have been acted by them, or for the present is or shall be ordained, we are bound to yield subjection and obedience unto in the Lord, as conceiving ourselves bound to defend both the persons of those thus chosen, and all civil laws made by them, with our persons, liberties, and estates, with all that is called ours, although we should suffer never so much from them in not actively submitting to some ecclesiastical laws, which might be conceived by them to be their duties to establish which we for the present could not see, nor our consciences could submit unto; yet are we bound to yield our persons to their pleasures.

50. And if God should provide such a mercy for us, as to incline the magistrates' hearts so far to tender our consciences, as that we might be protected by them from wrong, injury, oppression and molestation, which long we formerly have groaned under by the tyranny and oppression of the prelatical hierarchy, which God through mercy hath made this present King and Parliament wonderful, honorable, as an instrument in His hand, to throw down; and we thereby have had some breathing time, we shall, we hope, look at it as a mercy beyond our expectation, and conceive ourselves further engaged forever to bless God for it.

51. But if God withhold the magistrates' allowance and furtherance herein; yet we must notwithstanding proceed together in Christian communion, not daring to give place to suspend our practice, but to walk in obedience to Christ in the profession and holding forth this faith before mentioned, even in the midst of all trials and afflictions, not accounting our goods, lands, wives, children, fathers, mothers, brethren, sisters, yea, and our own lives dear unto us so we may finish our course with joy: remembering always we ought to obey God rather than men, and grounding upon the commandment, commission and promise of our Lord and Master Jesus Christ, who as He hath all power in heaven and earth, so also hath promised, if we keep His commandments which He hath given us, to be with us to the

end of the world: and when we have finished our course, and kept the faith, to give us the crown of righteousness, which is laid up for all that love His appearing, and to whom we must give an account of all our actions, no man being able to discharge us of the same.

52. And likewise unto all men is to be given whatsoever is their due; tributes, customs, and all such lawful duties, ought willingly to be by us paid and performed, our lands, goods, and bodies, to submit to the magistrate in the Lord, and the magistrate every way to be acknowledged, reverenced, and obeyed, according to godliness; not because of wrath only but for conscience sake. And finally, all men so to be esteemed and regarded, as is due and meet for their place, age, estate, and condition.

53. And thus we desire to give unto God that which is God's, and unto Caesar that which is Caesar's, and unto all men that which belongeth unto them, endeavoring ourselves to have always a clear conscience void of offence towards God and towards man. And if any take this that we have said to be heresy, then do we with the apostle freely confess, that after the way which they call heresy, worship we the God of our fathers, believing all things which are written in the law and in the prophets and apostles, desiring from our souls to disclaim all heresies and opinions which are not after Christ, and to be steadfast, unmovable, always abounding in the work of the Lord, as knowing our labor shall not be in vain in the Lord.

1 Corinthians 1:24:
Not that we have dominion over your faith,
but are helpers of your joy: for by faith we stand.

CHAPTER FOUR

Preface to the Second London Confession (1677)

Courteous reader: It is now many years since divers of us (with other sober Christians then living and walking in the way of the Lord that we profess) did conceive ourselves to be under a necessity of publishing a CONFESSION OF OUR FAITH for the information and satisfaction of those that did not thoroughly understand what our principles were, or had entertained prejudices against our profession by reason of the strange representation of them, by some men of note, who had taken very wrong measures, and accordingly led others into misapprehensions, of us, and them: and this was first put forth about the year, 1643, in the name of seven congregations then gathered in London; since which time, diverse impressions thereof have been dispersed abroad, and our end proposed, in good measure answered, inasmuch as many (and some of those men eminent, both for piety and learning) were thereby satisfied, that we were no way guilty of those heterodoxies and fundamental errors, which had too frequently been charged upon us without ground or occasion given on our part. And forasmuch as that CONFES-SION is not now commonly to be had; and also that many others have since embraced the same truth which is owned therein; it was judged necessary by us to join together in giving a testimony to the world; of our firm adhering to those wholesome principles, by the publication of this which is now in your hand.

And forasmuch as our method, and manner of expressing our sentiments in this doth vary from the former (although the substance of the matter is the same) we shall freely impart to you the reason and occasion thereof. One thing that greatly prevailed with us to undertake this work, was (not only to give a full account of ourselves to those Christians that differ from us about the subject of baptism, but also) the profit that might from thence arise unto those that have any account of our labors, in their instruction and establishment in the great truths of the Gospel; in the clear understanding and steady belief of which our comfortable walking with God, and fruitfulness before Him in all our ways is most nearly concerned. [And therefore we did conclude it necessary to express ourselves the most fully and distinctly, and also to fix on such a method as might be most comprehensive of those things which we designed to explain our sense and belief of; and finding no defect in this regard in that fixed on by the assembly, and after them by those of the congregational way, we did readily conclude it best to retain the same order in our present confession. And also when we observed that those last mentioned did, in their confession (for reasons which seemed of weight both to themselves and others), choose not only to express their mind in words concurrent with the former in sense, concerning all those articles wherein they were agreed, but also for the most part without any variation of the terms, we did in like manner conclude it best to follow their example, in making use of the very same words with them both, in those articles (which are very many) wherein our faith and doctrine is the same with theirs. And this we did, the more abundantly to manifest our consent with both, in all the fundamental articles of the Christian religion, as also with many others whose orthodox confessions have been published to the world on the behalf of the protestants in diverse nations and cities; and also to convince all that we have no itch to clog religion with new words, but to readily acquiesce in that form of sound words which hath been, in consent with the Holy Scriptures, used by others before us; hereby declaring before God, angels, and men, our hearty agreement with them, in that wholesome protestant doctrine, which, with so clear evidence of Scriptures they have asserted. Some things, indeed, are in some places added, some terms omitted, and some few changed; but these alterations are of that nature, as that we need not doubt any charge or suspicion of unsoundness in they indeed die in their sins; but will not their blood be required of those under whose care they were, who yet permitted them to go on without warning, yea led them into the paths of destruction? And will not the diligence of Christians with respect to the discharge of these duties, in ages past, rise up in judgment against, and condemn many of those who would be esteemed such now?

We shall conclude with our earnest prayer, that the God of all grace, will pour out those measures of His Holy Spirit upon us, that the profession of truth may be accompanied with the sound belief, and diligent practice of it by us; that His name may in all things be glorified, through Jesus Christ our Lord, Amen.

CHAPTER FIVE

Preface to the Second London Confession (1689)

We the ministers and messengers of, and concerned for, upwards of one hundred baptized congregations in England and Wales (denying Arminianism) being met together in London, from the third of the seventh month to the eleventh of the same, 1689, to consider of some things that might be for the glory of God, and the good of these congregations; have thought meet (for the satisfaction of all other Christians that differ from us in the point of baptism) to recommend to their perusal the confession of our faith, which confession we own, as containing the doctrine of our faith and practice, and do desire that the members of our churches respectively to furnish themselves therewith.

Hanserd Knollys	Pastor	Broken Wharf	London
William Kiffin	Do.	Devonshire-Sq	Do.
John Harris	Do.	Joiners' Hall	Do.
William Collins	Do.	Petty France	Do.
Hercules Collins	Do.	Wapping	Do.
Robert Steed	Do.	Broken Wharf	Do.
Leonard Harrison	Do.	Limehouse	Do.
George Barret	Do.	Mile End Green	Do.
Isaac Lamb	Do.	Pennington-St.	Do.
Richard Adams	Minister	Shad Thames	Southwark
Benjamin Keach	Pastor	Horse-lie-down	Do.
Andrew Gifford	Do.	Bristol, Fryars	Som. & Glouc.
Thomas Vaux	Do.	Broadmead	Do.
Thomas Winnel	Do.	Taunton	Do.
James Hitt	Preacher	Dalwood	Dorset
Richd. Tidmarsh	Minister	Oxford City	Oxon
William Facey	Pastor	Reading	Berks
Samuel Buttall	Minister	Plymouth	Devon
Christopher Price	Do.	Abergavenny	Monmouth
Daniel Finch	Do.	Kingsworth	Herts
John Ball		Riverton	Devon
Edmond White	Pastor	Evershall	Bedford
William Prichard	Do.	Blaenau	Monmouth

Paul Fruin	Minister	Warwick	Warwick
Richard Ring	Pastor	Southampton	Hants
John Tomkins	Minister	Abingdon	Berks
Toby Willis	Pastor	Bridgewater	Somset
John Carter		Steventon	Bedford
James Web		Devizes	Wilts
Richard Sutton	Pastor	Tring	Herts
Robert Knight	Do	Stukely	Bucks
Edward Price	Do.	Hereford City	Hereford
William Phips	Do.	Exon	Devon
William Hawkins	Do.	Dimmock	Gloucester
Samuel Ewer	Do.	Hempstead	Herts
Edward Man	Do.	Houndsditch	London
Charles Archer	Do.	Nook-Norton	Oxon

In the name and behalf of the whole assembly.

CHAPTER SIX

The Philadelphia Confession of Faith (1742)

Chapter 1:

Of the Holy Scriptures

1. The Holy Scripture is the only sufficient, certain, and infallible rule of all saving knowledge, faith, and obedience; although the light of nature and the works of creation and providence do so far manifest the goodness, wisdom, and power of God, as to leave men unexcusable; yet they are sufficient to give that knowledge of God and His will, which is necessary unto salvation. Therefore it pleased the Lord at sundry times and in divers manners, to reveal Himself, and to declare that His will unto His Church; and afterward, for the better preserving and propagation of the truth, and for the more sure establishment and

comfort of the Church against the corruption of the flesh, and the malice of Satan, and of the world, to commit the same wholly unto writing; which maketh the Holy Scriptures to be most necessary, those former ways of God's revealing His will unto His people being now ceased.

2. Under the name of Holy Scripture, or the Word of God written, are now contained all the books of the Old and New Testament, which are these:

OF THE OLD TESTAMENT: Genesis, Exodus, Leviticus, Numbers, Deuteronomy, Joshua, Judges, Ruth, 1 Samuel, 2 Samuel, 1 Kings, 2 Kings, 1 Chronicles, 2 Chronicles, Ezra, Nehemiah, Esther, Job, Psalms, Proverbs, Ecclesiastes, The Song of Songs, Isaiah, Jeremiah, Lamentations, Ezekiel, Daniel, Hosea, Joel, Amos, Obadiah, Jonah, Micah, Nahum, Habakkuk, Zephaniah, Haggai, Zechariah, Malachi.

OF THE NEW TESTAMENT: Matthew, Mark, Luke, John, The Acts of the Apostles, Paul's Epistles to the Romans, 1 Corinthians, 2 Corinthians, Galatians, Ephesians, Philippians, Colossians, 1 Thessalonians, 2 Thessalonians, 1 Timothy, 2 Timothy, to Titus, to Philemon, the Epistle to the Hebrews, the Epistle of James, the first and second Epistles of Peter, the first, second, and third Epistles of John, the Epistle of Jude, the Revelation.

All which are given by the inspiration of God, to be the rule of faith and life.

3. The books commonly called Apocrypha, not being of divine inspiration, are no part of the canon (or rule) of the Scripture, and therefore are of no authority to the Church of God, nor to be any otherwise approved or made us of, than other human writings.

4. The authority of the Holy Scripture, for which it ought to be believed, dependeth not upon the testimony of any or Church, but wholly upon God (who is Truth itself), the Author thereof; therefore it is to be received, because it is the Word of God.

5. We may be moved and induced by the testimony of the Church of God to an high and reverent esteem of the Holy Scriptures; and the heavenliness of the matter, the efficacy of the doctrine, and the majesty of the style, the consent of all the

parts, the scope of the whole (which is to give all glory to God), the full discovery it makes of the only way of man's salvation, and many other incomparable excellencies, and entire perfections thereof, are arguments whereby it doth abundantly evidence itself to be the Word of God; yet notwithstanding, our full persuasion, and assurance of the infallible truth, and divine authority thereof, is from the inward work of the Holy Spirit, bearing witness by and with the Word in our hearts.

6. The whole counsel of God concerning all things necessary for His own glory, man's salvation, faith, and life, is either expressly set down or necessarily contained in the Holy Scripture; unto which nothing at any time is to be added, whether by new revelation of the Spirit, or traditions of men.

Nevertheless we acknowledge the inward illumination of the Spirit of God, to be necessary for the saving understanding of such things as are revealed in the Word; and that there are some circumstances concerning the worship of God and government of the Church, common to human actions and societies, which are to be ordered by the light of nature, and Christian prudence, according to the general rules of the Word, which are always to be observed.

7. All things in Scripture are not alike plain in themselves, not alike clear unto all; yet those things which are necessary to be known, believed, and observed for salvation, are so clearly propounded and opened in some place of Scripture or other, that not only the learned but the unlearned, in a due use of ordinary means, may attain to a sufficient understanding of them.

8. The Old Testament in Hebrew (which was the native language of the people of God of old) and the New Testament in Greek (which at the time of the writing of it was most generally known to the nations), being immediately inspired by God, and by His singular care and providence kept pure in all ages are, therefore authentical; so as in all controversies of religion, the Church is finally to appeal unto them. But because these original tongues are not known to all the people of God, who have a right unto and interest in the Scriptures, and are commanded in the fear of God to read and search them, therefore they are to be

translated into the vulgar language of every nation, unto which they come, that the Word of God dwelling plentifully in all, they may worship Him in an acceptable manner, and through patience and comfort of the Scriptures may have hope.

9. The infallible rule of interpretation of Scripture is the Scripture itself. And therefore, when there is a question about the true and full sense of any Scripture (which is not manifold but one), it must be searched by other places that speak more clearly.

10. The supreme judge by which all controversies of religion are to be determined, and all decrees of councils, opinions of ancient writers, doctrines of men, and private spirits, are to be examined, and in whose sentence we are to rest, can be no other but the Holy Scripture delivered by the Spirit, into which Scripture so delivered our faith is finally resolved.

Chapter 2:

Of God and of the Holy Trinity

1. The Lord our God is but one only living and true God; whose subsistence is in and of Himself, infinite in being and perfection, whose essence cannot be comprehended by any but Himself; a most pure Spirit, invisible, without body, parts, or passions, who only hath immortality, dwelling in the light which no man can approach unto, who is immutable, immense, eternal, incomprehensible, Almighty, every way infinite, most holy, most wise, most free, most absolute, working all things according to the counsel of His own immutable and most righteous will for His own glory, most loving, gracious, merciful, longsuffering, abundant in goodness and truth, forgiving iniquity, transgression, and sin, the rewarder of them that diligently seek Him, and withal most just, and terrible in His judgments, hating all sin, and who will by no means clear the guilty.

2. God, having all glory, goodness, blessedness, in and of Himself, is alone in, and unto Himself all-sufficient, not standing in need of any creature which He hath made, nor deriving any glory from them, but only manifesting His own glory in, by,

unto, and upon them; He is the alone fountain of all being, of whom, through whom, and to whom are all things, and He hath most sovereign dominion over all creatures, to do by them, for them, or upon them, whatsoever Himself pleaseth; in His sight all things are open and manifest, His knowledge is infinite, infallible, and independent upon the creature, so as nothing is to Him contingent, or uncertain; He is most holy in all His counsels, in all His works, and in all His commands; to Him is due from angels and men, whatsoever worship, service, or obedience, as creatures they owe unto the Creator, and whatever He is further pleased to require of them.

3. In this divine and infinite Being there are three subsistences, the Father, the Word (or Son), and Holy Spirit, of one substance, power, and eternity, each having the whole divine essence, yet the essence undivided; the Father is of none, neither begotten nor proceeding, the Son is eternally begotten of the Father, the Holy Spirit proceeding from the Father and the Son; all infinite without beginning, therefore but one God, who is not to be divided in nature and being, but distinguished by several peculiar, relative properties, and personal relations; which doctrine of the Trinity is the foundation of all our communion with God, and comfortable dependence on Him.

Chapter 3:

Of God's Decrees

1. God hath decreed in Himself, from all eternity, by the most wise and holy counsel of His own will, freely and unchangeably, all things whatsoever come to pass; yet so as thereby is God neither the Author of sin nor hath fellowship with any therein, nor is violence offered to the will of the creature nor yet is the liberty or contingency of second causes taken away, but rather established; in which appears His wisdom in disposing all things, and power, and faithfulness in accomplishing His decree.

2. Although God knoweth whatsoever may, or can come to pass upon all supposed conditions: yet hath He not decreed any-

thing, because He foresaw it as future, or as that which would come to pass upon such conditions.

3. By the decree of God, for the manifestation of His glory, some men and angels are predestinated or foreordained to eternal life, through Jesus Christ, to the praise of His glorious grace; others being left to act in their sin to their just condemnation, to the praise of His glorious justice.

4. These angels and men thus predestinated, and foreordained, are particularly and unchangeably designed; and their number so certain, and definite, that it cannot be either increased or diminished.

5. Those of mankind that are predestinated to life, God, before the foundation of the world was laid, according to His eternal and immutable purpose and the secret counsel and good pleasure of His will, hath chosen in Christ unto everlasting glory, out of His mere free grace and love; without any other thing in the creature as a condition or cause moving him thereunto.

6. As God hath appointed the elect unto glory, so He hath, by the eternal and most free purpose of His will, foreordained all the means thereunto, wherefore they who are elected, being fallen in Adam, are redeemed by Christ, are effectually called unto faith in Christ, by His Spirit working in due season, are justified, adopted, sanctified, and kept by His power through faith, unto salvation; neither are any other redeemed by Christ, or effectually called, justified, adopted, sanctified, and saved, but the elect only.

7. The doctrine of this mystery of predestination is to be handled with special prudence and care: that men attending the will of God revealed in His Word and yielding obedience thereunto, may, from the certainty of their effectual vocation, be assured of their eternal election; so shall this doctrine afford matter of praise, reverence, and admiration of God, and of humility, diligence, and abundant consolation to all that sincerely obey the Gospel.

Chapter 4:

Of Creation

1. In the beginning it pleased God the Father, Son, and Holy Spirit, for the manifestation of the glory of His eternal power, wisdom, and goodness, to create or make the world, and all things therein, whether visible or invisible, in the space of six days, and all very good.

2. After God had made all other creatures, He created man, male and female, with reasonable and immortal souls, rendering them fit unto that life to God for which they were created, being made after the image of God, in knowledge, righteousness, and true holiness; having the law of God written in their hearts, and power to fulfil it; and yet under a possibility of transgressing, being left to the liberty of their own will, which was subject to change.

3. Besides the law written in their hearts, they received a command not to eat of the tree of knowledge of good and evil; which whilst they kept, they were happy in their communion with God, and had dominion over the creatures.

Chapter 5:

Of Divine Providence

1. God, the good Creator of all things, in His infinite power and wisdom doth uphold, direct, dispose, and govern all creatures and things, from the greatest even to the least, by His most wise and Holy providence, to the end for the which they were created, according unto His infallible foreknowledge, and the free and immutable counsel of His own will; to the praise of the glory of His wisdom, power, justice, infinite goodness, and mercy.

2. Although in relation to the foreknowledge and decree of God, the first Cause, all things come to pass immutably and infallibly; so that there is not anything befalls any by chance, or without His providence; yet by the same providence He

ordereth them to fall out according to the nature of second causes, either necessarily, freely, or contingently.

3. God in His ordinary providence maketh use of means; yet is free to work without, above, and against them at His pleasure.

4. The almighty power, unsearchable wisdom, and infinite goodness of God so far manifest themselves in His providence, that His determinate counsel extendeth itself even to the first fall, and all other sinful actions, both of angels and men; and that not by a bare permission, which also He most wisely and powerfully boundeth, and otherwise ordereth, and governeth, in a manifold dispensation to His most holy ends: yet so, as the sinfulness of their acts proceedeth only from the creatures, and not from God; who being most holy and righteous, neither is nor can be the Author or approver of sin.

5. The most wise, righteous, and gracious God doth oftentimes leave for a season His own children to manifold temptations and the corruptions of their own heart, to chastise them for their former sins, or to discover unto them the hidden strength of corruption and deceitfulness of their hearts; that they may be humbled; and to raise them to a more close and constant dependence for their support upon Himself; and to make them more watchful against all future occasions of sin, and for other just and holy ends. So that whosoever befalls any of His elect is by His appointment, for His glory and their good.

As for those wicked and ungodly men, whom God as a righteous judge, for former sin doth blind and harden; from them he not only withholdeth His grace, whereby they might have been enlightened in their understanding and wrought upon in their hearts; but sometimes also withdraweth the gifts which they had, and exposeth them to such objects as their corruptions make occasion of sin, and withal gives them over to their own lusts, the temptations of the world, and the power of Satan, whereby it comes to pass that they harden themselves, even under those means which God useth for the softening of others.

7. As the providence of God doth in general reach to all creatures, so after a more special manner it taketh care of His Church, and disposeth of all things to the good thereof.

Chapter 6:

Of the Fall of Man, of Sin, and of the Punishment Thereof

1. Although God created man upright and perfect, and gave him a righteous law, which had been unto life had he kept it, and threatened death upon the breach thereof, yet He did not long abide in this honor; Satan using the subtlety of the serpent to seduce Eve, then by her seducing Adam, who without any compulsion, did willfully transgress the law of their creation and the command given unto them, in eating the forbidden fruit, which God was pleased according to His wise and holy counsel to permit, having purposed to order it to His own glory.

2. Our first parents by this sin fell from their original righteousness and communion with God, and we in them, whereby death came upon all; all becoming dead in sin and wholly defiled in all the faculties and parts of soul and body.

3. They being the root, and by God's appointment, standing in the room and stead of all mankind, the guilt of the sin was imputed and corrupted nature conveyed to all their posterity, descending from them by ordinary generation, being now conceived in sin and by nature children of wrath, the servants of sin, the subjects of death, and all other miseries, spiritual, temporal, and eternal, unless the Lord Jesus set them free.

4. From this original corruption, whereby we are utterly indisposed, disabled, and made opposite to all good, and wholly inclined to all evil, do proceed all actual transgressions.

5. This corruption of nature, during this life, doth remain in those that are regenerated; and although it be through Christ pardoned, and mortified, yet both itself, and the first motions thereof, are truly and properly sin.

Chapter 7:

Of God's Covenant

1. The distance between God and the creature is so great, that although reasonable creatures do owe obedience unto Him as

their Creator, yet they could never have attained the reward of life, but by some voluntary condescension on God's part, which He hath been pleased to express, by way of covenant.

2. Moreover, man having brought himself under the curse of the law by his fall, it pleased the Lord to make a covenant of grace, wherein He freely offereth unto sinners life and salvation by Jesus Christ, requiring of them faith in Him, that they may be saved; and promising to give unto all those that are ordained unto eternal life, His Holy Spirit, to make them willing and able to believe.

3. This covenant is revealed in the Gospel; first of all to Adam in the promise of salvation by the seed of the woman, and afterwards by farther steps, until the full discovery thereof was completed in the New Testament; and it is founded in that eternal covenant transaction that was between the Father and the Son, about the redemption of the elect; and it is alone by the grace of this covenant, that all of the posterity of fallen Adam, that ever were saved, did obtain life and a blessed immortality; man being now utterly incapable of acceptance with God upon those terms, on which Adam stood in his state of innocence.

Chapter 8:

Of Christ the Mediator

1. It pleased God, in His eternal purpose, to choose and ordain the Lord Jesus, His only begotten Son, according to the covenant made between them both to be the mediator between God and man; the priest and king; head and Savior of His Church, the heir of all things, and judge of the world: unto whom He did from all eternity give a people to be His seed, and to be by Him in time redeemed, called, justified, sanctified, and glorified.

2. The Son of God, the second person in the Holy Trinity, being very and eternal God, the brightness of the Father's glory, of one substance and equal with Him: who made the world, who upholdeth and governeth all things He hath made; did, when the fullness of time was come, take upon Him man's nature, with

all the essential properties and common infirmities thereof; yet without sin; being conceived by the Holy Spirit in the womb of the Virgin Mary, the Holy Spirit coming down upon her, and the power of the Most High overshadowing her, and so was made of a woman, of the tribe of Judah, of the seed of Abraham and David, according to the Scriptures, so that two whole, perfect, and distinct natures were inseparably joined together in one person, without conversion, composition, or confusion; which person is very God, and very man, yet one Christ, the only mediator between God and man.

3. The Lord Jesus, in His human nature thus united to the divine in the person of the Son, was sanctified, and anointed with the Holy Spirit, above measure; having in Him all the treasures of wisdom and knowledge; in whom it pleased the Father, that all fullness should dwell; to the end, that being holy, harmless, undefiled, and full of grace and truth, He might be thoroughly furnished to execute the office of a mediator, and surety; which office He took not upon Himself, but was thereunto called by His Father, who also put all power and judgment in His hand, and gave Him commandment to execute the same.

4. This office the Lord Jesus did most willingly undertake, which that He might discharge He was made under the law and did perfectly fulfil it, and underwent the punishment due to us, which we should have borne and suffered, being made sin and a curse for us; enduring most grievous sorrows in His soul, and most painful sufferings in His body; was crucified, and died, and remained in the state of the dead; yet saw no corruption; on the third day He arose from the dead, with the same body in which He suffered; with which He also ascended into heaven; and there sitteth at the right hand of His Father, making intercession; and shall return to judge men and angels, at the end of the world.

5. The Lord Jesus, by His perfect obedience and sacrifice of Himself, which He through the eternal Spirit once offered up unto God, hath fully satisfied the justice of God, procured reconciliation, and purchased an everlasting inheritance in the kingdom of heaven for all those whom the Father hath given unto Him.

6. Although the price of redemption was not actually paid by Christ, till after His incarnation, yet the virtue, efficacy, and benefit thereof were communicated to the elect in all ages successively, from the beginning of the world, in and by those promises, types, and sacrifices wherein He was revealed, and signified to be the seed of the woman, which should bruise the serpent's head, and the Lamb slain from the foundation of the world; being the same yesterday, and today, and forever.

7. Christ in the work of mediation acteth according to both natures by each nature doing that which is proper to itself; yet by reason of the unity of the person, that which is proper to one nature is sometimes in Scripture attributed to the person denominated by the other nature.

8. To all those for whom Christ hath obtained eternal redemption, He doth certainly and effectually apply, and communicate the same, making intercession for them; uniting them to Himself by His Spirit revealing unto them, in and by the Word, the mystery of salvation, persuading them to believe and obey; governing their hearts by His Word and Spirit, and overcoming all their enemies by His almighty power and wisdom; in such manner and ways as are most consonant to His wonderful and unsearchable dispensation; and all of free and absolute grace, without any condition foreseen in them, to procure it.

9. This office of mediator between God and man, is proper only to Christ, who is the prophet, priest, and king of the Church of God; and may not be either in whole, or any part thereof transferred from Him to any other.

10. This number and order of offices is necessary; for in respect of our ignorance, we stand in need of His prophetical office; and in respect of our alienation from God and imperfection of the best of our services, we need His priestly office, to reconcile us, and present us acceptable unto God: and in respect of our adverseness and utter inability to return to God, and for our rescue and security from our spiritual adversaries, we need His kingly office to convince, subdue, draw, uphold, deliver, and preserve us to His heavenly kingdom.

Chapter 9:

Of Free Will

1. God hath indued the will of man with that natural liberty and power of acting upon choice, that it is neither forced, nor by any necessity of nature determined to do good or evil.

2. Man in his state of innocency, had freedom, and power, to will and to do that which was good, and well-pleasing to God; but yet was mutable, so that he might fall from it.

3. Man, by his fall into a state of sin, hath wholly lost all ability of will to any spiritual good accompanying salvation; so as a natural man, being altogether averse from that good, and dead in sin, is not able, by his own strength, to convert himself, or to prepare himself thereunto.

4. When God converts a sinner, and translates him into the state of grace, He freeth him from his natural bondage under sin, and by His grace alone enables him freely to will and to do that which is spiritually good; yet so as that, by reason of his remaining corruptions, he doth not perfectly nor only will that which is good, but doth also will that which is evil.

5. The will of man is made perfectly and immutably free to God alone in the state of glory only.

Chapter 10:

Of Effectual Calling

1. Those whom God hath predestinated unto life He is pleased, in His appointed and accepted time, effectually to call by His Word and Spirit, out of that state of sin and death in which they are by nature, to grace and salvation by Jesus Christ; enlightening their minds, spiritually and savingly, to understand the things of God; taking away their heart of stone, and giving unto them a heart of flesh; renewing their wills, and by His almighty power determining them to that which is good, and effectually drawing them to Jesus Christ; yet so as they come most freely, being made willing by His grace.

2. This effectual call is of God's free and special grace alone, not from anything at all foreseen in man, nor from any power or agency in the creature, co-working with His special grace, the creature being wholly passive therein, being dead in sins and trespasses, until, being quickened and renewed by the Holy Spirit, he is thereby enabled to answer this call, and to embrace the grace offered and conveyed in it, and that by no less power than that which raised up Christ from the dead.

3. Elect infants dying in infancy, are regenerated and saved by Christ through the Spirit; who worketh when, and where, and how He pleaseth; so also are all other elect persons, who are incapable of being outwardly called by the ministry of the Word.

4. Others not elected, although they may be called by the ministry of the Word; and may have some common operations of the Spirit, yet not being effectually drawn by the Father, they neither will nor can truly come to Christ; and therefore cannot be saved: much less can men that receive not the Christian religion be saved; be they never so diligent to frame their lives according to the light of nature and the law of that religion they do profess.

Chapter 11:

Of Justification

1. Those whom God effectually calleth, He also freely justifieth, not by infusing righteousness into them, but by pardoning their sins, and by accounting and accepting their persons as righteous; not for anything wrought in them, or done by them, but for Christ's sake alone, not by imputing faith itself, the act of believing, or any other evangelical obedience to them, as their righteousness; but by imputing Christ's active obedience unto the whole law, and passive obedience in His death, for their whole and sole righteousness, the receiving, and resting on Him, and His righteousness, by faith; which faith they have not of themselves, it is the gift of God.

2. Faith thus receiving and resting on Christ, and His righteousness, is the alone instrument of justification: yet it is not

alone in the person justified, but is ever accompanied with all other saving graces, and is no dead faith, but worketh by love.

3. Christ, by His obedience and death, did fully discharge the debt of all those that are justified; and by the sacrifice of Himself, in the blood of His cross, undergoing in their stead the penalty due unto them, make a proper, real, and full satisfaction to God's justice in their behalf; yet inasmuch as He was given by the Father for them, and His obedience and satisfaction accepted in their stead, and both freely, not for anything in them, their justification is only of free grace, that both the exact justice and rich grace of God might be glorified in the justification of sinners.

4. God did from all eternity decree to justify all the elect, and Christ did in the fullness of time die for their sins, and rise again for their justification; nevertheless they are not justified personally, until the Holy Spirit doth in due time actually apply Christ unto them.

5. God doth continue to forgive the sins of those that are justified, and although they can never fall from the state of justification, yet they may by their sins fall under God's fatherly displeasure; and in that condition, they have not usually the light of His countenance restored unto them, until they humble themselves, confess their sins, beg pardon, and renew their faith and repentance.

6. The justification of believers under the Old Testament, was in all these respects one and the same with the justification of believers under the New Testament.

Chapter 12:

Of Adoption

All those that are justified, God vouchsafed in and for the sake of His only Son Jesus Christ, to make partakers of the grace of adoption; by which they are taken into the number, and enjoy the liberties, and privileges of children of God; have His name put upon them, receive the spirit of adoption, have access to the throne of grace with boldness; are enabled to cry, Abba, Father;

are pitied, protected, provided for, and chastened by Him, as by a father; yet never cast off, but sealed to the day of redemption, and inherit the promises, as heirs of everlasting salvation.

Chapter 13:

Of Sanctification

1. They who are united to Christ, effectually called, and regenerated, having a new heart and a new spirit created in them, through the virtue of Christ's death and resurrection; are also further sanctified, really, and personally, through the same virtue, by His Word and Spirit dwelling in them; the dominion of the whole body of sin is destroyed, and the several lusts thereof are more and more weakened and mortified; and they more and more quickened, and strengthened in all saving graces, to the practice of all true holiness, without which no man shall see the Lord.

2. This sanctification is throughout, in the whole man, yet imperfect in this life; there abideth still some remnants of corruption in every part, whence ariseth a continual, and irreconcilable war; the flesh lusting against the spirit, and the spirit against the flesh.

3. In which war, although the remaining corruption for a time may much prevail, yet, through the continual supply of strength, from the sanctifying Spirit of Christ, the regenerate part doth overcome; and so the saints grow in grace, perfecting holiness in the fear of God pressing after an heavenly life, in evangelical obedience to all the commands which Christ, as head and king, in His Word hath prescribed to them.

Chapter 14:

Of Saving Faith

1. The grace of faith, whereby the elect are enabled to believe to the saving of their souls, is the work of the Spirit of Christ in their hearts, and is ordinarily wrought by the ministry of the

Word; by which also, and by the administration of baptism, and the Lord's supper, prayer, and other means appointed of God, it is increased and strengthened.

2. By this faith, a Christian believeth to be true whatsoever is revealed in the Word, for the authority of God Himself; and also apprehendeth an excellency therein above all other writings, and all things in the world; as it bears forth the glory of God in His attributes, the excellency of Christ in His nature and offices, and the power and fullness of the Holy Spirit in His workings and operations; and so is enabled to cast his soul upon the truth thus believed. And also acteth differently upon that which each particular passage thereof containeth; yielding obedience to the commands, trembling at the threatenings, and embracing the promises of God, for this life and that which is to come. But the principal acts of saving faith have immediate relation to Christ, accepting, receiving, and resting upon Him alone, for justification, sanctification, and eternal life, by virtue of the covenant of grace.

3. This faith, although it be different in degrees, and may be weak, or strong, yet it is in the least degree of it different in the kind, or nature of it (as is all other saving grace) from the faith and common grace of temporary believers; and therefore though it may be many times assailed, and weakened, yet it gets the victory, growing up in many, to the attainment of a full assurance through Christ, who is both the Author and Finisher of our faith.

Chapter 15:

Of Repentance Unto Life and Salvation

1. Such of the elect as are converted at riper years, having sometime lived in the state of nature, and therein served divers lusts and pleasures, God in their effectual calling giveth them repentance unto life.

2. Whereas there is none that doth good, and sinneth not, and the best of men may, through the power and deceitfulness of their corruption dwelling in them, with the prevalency of temp-

tation, fall into great sins and provocations, God hath in the covenant of grace mercifully provided that believers so sinning and falling be renewed through repentance unto salvation.

3. This saving repentance is an evangelical grace, whereby a person, being by the Holy Spirit made sensible of the manifold evils of his sin, doth, by faith in Christ, humble himself for it with godly sorrow, detestation of it, and self-abhorrency; praying for pardon and strength of grace, with a purpose and endeavor by supplies of the Spirit to walk before God unto all well-pleasing in all things.

4. As repentance is to be continued through the whole course of our lives, upon the account of the body of death, and the motions thereof; so it is every man's duty to repent of his particular known sins particularly.

5. Such is the provision which God hath made through Christ in the covenant of grace, for the preservation of believers unto salvation, that although there is no sin so small but it deserves damnation; yet there is no sin so great, that it shall bring damnation on them that repent; which makes the constant preaching of repentance necessary.

Chapter 16:

Of Good Works

1. Good works are only such as God hath commanded in His Holy Word, and not such as without the warrant thereof are devised by men, out of blind zeal or upon any pretense of good intentions.

2. These good works, done in obedience to God's commandments, are the fruits and evidences of a true and lively faith; and by them believers manifest their assurance, edify their brethren, adorn the profession of the Gospel, stop the mouths of the adversaries, and glorify God, whose workmanship they are, created in Christ Jesus thereunto, that having their fruit unto holiness, they may have the end eternal life.

3. Their ability to do good works is not at all of themselves, but wholly from the Spirit of Christ; and that they may be

enabled thereunto, besides the graces they have already received, there is necessary an actual influence of the same Holy Spirit, to work in them to will and to do of His good pleasure; yet are they not hereupon to grow negligent, as if they were not bound to perform any duty, unless upon a special motion of the Spirit, but they ought to be diligent in stirring up the grace of God that is in them.

4. They who in their obedience attain to the greatest height which is possible in this life, are so far from being able to super-erogate and to do more than God requires, as that they fall short of much which in duty they are bound to do.

5. We cannot by our best works merit pardon of sin or eternal life at the hand of God, by reason of the great disproportion that is between them and the glory to come, and the infinite distance that is between us and God, whom by them we can neither profit nor satisfy; for the debt of our former sins; but when we have done all we can, we have done but our duty, and are unprofitable servants; and because as they are good they proceed from His Spirit, and as they are wrought by us they are defiled and mixed with so much weakness and imperfection, that they cannot endure the severity of God's judgment.

6. Yet, notwithstanding, the persons of believers being accepted through Christ, their good works also are accepted in Him; not as though they were in this life wholly unblamable and unreprovable in God's sight, but that He, looking upon them in His Son, is pleased to accept and reward that which is sincere, although accompanied with many weaknesses and imperfections.

7. Works done by unregenerate men, although for the matter of them they may be things which God commands, and of good use both to themselves and others; yet because they proceed not from a heart purified by faith, nor are done in a right manner according to the Word, nor to a right end, the glory of God, they are therefore sinful and cannot please God, nor make a man meet to receive grace from God; and yet their neglect of them is more sinful and displeasing to God.

Chapter 17:

Of Perseverance of the Saints

1. Those whom God hath accepted in the Beloved, effectually called and sanctified by His Spirit, and given the precious faith of His elect unto, can neither totally nor finally fall from the state of grace; but shall certainly persevere therein to the end and be eternally saved seeing the gifts and callings of God are without repentance (whence He still begets and nourisheth in them faith, repentance, love, joy, hope, and all the graces of the Spirit unto immortality); and though many storms and floods arise and beat against them, yet they shall never be able to take them off that foundation and rock which by faith they are fastened upon; notwithstanding, through unbelief and the temptations of Satan, the sensible sight of the light and love God may for a time be clouded and obscured from them, yet He is still the same, and they shall be sure to be kept by the power of God unto salvation, where they shall enjoy their purchased possession, they being engraven upon the palm of His hands, and their names having been written in the book of life from all eternity.

2. This perseverance of the saints depends not upon their own free will, but upon the immutability of the decree of election, flowing from the free and unchangeable love of God the Father; upon the efficacy of the merit and intercession of Jesus Christ and union with Him, the abiding of His Spirit, and the seed of God within them, and the nature of the covenant of grace; from all which ariseth also the certainty and infallibility thereof.

3. And though they may, through the temptation of Satan and of the world, the prevalency of corruption remaining in them, and the neglect of the means of their preservation fall in grievous sins, and for a time continue therein, whereby they incur God's displeasure, and grieve His Holy Spirit, come to have their graces and comforts impaired, have their hearts hardened and their consciences wounded, hurt, and scandalize others, and bring temporal judgments upon themselves, yet they shall renew

their repentance and be preserved, through faith in Christ Jesus, to the end.

Chapter 18:

Of the Assurance of Grace and Salvation

1. Although temporary believers and other unregenerate men, may vainly deceive themselves with false hopes and carnal presumptions of being in the favor of God, and in a state of salvation, which hope of theirs shall perish; yet such as truly believe in the Lord Jesus, and love Him in sincerity, endeavoring to walk in all good conscience before Him, may in this life be certainly assured that they are in the state of grace; and may rejoice in the hope of the glory of God, which hope shall never make them ashamed.

2. This certainty is not a bare conjectural and probable persuasion, grounded upon a fallible hope, but an infallible assurance of faith, founded on the blood and righteousness of Christ revealed in the Gospel; and also upon the inward evidence of those graces of the Spirit unto which promises are made, and on the testimony of the Spirit of adoption, witnessing with our spirits that we are the children of God; and as a fruit thereof, keeping the heart both humble and holy.

3. This infallible assurance doth not so belong to the essence of faith, but that a true believer may wait long, and conflict with many difficulties, before he be partaker of it; yet being enabled by the Spirit, to know the things which are freely given him of God, he may without extraordinary revelation in the right use of means attain thereunto; and therefore it is the duty of every one to give all diligence to make their calling and election sure, that thereby his heart may be enlarged in peace and joy in the Holy Spirit, in love and thankfulness to God, and in strength and cheerfulness in the duties of obedience, the proper fruits of this assurance; so far is it from inclining men to looseness.

4. True believers may have the assurance of their salvation divers ways shaken, diminished, and intermitted; as by negligence in preserving of it, by falling into some special sin, which

woundeth the conscience, and grieveth the Spirit, by some sudden or vehement temptation, by God's withdrawing the light of His countenance, and suffering even such as fear Him to walk in darkness and to have no light; yet are they never destitute of the seed of God, and life of faith, that love of Christ and the brethren, that sincerity of heart, and conscience of duty, out of which, by the operation of the Spirit, this assurance may in due time be revived, and by the which in the meantime they are preserved from utter despair.

Chapter 19:

Of the Law of God

1. God gave to Adam a law of universal obedience written in his heart, and a particular precept of not eating the fruit of the tree of knowledge of good and evil, by which He bound him, and all his posterity to personal, entire, exact and perpetual obedience; promised life upon the fulfilling, and threatened death upon the breach of it, and endued him with power and ability to keep it.

2. The same law that was first written in the heart of man continued to be a perfect rule of righteousness after the fall, and was delivered by God upon Mount Sinai in ten commandments, and written in two tables, the four first containing our duty towards God, and the other six our duty to man.

3. Besides this law, commonly called moral, God was pleased to give to the people of Israel ceremonial laws, containing several typical ordinances, partly of worship, prefiguring Christ, His graces, actions, sufferings, and benefits; and partly holding forth divers instructions of moral duties; all which ceremonial laws being appointed only to the time of reformation, are by Jesus Christ the true Messiah and only lawgiver, who was furnished with power from the Father for that end, abrogated and taken away.

4. To them also He gave sundry judicial laws, which expired together with the state of that people, not obliging any now by virtue of that institution; their general equity only being for moral use.

5. The moral law doth forever bind all as well justified persons as others, to the obedience thereof, and that not only in regard of the matter contained in it, but also in respect of the authority of God, the Creator, who gave it; neither doth Christ in the Gospel any way dissolve, but much strengthen this obligation.

6. Although true believers be not under the law, as a covenant of works to be thereby justified or condemned, yet it is of great use to them, as well as to others, in that, as a rule of life, informing them of the will of God and their duty, it directs and binds them to walk accordingly; discovering also the sinful pollutions of their natures, hearts, and lives, so as examining themselves thereby, they may come to further conviction of, humiliation for, and hatred against, sin, together with a clearer sight of the need they have of Christ and the perfection of His obedience; it is likewise of use to the unregenerate, to restrain their corruption, in that it forbids sin; and the threatenings of it serve to show what even their sins deserve, and what afflictions in this life they may expect for them, although freed from the curse and rigor thereof. The promises of it likewise show them God's approbation of obedience, and what blessings they may expect upon the performance thereof, though not as due to them by the law as a covenant of works; so as man's doing good and refraining from evil, because the law encourageth to the one and deterreth from the other, is no evidence of His being under the law and not under grace.

7. Neither are the forementioned uses of the law contrary to the grace of the Gospel, but do sweetly comply with it, the spirit of Christ subduing and enabling the will of man to do that freely and cheerfully, which the will of God revealed in the law requireth to be done.

Chapter 20:

Of the Gospel, and of the Extend of the Grace Thereof

1. The covenant of works being broken by sin, and made unprofitable unto life, God was pleased to give forth the promise of Christ, the seed of the woman, as the means of calling the

elect, and begetting in them faith and repentance; in this promise, the Gospel, as to the substance of it, was revealed, and therein effectual, for the conversion and salvation of sinners.

2. This promise of Christ, and salvation by Him, is revealed only by the Word of God; neither do the works of creation, or providence, with the light of nature, make discovery of Christ, or of grace by Him, so much as in a general or obscure way; much less that men, destitute of the revelation of Him by the promise or Gospel should be enabled thereby to attain saving faith or repentance.

3. This revelation of the Gospel unto sinners, made in divers times, and by sundry parts, with the addition of promises and precepts, for the obedience required therein, as to the nations and persons to whom it is granted, is merely of the sovereign will and good pleasure of God, not being annexed by virtue of any promise, to the due improvement of men's natural abilities, by virtue of common light received without it, which none ever did make, or can so do: and therefore in all ages the preaching of the Gospel hath been granted unto persons and nations, as to the extent or straightening of it, in great variety, according to the counsel of the will of God.

4. Although the Gospel be the only outward means of revealing Christ and saving grace, and is as such abundantly sufficient thereunto, yet that men who are born in trespasses may be born again, quickened, or regenerated, there is moreover necessary an effectual, insuperable work of the Holy Spirit upon the whole soul, for the producing in them a new spiritual life; without which no other means will effect their conversion unto God.

Chapter 21:

Of Christian Liberty, and Liberty of Conscience

1. The liberty which Christ hath purchased for believers under the Gospel, consists in their freedom from the guilt of sin, the condemning wrath of God, the rigor and curse of the law,

and in their being delivered from this present evil world, bondage to Satan, and dominion of sin, from the evil of afflictions, the fear, and sting of death, the victory of the grace, and everlasting damnation; as also in their free access to God, and their yielding obedience unto Him, not out of a slavish fear, but a child-like love and willing mind.

All which were common also to believers under the law for the substance of them; but under the New Testament, the liberty of Christians is further enlarged in their freedom from the yoke of the ceremonial law, to which the Jewish Church was subjected, and in greater boldness of access to the throne of grace, and in fuller communications of the free Spirit of God, than believers under the law did ordinarily partake of.

2. God alone is Lord of the conscience, and hath left it free from the doctrines and commandments of men which are in any thing contrary to His Word or not contained in it. So that to believe such doctrines, or obey such commands out of conscience, is to betray true liberty of conscience; and the requiring of an implicit faith, and absolute and blind obedience, is to destroy liberty of conscience and reason also.

3. They who, upon pretense of Christian liberty, do practice any sin, or cherish any sinful lust, as they do thereby pervert the main design of the grace of the Gospel to their own destruction, so they wholly destroy the end of Christian liberty; which is, that being delivered out of the hands of all our enemies, we might serve the Lord without fear, in holiness and righteousness before Him, all the days of our life.

Chapter 22:

Of Religious Worship and the Sabbath Day

1. The light of nature shows that there is a God, who hath lordship and sovereignty over all; is just, good, and doth good unto all; and is therefore to be feared, loved, praised, called upon, trusted in, and service with all the heart and all the soul and with all the might. But the acceptable way of worshipping the true God is instituted by Himself, and so limited by His own

revealed will, that He may not be worshipped according to the imaginations and devices of men, or the suggestions of Satan, under any visible representations, or any other way not pre-scribed in the Holy Scriptures.

2. Religious worship is to be given to God the Father, Son, and Holy Spirit, and to Him alone; not to angels, saints, or any other creatures; and since the fall, not without a mediator, nor in the mediation of any other but Christ alone.

3. Prayer, with thanksgiving, being one special part of natural worship, is by God required of all men. But that it may be accepted, it is to be made in the name of the Son, by the help of the Spirit, according to His will; with understanding, reverence, humility, fervency, faith, love, and perseverance; and when with others, in a known tongue.

4. Prayer is to be made for things lawful, and for all sorts of men living, or that shall live hereafter; but not for the dead, nor for those of whom it may be known, that they have sinned the sin unto death.

5. The reading of the Scriptures, preaching, and hearing the Word of God, teaching and admonishing one another in psalms, hymns, and spiritual songs, singing with grace in our hearts to the Lord; as also the administration of baptism and the Lord's supper, are all parts of religious worship of God, to be per-formed in obedience to Him, with understanding, faith, rever-ence, and godly fear; moreover, solemn humiliation, with fastings, and thanksgivings, upon special occasions, ought to be used in an holy and religious manner.

6. Neither prayer, nor any other part of religious worship, is now, under the Gospel, tied unto, or made more acceptable by, any place in which it is performed, or towards which it is directed; but God is to be worshipped every where in Spirit and in truth; as in private families daily, and in secret each one by himself, so more solemnly in the public assemblies, which are not carelessly, nor wilfully, to be neglected or forsaken, when God by His Word or providence calleth thereunto.

7. As it is of the law of nature, that in general a proportion of time, by God's appointment, be set apart for the worship of

God, so by His Word, in a positive, moral, and perpetual commandment, binding all men in all ages, He hath particularly appointed one day in seven for a sabbath to be kept holy unto Him, which from the beginning of the world, to the resurrection of Christ, was the last day of the week, and from the resurrection of Christ was changed into the first day of the week, which is called the Lord's day; and is to be continued to the end of the world, as the Christian sabbath; the observation of the last day of the week being abolished.

8. The sabbath is then kept holy unto the Lord, when men, after a due preparation of their hearts, and ordering their common affairs aforehand, do not only observe an holy rest all the day, from their own works, words, and thoughts, about their world employment, and recreations, but also are taken up the whole time in the public and private exercises of His worship, and in the duties of necessity and mercy.

Chapter 23:

We believe that (Acts 16:25, Eph. 5:19; Col. 3:16) singing the praises of God, is a holy ordinance of Christ, and not a part of natural religion, or a moral duty only; but that it is brought under divine institution, it being enjoined on the churches of Christ to sing psalms, hymns, and spiritual songs; and that the whole church in their public assemblies, as well as private Christians, ought to (Heb. 2:12, Jam. 5:13) sing God's praises according to the best light they have received. Moreover, it was practiced in the great representative church, by (Matt. 26:30, Matt. 14:26) our Lord Jesus Christ with His disciples, after He had instituted and celebrated the sacred ordinance of His Holy Supper, as a commemorative token of redeeming love.

Chapter 24:

Of Lawful Oaths and Vows

1. A lawful oath is a part of religious worship, wherein the person swearing in truth, righteousness, and judgment, sol-

emnly calleth God to witness what he sweareth and to judge him according to the truth or falseness thereof.

2. The name of God only is that by which men ought to swear; and therein it is to be used, with all holy fear and reverence; therefore to swear vainly or rashly by that glorious and dreadful name, or to swear at all by any other thing, is sinful, and to be abhorred; yet as in matter of weight and moment, for confirmation of truth, and ending all strife, an oath is warranted by Word of God; so a lawful oath being imposed, by lawful authority, in such matters, ought to be taken.

3. Whosoever taketh an oath, warranted by the Word of God, ought duly to consider the weightiness of so solemn an act, and therein to avouch nothing, but what he knoweth to be truth; for that by rash, false, and vain oaths, the Lord is provoked, and for them this land mourns.

4. An oath is to be taken in the plain and common sense of the words, without equivocation or mental reservation.

5. A vow, which is not to be made to any creature, but to God alone, is to be made and performed with all religious care and faithfulness; but popish monastical vows, of perpetual single life, professed poverty, and regular obedience, are so far from being degrees of higher perfection that they are superstitious and sinful snares, in which no Christian may entangle himself.

Chapter 25:

Of the Civil Magistrate

1. God, the supreme Lord, and King of all the world, hath ordained civil magistrates to be under Him, over the people, for His own glory, and the public good; and to this end hath armed them with the power of the sword, for defense and encouragement of them that do good, and for the punishment of evil doers.

2. It is lawful for Christians to accept and execute the office of a magistrate, when called thereunto; in the management whereof, as they ought especially to maintain justice and peace, according to the wholesome laws of each kingdom and com-

monwealth; so for that end they may lawfully now under the New Testament wage war, upon just and necessary occasions.

3. Civil magistrates being set up by God for the ends aforesaid, subjection in all lawful things commanded by them ought to be yielded by us in the Lord, not only for wrath, but for conscience's sake; and we ought to make supplications and prayers for kings and all that are in authority, that under them we may live a quiet and peaceable life, in all godliness and honesty.

Chapter 26:

Of Marriage

1. Marriage is to be between one man and one woman; neither is it lawful for any man to have more than one wife, nor for any woman to have more than one husband at the same time.

2. Marriage was ordained for the mutual help of husband and wife, for the increase of mankind with a legitimate issue, and for the preventing of uncleanness.

3. It is lawful for all sorts of people to marry, who are able with judgment to give their consent; yet it is the duty of Christians to marry [only] in the Lord; and therefore such as profess the true religion should not marry with infidels or idolaters; neither should such as are godly be unequally yoked, by marrying with such as are wicked in their life or maintain damnable heresy.

4. Marriage ought not to be within the degrees of consanguinity or affinity, forbidden in the Word; nor can such incestuous marriage ever be made lawful by any law of man or consent of parties, so as those persons may live together as man and wife.

Chapter 27:

Of the Church

1. The catholic or universal Church, which with respect to the internal work of the Spirit, and truth of grace, may be called invisible, consists of the whole number of the elect, that have been, are, or shall be gathered into one, under Christ, the head

thereof; and is the spouse, the body, the fullness of Him that fil-leth all in all.

2. All persons throughout the world, professing the faith of the Gospel, and obedience unto God by Christ according unto it, not destroying their own profession by any errors averting the foundation, or unholiness of conversation, are and may be called visible saints; and of such ought all particular congrega-tions to be constituted.

3. The purest churches under heaven are subject to mixture and error; and some have so degenerated as to become no churches of Christ, but synagogues of Satan; nevertheless Christ always hath had, and ever shall have a kingdom in this world to the end thereof, of such as believe in Him, and make professions of His name.

4. The Lord Jesus Christ is the head of the Church, in whom, by the appointment of the Father, all power for the calling, insti-tution, order, or government of the Church, is invested in a supreme and sovereign manner; neither can the pope of Rome, in any sense, be head thereof, but is [no other] than antichrist, that man of sin and son of perdition, that exalteth himself in the Church against Christ, and all that is called God; whom the Lord shall destroy with the brightness of His coming.

5. In the execution of this power wherewith he is so entrusted, the Lord Jesus calleth out of the world unto Himself, through the ministry of His Word, by His Spirit, those that are given unto Him by His Father, that they may walk before Him in all the ways of obedience, which He prescribeth to them in His Word. Those thus called, He commandeth to walk together in particular societies, or churches, for their mutual edification, and the due performance of that public worship, which He requireth of them in the world.

6. The members of these churches are saints by calling, visibly manifesting and evidencing (in and by their profession and walk-ing) their obedience unto that call of Christ; and do willingly consent to walk together according to the appointment of Christ, giving up themselves to the Lord and one to another, by

the will of God, in professed subjection to the ordinances of the Gospel.

7. To each of these churches thus gathered, according to His mind declared in His Word, He hath given all that power and authority, which is any way needful, for their carrying on that order in worship and discipline, which He hath instituted for them to observe, with commands and rules for the due and right exerting and executing of that power.

8. A particular Church gathered, and completely organized, according to the mind of Christ, consists of officers and members: and the officers appointed by Christ to be chosen and set apart by the Church (so called and gathered) for the peculiar administration of ordinances and execution of power or duty, which He entrusts them with or calls them to, to be continued to the end of the world, are bishops or elders, and deacons

9. The way appointed by Christ for the calling of any person, fitted and gifted by the Holy Spirit, unto the office of bishop or elder in the Church is, that he be chosen thereunto by the common suffrage of the Church itself; and solemnly set apart by fasting and prayer, with imposition of hands of the eldership of the Church, if there be any before constituted therein: and of a deacon, that he be chosen by the like suffrage, and set apart by prayer, and the imposition of hands.

10. The work of pastors being constantly to attend the service of Christ in His Churches, in the ministry of the Word and prayer, with watching for their souls, as they that must give an account to Him, it is incumbent on the churches to whom they minister, not only to give them all due respect, but also to communicate to them of all their good things, according to their ability, so as they may have a comfortable supply, without being themselves entangled in secular affairs; and may also be capable of exercising hospitality towards others; and this is required by the law of nature and by the express order of our Lord Jesus, who hath ordained, that they that preach the Gospel should live of the Gospel.

11. Although it be incumbent on the bishops or pastors of the churches to be instant in preaching the Word by way of office,

yet the work of preaching the Word is not so peculiarly confined to them, but that others also gifted and fitted by the Holy Spirit for it, and approved and called by the Church may and ought to perform it.

12. As all believers are bound to join themselves to particular churches, when and where they have opportunity so to do; so all that are admitted unto the privileges of a church, are also under the censures and government thereof, according to the rule of Christ.

13. No church members, upon any offense taken by them, having performed their duty required of them towards the person they are offended at, ought to disturb any church order, or absent themselves from the assemblies of the Church or administration of any ordinances, upon the account of such offense at any of their fellow members, but to wait upon Christ, in the further proceeding of the Church .

14. As each church and all the members of it are bound to pray continually for the good and prosperity of all the Churches of Christ, in all places, and upon all occasions to further it, (every one within the bounds of their places and callings, in the exercise of their gifts and graces) so the churches (when planted by the providence of God so as they may enjoy opportunity and advantage for it) ought to hold communion amongst themselves for their peace, increase of love, and mutual edification.

15. In cases of difficulties or differences, either in point of doctrine or administration, wherein either the Churches in general are concerned, or any one church, in their peace, union, and edification; or any member or members of any church are injured, in or by any proceedings in censures not agreeable to truth and order: it is according to the mind of Christ, that many churches holding communion together, do by their messengers meet to consider and give their advice in or about that matter in difference, to be reported to all the Churches concerned; howbeit, these messengers assembled, are not entrusted with any Church power properly so called; or with any jurisdiction over the Churches themselves, to exercise any censures either over

any Churches or persons; or to impose their determination on the Churches or officers.

Chapter 28:

On the Communion of Saints

1. All saints that are united to Jesus Christ their Head, by His Spirit and faith, although they are not made thereby one person with Him, have fellowship in His graces, sufferings, death, resurrection, and glory; and being united to one another in love, they have communion in each other's gifts and graces, and are obliged to the performance of such duties, public and private, in an orderly way as do conduce to their mutual good, both in the inward and outward man.

2. Saints by profession are bound to maintain an holy fellowship and communion in the worship of God, and in performing such other spiritual services as tend to their mutual edification; as also in relieving each other in outward things, according to their several abilities and necessities; which communion, according to the rule of the Gospel, though especially to be exercised by them, in the relations wherein they stand, whether in families or Churches, yet, as God offereth opportunity, is to be extended to all the household of faith, even all those who in every place call upon the name of the Lord Jesus; nevertheless their communion one with another as saints, doth not take away or infringe the title or propriety which each man hath in his goods and possessions.

Chapter 29:

Of Baptism and the Lord's Supper

1. Baptism and the Lord's supper are ordinances of positive and sovereign institution, appointed by the Lord Jesus, the only lawgiver, to be continued in His Church to the end of the world.

2. These holy appointments are to be administered by those only who are qualified, and thereunto called, according to the commission of Christ.

Chapter 30:

Of Baptism

1. Baptism is an ordinance of the New Testament, ordained by Jesus Christ to be unto the party baptized a sign of his fellowship with Him in His death and resurrection; of his being engrafted into Him; of remission of sins; and of His giving up unto God, through Jesus Christ, to live and walk in newness of life.

2. Those who do actually profess repentance towards God, faith in and obedience to our Lord Jesus, are the only proper subjects of this ordinance.

3. The outward element to be used in this ordinance is water, wherein the party is to be baptized in the name of the Father and of the Son and of the Holy Spirit.

4. Immersion, or dipping of the person in water, is necessary to the due administration of this ordinance.

Chapter 31:

We believe that laying on of hands (with prayer) upon baptized believers, as such, is an ordinance of Christ, and ought to be submitted unto by all such persons that are admitted to partake of the Lord's Supper; and that the end of this ordinance is not for the extraordinary gifts of the Spirit, but for a farther reception of the Holy Spirit of promise, or for the addition of the graces of the Spirit, and the influences thereof; to confirm, strengthen, and comfort them in Christ Jesus; it being ratified and established by the extraordinary gifts of the Spirit in the primitive times, to abide in the Church, as meeting together on the first day of the week was, that being the day of worship, or Christian Sabbath, under the gospel; and as preaching the Word was, and as baptism was, and prayer was, and singing psalms was, so this of laying on of hands was, for as the whole gospel was confirmed by signs and wonders, and divers miracles and gifts of the Holy Ghost in general, so was every ordinance in like manner confirmed in particular.

Chapter 32:

Of the Lord's Supper

1. The supper of the Lord Jesus was instituted by Him the same night wherein He was betrayed, to be observed in His Churches unto the end of the world, for the perpetual remembrance, and showing forth the sacrifice of Himself in His death, confirmation of the faith of believers in all the benefits thereof, their spiritual nourishment and growth in Him, their further engagement in and to all duties which they owe unto Him, and to be a bond and pledge of their communion with Him and with each other.

2. In this ordinance Christ is not offered up to His Father, nor any real sacrifice made at all, for remission of sin of the quick or dead, but only a memorial of that one offering up of Himself by Himself upon the cross, once for all; and a spiritual oblation of all possible praise unto God for the same. So that the popish sacrifice of the mass (as they call it) is most abominable, injurious to Christ's own only sacrifice, the alone propitiation for all the sins of the elect.

3. The Lord Jesus hath, in this ordinance, appointed His ministers to pray, and bless the elements of bread and wine, and thereby to set them apart from a common to an holy use, and to take and break the bread; to take the cup, and (they communicating also themselves) to give both to the communicants.

4. The denial of the cup to the people, worshipping the elements, the lifting them up, or carrying them about for adoration, and reserving them for any pretended religious use are all contrary to the nature of this ordinance, and to the institution of Christ.

5. The outward elements in this ordinance, duly set apart to the uses ordained by Christ, have such relation to Him crucified, as that truly, although in terms used figuratively, they are sometimes called by the name of the things they represent, to wit, the body and blood of Christ, albeit in substance and nature they still remain truly and only bread and wine as they were before.

6. That doctrine which maintains a change of the substance of bread and wine, into the substance of Christ's body and blood (commonly called transubstantiation) by consecration of a priest, or by any other way, is repugnant not to Scripture alone, but even to common sense and reason, overthroweth the nature of the ordinance, and hath been and is the cause of manifold superstitions, yea, of gross idolatries.

7. Worthy receivers, outwardly partaking of the visible elements in this ordinance, do then also inwardly by faith, really and indeed, yet not carnally and corporally, but spiritually receive, and feed upon Christ crucified, and all the benefits of His death; the body and blood of Christ being then not corporally or carnally, but spiritually present to the faith of believers in that ordinance, as the elements themselves are to their outward senses.

8. All ignorant and ungodly persons, as they are unfit to enjoy communion with Christ, so are they unworthy of the Lord's table, and cannot, without great sin against Him, while they remain such, partake of these holy mysteries or be admitted thereunto; yea, whosoever shall receive unworthily, are guilty of the body and blood of the Lord, eating and drinking judgment to themselves.

Chapter 33:

Of the State of Man after Death, and of the Resurrection of the Dead

1. The bodies of men after death return to dust and see corruption; but their souls, (which neither die nor sleep) having an immortal subsistence, immediately return to God who gave them: the souls of the righteous, being then made perfect in holiness, are received into paradise, where they are with Christ, and behold the face of God, in light and glory, waiting for the full redemption of their bodies; and the souls of the wicked are cast into hell, where they remain in torment and utter darkness, reserved to the judgment of the great day; besides these two

places for souls separated from their bodies, the Scripture acknowledgeth none.

2. At the last day, such of the saints are found alive shall not sleep, but be changed; and all the dead shall be raised up with the selfsame bodies, and none other; although with different qualities, which shall be united again to their souls for ever.

3. The bodies of the unjust shall, by the power of Christ, be raised to dishonor; the bodies of the just, by His spirit, unto honor, and be made conformable to His own glorious body.

Chapter 34:

Of the Last Judgment

1. God hath appointed a day wherein He will judge the world in righteousness, by Jesus Christ, to whom all power and judgment is given of the Father; in which day not only the apostate angels shall be judged, but likewise all persons that have lived upon the earth shall appear before the tribunal of Christ to give an account of their thoughts, words, and deeds, and to receive according to what they have done in the body, whether good or evil.

2. The end of God's appointing this day, is for the manifestation of the glory of His mercy, in the eternal salvation of the elect; and of His justice, in the eternal damnation of the reprobate, who are wicked and disobedient; for then shall the righteous go into everlasting life, and receive that fullness of joy and glory, with everlasting reward, in the presence of the Lord: but the wicked, who know not God and obey not the Gospel of Jesus Christ, shall be cast into eternal torments, and punished with everlasting destruction, from the presence of the Lord, and from the glory of His power.

3. As Christ would have us to be certainly persuaded that there shall be a day of judgment, both to deter all men from sin, and for the greater consolation of the godly in their adversity, so will He have that day unknown to men, that they may shake off all carnal security, and be always watchful, because they know

not at what hour the Lord will come, and may ever be prepared to say, "Come, Lord Jesus; Come quickly." Amen.

CHAPTER SEVEN

The Orthodox Creed (1679)

Article 1

Of the Essence of God

We verily believe that there is but one only living and true God whose subsistence is in and of Himself, whose essence cannot be comprehended by any but Himself; a most pure, spiritual, or invisible substance; who hath an absolute, independent, unchangeable, and infinite being without matter or form, body, part, or passions.

"For I am the Lord, I change not. God is a spirit. Now unto the King eternal, immortal, invisible, the only wise God be honor and glory forever and ever, Amen. Ye heard a voice, but saw no similitude." (Mal. 3:6; John 4:24; I Tim. 1:17; Deut. 14:12)

Of the Divine Attributes in God

Every particle of being in heaven and earth leads us to the infinite being of beings, namely God, who is simplicity (one mere and perfect act, without all composition, and an immense sea of perfections); who is the only eternal being, everlasting without time, whose immense presence is always everywhere present, having immutability without any alteration in being or will; in a word, God is infinite, of universal, unlimited, and incomprehensible perfection, most holy, wise, just, and good; whose wisdom is His justice, whose justice is His holiness, and whose wisdom, justice, and holiness is Himself. Most merciful, gracious, faithful, and true, a full fountain of love, and who is that perfect, sovereign, divine will, the Alpha of supreme being.

"Is it true, indeed, that God will dwell on the earth? Behold, the heaven, and heaven of heavens, cannot contain Thee: how much less this house which I have built. Great is the Lord, and worthy to be praised, and His greatness is incomprehensible" (Job 33:13; 1 Kings 8:27; Ps. 145:3).

Of the Holy Trinity

In this divine and infinite being, or unity of the Godhead, there are three persons or subsistences, the Father, the Word, or Son, and the Holy Spirit, of one substance, power, eternity, and will, each having the whole divine essence, yet the essence undivided. The Father is of none, neither begotten nor proceeding; the Son is eternally begotten of the Father; the Holy Ghost is of the Father and the Son, proceeding. All infinite, without beginning, therefore but one God, who is indivisible, and not to be divided in nature or being, but distinguished by several properties and personal relations; and we worship and adore a Trinity in unity, and a unity in Trinity, three Persons and but one God; which doctrine of the Trinity is the foundation of all our communion with God and comfortable dependence on Him.

"And there are three that bare record in heaven, the Father, the Word, and the Holy Spirit, and these three are one. Baptizing them in the name of the Father, Son, and Holy Ghost." (1 John 5:7; Matt. 28:19).

Article 4

Of the Divine Nature, or Godhead of Christ

We confess and believe that the Son of God, or the eternal Word, is very and true God, having His personal subsistence of the Father alone, and yet forever of Himself as God; and of the Father as the Son, the eternal Son of an eternal Father; not later in beginning. There was never any time when He was not, not less in dignity, not other in substance, begotten without diminution of His Father that begat, of one nature and substance with the Father; begotten of the Father, while the Father communicated wholly to the Son, which He retained wholly in Himself, because both were infinite, without inequality of nature, without division of essence, neither made, nor created, nor adopted, but begotten before all time; not a metaphorical or subordinate God; not a God by office, but a God by nature, co-equal, co-essential, and co-eternal with the Father and the Holy Ghost.

"Jesus said unto them, 'Verily, verily, I say unto you, before Abraham was, I am.' Jesus Christ the same yesterday and today and forever. David therefore calleth Him Lord, how is He then His Son?" (John 8:58; Heb. 13:8; Luke 20:44)

Article 5

Of the Second Person of the Holy Trinity, Taking Our Flesh

We believe that the only begotten Son of God, the second person in the sacred Trinity, took to Himself a true, real, and fleshly body, and reasonable soul, being conceived in the fullness of time, by the Holy Ghost, and born of the virgin Mary, and became very and true man like unto us in all things, even in our infirmities, sin only excepted, as appeareth by His conception, birth, life, and death. He was of a woman, and by the power of the Holy Ghost, in a supernatural and miraculous manner, was formed of the only seed, or substance of the virgin Mary, in which respect He hath the name of the Son of man, and is the true Son of David, the fruit of the virgin's womb, to that end He might die for Adam (Gen. 26:17; Heb. 2:16).

Article 6

Of the Union of the Two Natures in Christ

We believe the person of the Son of God, being a person from all eternity existing, did assume the most pure nature of man, wanting all personal existing of its own, into the unity of His person, or Godhead, and made it His own; the properties of each nature being preserved, and this inseparable and indissolvable union of both natures, and was made by the Holy Ghost, sanctifying our nature in the virgin's womb, without change of either nature, or mixture of both, and of two natures is one Christ, God-man, or Immanuel, God with us. Which mystery exceeds the conception of men, and is the wonder of angels, one only Mediator, Jesus Christ, the Son of God.

Article 7

Of the Communication of Properties

We believe that the two natures in Christ continue still distinct in substance, properties, and actions, and remain one and the same Christ: For the properties of the Godhead cannot agree to the properties of the manhood, nor the properties of the manhood to the properties of the Godhead; for as the Godhead or divine nature cannot thirst, or be hungry, no more can the manhood be in all, or many places at once. Therefore, we believe, the Godhead was neither turned nor transfused into the manhood, nor the manhood into the Godhead, but both, the divine nature keepeth entire all His essential properties to its self, so that the humanity is neither omnipotent, omniscient, nor omnipresent: And the human also keepeth His properties, though often that which is proper to the one nature, is spoken of the person denominated from the other, which must be understood by the figure synecdoche (a part being taken for the whole, by reason of the union of both natures into one person).

"Hereby perceive we love of God, because He laid down His life for us" (1 John 3:16).

Article 8

Of the Holy Spirit

We believe that there is one Holy Spirit, the third Person subsisting in the sacred Trinity, one with the Father and Son, who is very and true God, of one substance or nature with the Father and Son, co-equal, co-eternal, and co-essential with the Father and Son, to whom with the Father and Son, three Persons, and but one eternal and almighty God, be by all the hosts of saints and angels, ascribed eternal glory and hallelujahs. Amen.

Article 9

Of Predestination and Election

The decrees of God are founded on infinite wisdom, and situate in eternity, and are crowned with infallibility, as to the event. Now predestination unto life is the everlasting purpose of God, whereby before the foundation of the world was laid, He hath constantly decreed in His counsel secret to us to deliver from curse and damnation those whom He hath chosen in Christ, and bring them to everlasting salvation as vessels made to honor through Jesus Christ, whom He elected before the foundation of the world, and is called God's elect, in whom His soul delighteth, being the Lamb foreordained and so predesti-

nated unto the superlative glory of the hypostatical union. And
this not for any foreseen holiness in His human nature, with all
that did flow out of the hypostatical union, being elected of
mere grace, as are all the members of His mystical body. And
God the Father gave this His elected and beloved Son, for a covenant to the people, and said that His covenant shall stand fast
with Him; and His seed shall endure forever. And albeit God the
Father be the efficient cause of all good things He intended to
us, yet Christ is the meriting cause of all those good things God
intended to us in election (repentance, faith, and sincere obedience to all God's commandments). And so God the Father, that
He might bring about the eternal salvation of His elect, chose
the man Christ, with respect to His human nature, out of the
fallen lump of mankind, which in the fullness of time, He made
of a woman, made under the law, to redeem those that were
under it, that we might receive the adoption of sons. And
though Christ came from Adam, as Eve did, yet not by Adam, as
Cain did (by natural propagation). Therefore without any stain
of sin, and this second Adam, being by God's eternal decree,
excepted out of the first covenant, as being neither God the
Father, who was justly offended, nor yet sinful Adam, who had
offended Him in breaking of it. Therefore Christ, the second
Adam, was a fit Mediator between God and man, to reconcile
both in Himself, by the shedding and sprinkling of His blood,
according to God's eternal purpose in electing of Christ, and of
all that do, or shall believe in Him, which eternal election or
covenant transaction between the Father and Son is very consistent with His revealed will in the Gospel; for we ought not to
oppose the grace of God in electing of us, nor yet the grace of
the Son in dying for all men and so for us, not yet the grace of
the Holy Ghost in propounding the Gospel and persuading us
to believe it. For until we do believe, the effects of God's displeasure are not taken from us; for the wrath of God abideth on
all them that do not believe in Christ; for the actual declaration
in the court of conscience is by faith as an instrument, not for
faith as a meriting cause: for Christ is the meriting cause of eternal life to all that believe, but not of God's will to give eternal

life to them, nor yet of God's decree to save us, albeit we are chosen in Christ before the foundation of the world. Now faith is necessary as the way of our salvation, as an instrumental cause: but the active and passive obedience of Christ is necessary as a meriting cause of our salvation; therefore God's eternal decree doth not oppose His revealed will in the Gospel, it being but one, not two diverse or contrary wills. For His decree as King, decreeth the event, or what shall be done infallibly; but His command as a lawgiver, sheweth not what shall be done, but what is the duty of man to do, and leave undone. Therefore God hath, we believe, decreed that faith as the means and salvation as the end shall be joined together, that where one is the other must be also, for it is written, he that believeth shall be saved; also, believe in the Lord Jesus Christ, and thou shalt be saved. Now here is a great mystery indeed, for God so administereth His absolute decree that He leaveth us much place for an efficacious conditional dispensation, as if the decree itself were conditional.

Article 10

Of Preterition or Reprobation

We do believe, that known unto God are all His works from eternity; therefore He foresaw Adam's fall, but did not decree it, yet foreseeing it in His eternal counsel and wisdom, did elect and choose Jesus Christ, and all that do or shall believe in Him, out of that fallen lump of mankind. And hath manifested His love and grace by Jesus Christ, His elect or beloved Son, through the Gospel means, to all; and hath given us His Word and oath, to assure us that He desires not the death of the wicked, but rather that they repent or return to Him and live, and if any do perish, their destruction is of themselves: and hath decreed to punish all those wicked or ungodly, disobedient, and unbelieving or impenitent sins, that have or shall despise His grace, love, and wooings, or strivings of the Holy Ghost, or long-suffering, whether by a total and continued rejection of grace or by an universal and final apostasy; and such persons, so living and dying, shall be punished with everlasting destruction in hell fire, with the fallen angels or devils and shall be fixed in an irrecoverable state of damnation, irrevocable under the wrath of God, they being the proper objects of it; and shall remain under His inexpressible wrath and justice, in inconceivable torment, soul and body, to all eternity.

Article 11

Of Creation

In the beginning it pleased God the Father, Son, and Holy Ghost according to His eternal and immutable decree for the manifestation of the glory of His eternal power, wisdom, and goodness, to create or make out of nothing, the world, and all things therein, whether visible or invisible, and created man male and female, with a fleshly body and a reasonable and invisible, or spiritual, angelical, and immortal soul, made after the image of God, in knowledge, righteousness, and true holiness, having the law written in His heart and power or liberty of will to fulfil it, yet mutable, or under a possibility of transgressing, being left to the liberty of their own will, which was subject to change; and also gave them command not to eat of the tree of knowledge of good and evil, and while they kept this command, they enjoyed most happy communion with God, and had dominion over the creatures. And all this wonderful work of creation, both in heaven and in earth, was finished in the space of six days and all very good, and though reason cannot conceive nor comprehend it, yet God's Word hath plainly revealed it and faith believes it.

Article 12

Of Divine Providence

The Almighty God that created all things and gave them their being by His infinite power and wisdom, doth sustain and uphold and move, direct, dispose, and govern all creatures and things from the greatest to the least, according to the counsel of

His own good will and pleasure, for His own glory and His creatures, good.

Article 13

Of the First Covenant

The first covenant was made between God and man, before man had sinned in eating of the forbidden fruit in which covenant God required of man perfect obedience to all the commands thereof, and in case He did so obey He promised to be his God. And on the other part, man promised to perform entire and perfect obedience to all God's Holy commands in that covenant, by that strength wherewith God endowed him in his first creation; by the improvement of which he might have attained unto eternal life without faith, in the blood of the mediator of the new covenant of grace; but he sinning against this covenant, which consisted in two roots (to love God above all things, and his neighbor as himself); it being the substance of that law which was afterwards written in two tables of stone and delivered unto Moses upon Mount Sinai, and fell under the just sentence of eternal death, which was the punishment that God had appointed for the breach of it. And under this righteous judgment of God, Adam and his natural posterity had forever remained, as the fallen angels do, had not God of His infinite grace and love provided His Son to take unto Himself our nature and so became a fit Mediator between God the Father, who was offended, and man, who had offended Him in breaking His Holy law and covenant.

Article 14

Of the Fall of Man, of His Sin, and of the Punishment Thereof

The first man, Adam, in eating voluntarily of the forbidden fruit, incurred the curse of God upon himself, and all his posterity that came of him by natural propagation (corporal and spiritual death, in body and soul eternally); but this covenant was not only made with him, but with his seed also, which should descend from his loins by natural generation; he standing as a public person in the stead of all mankind. And, as St. Paul saith, by him came sin and death by sin, and so deprived himself and all his posterity of that original righteousness which God created him in.

Article 15

Of Original, or Birth, Sin

Original sin is the fault and corruption of the nature of every man that naturally descendeth from Adam by natural generation, by means of which man has not only lost that original righteousness that God created him in, but is naturally inclined to all manner of evil, being conceived in sin and brought forth in iniquity; and, as St. Paul saith, the flesh lusteth against the spirit. And therefore every man justly deserveth God's wrath and damnation. And this concupiscence, or indwelling lust, remaineth even in the regenerate, that they cannot love nor obey God perfectly in this life, according to the tenor of the first covenant.

Article 16

Of the New Covenant of Grace

The first covenant being broken by man's disobedience and by his sin, he was excluded from the favor of God and eternal life, in which deplorable condition of his, God being pleased out of His free grace and love to fallen man, in order to his recovery out of this sinful and deplorable estate, hath freely offered him a second, or a new covenant of grace, which new covenant of grace if Jesus Christ, in remission of sins, through faith in His blood, which God hath promised to give to all them that do obey and submit to the conditions of this covenant, which covenant of grace and eternal salvation annexed to it, is freely and fully offered unto all men upon the terms of the Gospel (repentance and faith). And the benefits of this covenant, by God's free grace through the redemption that is in Jesus Christ whom God has set forth to be a propitiation through faith in His blood, to declare His righteousness for the remission of sins that are past through the forbearance of God, that he might be just, and the justifier of him that believeth in Jesus. Therefore, we conclude, that a man is justified by faith without the deeds of the law; for by faith we receive that righteousness that the law, or the first covenant, required of the first Adam; which righteousness Christ hath fulfilled in our nature which He took of the virgin Mary, by His active obedience and is, by God's free donation, made over to us by imputation; for He hath made Him to us wisdom, righteousness, and sanctification. For as by one man's disobedience, many were made sinners, so by the obedience of one, that is Christ, shall many be made righteous. For Christ hath not only fulfilled the sanction of the law (to love God with all his heart and his neighbor as himself), but hath also voluntarily suffered the curse of the law, being made a curse for us that we might receive the blessing of Abraham and the promise of the Spirit through faith in His blood. And now, albeit the essential righteousness of Christ, as He is God equal with His Father, be not imputed unto us, not yet His person righteousness, as He was or is man, only, yet we believe His mediatorial righteousness, as God man, is imputed, reckoned, or made over to us, upon the terms of this new covenant of grace; and so being justified by His grace, we are thereby made heirs according to the hope of eternal life: for, as St. Paul saith, "If righteousness come by the law, then Christ is dead in vain" (Gal. 2:21).

Article 17

Of Christ and His Mediatorial Office

It pleased God, in His eternal purpose, to choose and ordain the Lord Jesus Christ, His only begotten Son, according to the covenant made between them both, to be the alone Mediator between God and man (God the Father, who was by Adam's sin justly offended, and Adam, our common parent, the person offending). Now in order to reconcile God to man and man to God, who were at a distance, Christ Jesus, the second Person in the Trinity, being very God, of the same substance with His Father, did, when the fullness of time was come, take unto Him man's nature, with all the essential properties, and common infirmities, sin only excepted, being made of a woman of the seed of Abraham and David; and although He came from Adam and had truly the nature of man, yet not by Adam; and the person of Christ took our nature into union with the divine nature, but He did not take the person of Adam which sinned, therefore we believe He was neither the covenantee, nor yet the coventanter, and so, by consequence, neither the creditor nor the debtor. And being concerned by this office or appointment of the Father to make peace, it plainly appears, that He is the only fit Mediator between God and man, who is very God and very man; yet one Christ, who was sanctified, and anointed with the Holy Spirit above measure and was superlatively and admirably fitted for, and called unto this office by His Father, who put all judgment into His hand, and power to execute the same, and He willingly understood the same; and being made under the law, did perfectly fulfil or keep it, and underwent the punishment due to us, which we should have suffered; for sin and the punishment of it, being reckoned or imputed to Him, He being made a curse for us and underwent and trod the winepress of His Father's wrath for us, in dolorous pangs and agony of soul and painful sufferings in His body, was crucified, dead, and buried, or remained in the state of the dead, yet saw no corruption and on the third day He arose from the dead, with the same body in which He suffered, with which He also ascended, and there sitteth at the right hand of His Father, making intercession for His saints, and shall return to judge men and angels at the end of the world. And the same Lord Jesus, by His perfect obedience to the whole law, and sacrifice of Himself, which He, through the eternal Spirit offered up unto the Father, hath fully satisfied the justice of God and reconciled Him to us; and hath purchased an everlasting inheritance in the kingdom of heaven, for all those that the Father hath given unto Him, and now, by a continued act of intercession in heaven, doth apply the benefits He hath purchased unto the elect. And in this office of Mediator, He hath the dignity of three offices (Priest, Prophet, and King): all which offices are necessary for the benefit of His church and without which we can never be saved. For, in respect of our ignorance, we stand in need of His prophetical office, and in respect of our alienation from God, and imperfect services, and God's wrath and justice, we stand in need of His priestly office, to reconcile God to us, and us to God; and in respect of our bondage to sin and Satan, and adverseness to return to God, we need His kingly office to subdue our enemies and deliver us captives out of the kingdom and power of sin, and preserve us to His heavenly kingdom. And thus, in our nature, He living the life of the law, and suffering the penalty due to us, continually presents us at the throne of grace; so is a most wonderful and complete Mediator for His elect.

Article 18

Of Christ Dying for All Mankind

God the Father, out of His royal bounty and fountain of love, when all mankind was fallen by sin, in breaking of the first covenant of works made with them in Adam, did choose Jesus Christ, and sent Him into the world to die for Adam, or fallen man. And God's love is manifest to all mankind, in that He is not willing, as himself hath sworn, and abundantly declared in His Word, that mankind should perish eternally, but would have all to be saved and come to the knowledge of the truth. And Christ died for all men, and there is a sufficiency in His death and merits for the sins of the whole world, and hath appointed the Gospel to be preached unto all and hath sent forth His Spirit to accompany the Word in order to beget repentance and faith: so that if any do perish, it's not for want of the means of grace manifested by Christ to them, but for the non-improvement of the grace of God, offered freely to them through Christ in the Gospel.

Article 19

Of the Agreement Between the Old and New Testament

The Gospel, or new covenant, was held forth or preached to the father, from Adam to Christ's coming in the flesh, though it was revealed by sundry degrees and in diverse manners, in types and shadows, darkly; yet it was the same Gospel, the same Christ, the same faith for kind, and the very same covenant, that they were justified and saved by, before Christ took flesh of the virgin, that we have now, and is to continue to the end of the world. For as the church of the Jews, in their Gospel types, had a priest and an altar, and a lamb and a fire, and without all these no sacrifice could or was accepted of God, then, nor now, without faith in the anti-type, Christ, whose human nature is the true lamb, the union of natures, the High Priest, the divine nature, the altar, and the Holy Ghost, the heavenly fire. And again, the blood shed upon the brazen altar, may be applied to our justification, and the sprinkling of it upon the incense altar, may be applied to the work of sanctification of Christ's Spirit, sprinkling His blood upon us. And the blood that was carried within the veil, into the most Holy place, is applied to our glorification in heaven. And as they had in their church the ark, a figure of Christ's presence, so have we the promise of His presence to the end of the world. And as they had the tables of the old covenant or law, in the ark, so have we the law fulfilled by Christ; and meeting God in Christ, it's handed forth by Christ now to us, as the only rule of our sanctification and obedience through His grace. And as they had the manna to nourish them in the wilderness Canaan; so have we the sacraments to nourish us in the church, and in our wilderness-condition, till we come to heaven. And as they had the rod that corrected them; so have we the church censures now to correct us, when we offend His law; and their burnt offerings may be applied to Christ, killing of original sin in us, and their sin offering may be applied to Christ, killing or taking away our actual sins, and their peace offering may be applied to our reconciliation with God in Christ by His Spirit, and so all the rest of those Gospel-anti-types may be applied. And thus the Old and New Testament, like the faces of the cherubims, look one toward another, and hold forth the self-same Gospel, salvation to them and us.

Article 20

Of Free-Will in Man

God hath endued the will of man with that natural liberty and power of acting upon choice, that it's neither forced, nor by any necessity of nature determined to do good or evil: but man, in the state of innocency, had such power and liberty of will to choose and perform that which was acceptable and well-pleasing to God, according to the requirement of the first covenant; but he falling from his state of innocency, wholly lost all ability, or liberty of will, to any spiritual good, for his eternal salvation, his will being now in bondage under sin and Satan, and therefore not able of his own strength to convert himself nor prepare himself thereunto, without God's grace, taketh away the enmity out of his will, and by his special grace, freeth him from his natural bondage under sin, enabling him to will freely and sincerely, that which is spiritually good, according to the tenure of the new covenant of grace in Christ, though not perfectly, according to the tenure of the first covenant, which perfection of will is only attainable in the state of glory, after the redemption or resurrection of our fleshly bodies.

Article 21

Of Vocation and Effectual Calling

Vocation, or calling, general or common, is, when God by the means of His Word and Spirit, freely of His own grace and goodness, doth ministerially acquaint mankind with His gracious good purpose of salvation by Jesus Christ; inviting and wooing them to come to Him, and to accept of Christ revealing unto them the Gospel covenant, and those that are cordial hearts do improve this common grace, be in time worketh unfeigned faith and sincere repentance in them; and by His grace they come to accept of Christ as their only Lord and Savior, with their whole heart; and God becomes their Father in Christ, and they being then effectually called, are by faith united to Jesus Christ by grace unto salvation.

Article 22

Of Evangelical Repentance

Unfeigned repentance is an inward and true sorrow of heart for sin, with sincere confession of the same to God, especially that we have offended so gracious a God and so loving a Father, together with a settled purpose of heart and a careful endeavor to leave all our sins, and to live a more holy and sanctified life according to all God's commands. Or it is a turning or change of the whole man to God, with endeavor, through His grace, to mortify the indwelling lust or corruptions and obtain a great reformation both in the outward and inward man, according to the will of God, and this repentance, for the nature of it, must be continued throughout the whole course of our lives and is wrought in us by the Spirit of God; by the ministry of the law and Gospel, in order to our obedience to Christ, or being baptized in His name, but this repentance unto life is not wrought without faith in the soul; for by faith we receive that grace, that perfects or carrieth on the work of repentance in the soul, from first to last.

Article 23

Of Justifying and Saving Faith

Faith is an act of the understanding, giving a firm assent to the things contained in the Holy Scriptures. But justifying faith is a grace or habit, wrought in the soul by the Holy Ghost, through preaching the Word of God, whereby we are enabled to believe, not only that the Messiah is offered to us, but also to take and receive Him, as a Lord and Savior, and wholly and only to rest unto Christ for grace and eternal salvation.

Article 24

Of Justification by Christ

Justification is a declarative or judicial sentence of God the Father, whereby He of His infinite love and free grace, for the alone and mediatorial righteousness of His own Son, performed in our nature and stead, which righteousness of God man, the Father imputing to us, and by effectual faith, received and embraced by us, doth free us by judicial sentence from sin and death, and accept us righteous in Christ our surety, unto eternal life; the active and passive obedience of Christ being the accomplishment of all that righteousness and sufferings the law or justice of God required, and this being perfectly performed by our Mediator, in the very nature of us men, and accepted by the Father in our stead, according to that eternal covenant-transaction, between the Father and the Son. And hereby we have deliverance from the guilt and punishment of all our sins, and are accounted righteous before God, at the throne of grace, by the lone righteousness of Christ the Mediator, imputed, or reckoned unto us through faith; for we believe there are six necessary causes of man's justification or salvation: First, the efficient cause of our justification is God's free grace. Secondly, the meritorious cause is the blood of Christ. Thirdly, the material cause is Christ's active obedience. Fourthly, the imputation of Christ, His obedience for us is the formal cause. Fifthly, the instrumental cause is faith. Sixthly, God's glory and man's salvation is the final cause. Now we principally apply the first and last to God the Father; the second and third to Christ the Mediator; the fourth and fifth to the blessed Comforter, the Holy Ghost; hence it is we are baptized in the name of the Father, of the Son, and Holy Ghost, and so we worship a trinity in unity and unity in trinity.

Article 25

Of Reconciliation and Sonship by Christ

Two privileges flow out of our justification by faith in Christ, our reconciliation and adoption, or sonship. Reconciliation is a gracious privilege, whereby we that were enemies are made friends; or we that were enemies, rebels, and aliens are received into favor or brought near to God through faith in Christ Jesus. And adoption is that power and privilege to be the sons of God through faith in Christ our surety, who being the eternal Son of God, became by incarnation our brother, that by Him God might bring many sons unto glory, according to His eternal decree of preserving the human nature of Christ that it never fell in Adam. And so we are, by faith according to God's free grace and Christ's purchase or redemption and the Holy spirit's application of it to us, made heirs and joint heirs with Christ, our elder Brother, of the same kingdom, and stupendous and unutterable glory forever and ever.

Article 26

Of Sanctification and Good Works

Those that are united unto Christ by effectual faith are regenerated and have a new heart and spirit created in them through the virtue of Christ His death, resurrection and inter-cession and by the efficacy of the Holy Spirit, received by faith and are sanctified by the Word and Spirit of truth, dwelling in them, by destroying and pulling down the strong holds, or dominion of sin and lust and more and more quickened and strengthened in all saving graces in the practice of holiness without which no man shall see the Lord. And this sanctifica-tion is throughout the whole man, though imperfect in this life, there abiding still in the best saints, some remnants of corrup-tion, which occasions a continual war in the soul, the flesh lust-ing against the spirit and the spirit against the flesh; yet through the continual supply of strength from Christ, which flows from Him to believers by means of the covenant of grace or hypostatical union with our nature, the regenerate part doth overcome, pressing after a heavenly life in evangelical obedience to all the commands that Christ, their King, and Lawgiver, hath commanded them in His Word or Holy Scriptures, which are the only rule and square of our sanctification and obedience in all good works and piety. And since our only assistance to good works, such as God hath commanded, is of God, who worketh in us both to will and to do, we have no cause to boast, nor ground to conclude, we merit anything thereby, we receiving all of free and undeserved grace, and when we have done the most, yet we are unprofitable servants and do abundantly fall short; and the best duties that we can now perform will not abide the judgment of God. Neither do any good works whatsoever, that are done by unregenerate men or without faith in and love to Christ, please God or are accepted of Him. Yet good works are of great advantage, being done in faith and love and wrought by the Holy spirit and are to be done by us, to show our thankfulness to God, for the grace of the new covenant by Christ and to fit us more and more for glory. And in this sense the ten commandments, as handed forth by Christ, the Mediator, are a rule of life to a believer, and show us our duty to God and man, as also our need of the grace of God and merit of Christ.

Article 27

Of Baptism and the Lord's Supper

Those two sacraments (baptism and the Lord's Supper) are ordinances of positive, sovereign, and Holy institution, appointed by the Lord Jesus Christ, the only Lawgiver, to be continued in His church to the end of the world; and to be administered by those only who are rightly qualified and thereunto called according to the command of Christ.

Article 28

Of the Right Subject and Administration of Holy Baptism

Baptism is an ordinance of the New Testament, ordained by Jesus Christ to be unto the party baptized, or dipped, a sign of our entrance into the covenant of grace and ingrafting into Christ and into the body of Christ, which is His church; and of remission of sin in the blood of Christ and of our fellowship with Christ in His death and resurrection, and of our living or rising to newness of life. And orderly none ought to be admitted into the visible church of Christ without being first baptized; and those which do really profess repentance towards God and faith in and obedience to our Lord Jesus Christ, are the only proper subjects of this ordinance, according to our Lord's holy institution and primitive practice; and ought by the minister or administrator to be done in a solemn manner, in the name of the Father, Son, and Holy Ghost, by immersion or dipping of the person in the element of water; this being necessary to the due administration of this holy sacrament, as Holy Scripture shows and the first and best antiquity witnesseth for some centuries of years. But the popish doctrine which they teach and believe, that those infants that die without baptism, or have it not actually or in desire, are not, nor cannot be saved, we do not believe. Nor yet their practice of admitting persons only upon an implicit faith of the church, nor their superstitious and popish ceremonies of salt and spittle and breathing on the face of the party baptized, together with their chrisoms and hallowed lights. Neither do we believe that infants dying in infancy, without baptism, go to purgatory or "limbus infantum" as they erroneously teach. Nor do we believe that the Pope of Rome or any other persons whomsoever, have power to alter or change this ordinance of Christ, as they have done by this superstitious and such like idolatrous inventions and practices of the Romish church. All which superstitions of theirs, the contrary to Christ's institution, or the apostles practice of holy baptism.

Article 29

Of the Invisible Catholic Church of Christ

There is one holy catholic church, consisting of, or made up of the whole number of the elect, that have been, are, or shall be gathered, in one body under Christ, the only Head thereof; which church is gathered by special grace and the powerful and internal work of the Spirit; and are effectually united unto Christ their Head, and can never fall away.

Article 30

Of the Catholic Church as Visible

Nevertheless, we believe the visible church of Christ on earth is made up of several distinct congregations, which make up that one catholic church or mystical body of Christ. And the marks by which she is known to be the true spouse of Christ are these: Where the Word of God is rightly preached and the sacraments truly administered, according to Christ's institution and the practice of the primitive church; having discipline and government duly executed, by ministers or pastors of God's appointing, and the church's election, that is a true constituted church; to which church and not elsewhere, all persons that seek for eternal life should gladly join themselves. And although there may be many errors in such a visible church or congregations, they being not infallible, yet those errors being not fundamental and the church in the major or governing part being not guilty, she is not thereby unchurched; nevertheless she ought to detect those errors and to reform according to God's Holy Word and from such visible church or congregations, no man ought, by any pretense whatever, schismatically to separate.

Article 31

Of Officers in the Church of Christ

The visible church of Christ, being completely gathered and organized, according to the mind of Christ, consists of officers and members; and the officers, appointed by Christ, to be chosen by His church, for the peculiar administration of ordinances and execution of the power and duty Christ hath enjoined them to the end of the world, are these three: Bishops, or messengers; and elders, or pastors; and deacons, or overseers of the poor; and the way appointed by Christ for the calling of any person fitted and gifted by the Holy Ghost unto the office of bishop or messenger in the churches is, that he be chosen thereunto by the common suffrage of the church and solemnly set apart by fasting and prayer, with imposition of hands by the bishops of the same function, ordinarily, and those bishops so ordained, have the government of those churches, that had suffrage in their election and no other ordinarily; as also to preach the Word or Gospel to the world or unbelievers. And the particular pastor, or elder, in like manner is to be chosen by the common suffrage of the particular congregation, and ordained by the bishop or messenger God hath placed in the church He hath charge of; and the elder, so ordained, is to watch over that particular church; and he may not ministerially act in any other church before he be sent, neither ought his power or office anyway to infringe the liberty or due power or office of his bishop, God being a God of order, having ordained things most harmoniously, tending every way to unity. The deacons are in like manner to be chosen by election and ordination, and are in their particular congregations, to receive the charity and free benevolence of the people; and the bishops and elders so chosen and ordained, to the world of God, ought to be enabled and capacitated thereunto by a sufficient and honorable maintenance of the people that chosen them, answerable to the dignity of their places, and charge committed to them, without which they cannot discharge their duty, as they ought to do, in studying to divide the Word of God aright, as St. Paul adviseth Timothy, and also to give themselves wholly to it; and this maintenance is to be given out of the labors, profits and estates of the people, by equality and proportionable to their ability in liberality, God having reserved a portion for all His laborers, out of all the members' worldly goods and possessions.

Article 32

Of Prayer with Laying on of Hands

Prayer, with imposition of hands by the bishop or elder on baptized believers, as such, for the reception of the Holy promised Spirit of Christ, we believe is a principle of Christ's doctrine and ought to be practiced and submitted to by every baptized believer in order to receive the promised Spirit of the Father and Son.

Article 33

Of the End and Right
Administration of the Lord's Supper

The supper of the Lord Jesus was instituted by Him the same night wherein He was betrayed; to be observed in His church to the end of the world for the perpetual remembrance and showing forth the sacrifice of Himself in His death; and for the confirmation of the faithful believers in all the benefits of His death and resurrection and spiritual nourishment and growth in Him; sealing unto them their continuance in the covenant of grace and to be a band and pledge of communion with Him, and an obligation of obedience to Christ, both passively and actively, as also of our communion and union each with other, in the participation of this Holy sacrament. And the outward elements of bread and wine, after they are set apart by the hand of the minister from common use and blessed or consecrated by the Word of God and prayer the bread being broken and wine poured forth signify to the faithful, the body and blood of Christ, or holdeth forth Christ, and Him crucified; and the minister distributing the bread and wine to the communicants, who are to take or receive both the bread and wine at the hands of the ministers applying it by faith, with thanksgiving to God the Father, for so great a benefit, and no unbaptized, unbelieving, or open profane or wicked heretical persons ought to be admitted to this ordinance to profane it.

Neither is that popish doctrine of transubstantiation to be admitted of, nor adoration of the unbloody sacrifice of the mass, as they call it, together with their denying of the cup to the laity, and many more idolatrous and superstitious practices, decreed in the popish councils of Lateran and Trent. In opposition to which, and such like idolatry of Rome, many of our worthy and famous ancients and renowned protestants, lost their lives by fire and faggot in England, whose spirits we hope are now in heaven as worthy martyrs and witnesses of Christ, in bearing a faithful testimony to this holy ordinance of their Lord and Master. Neither may we admit of consubstantiation, it being not consonant to God's Word. Nor are little infants, that cannot examine themselves, nor give account of their faith, nor understand what is signified by the outward signs of bread and wine to be admitted to this sacrament. Though St. Austin taught so from John 6:63, and many of the Greek churches so believe and practice to this day. And this holy ordinance ought to be celebrated among the faithful with examination of themselves (of their faith and love and knowledge of these holy and divine mysteries), lest they eat and drink their own damnation, for profaning of God's holy ordinance, as many, we fear, have done, and yet do at this day; whose hard and blind hearts the Lord in mercy open, if it be His blessed will.

Article 34

Of the Discipline and Government of the Church of Christ

We believe that the great King and Lawgiver, Christ, the universal and only Head of His church, hath given to His visible church a subordinate power, or authority, for the well-being, ordering, and governing of it, for His own glory and the church's profit and good, the executive part of which derivative power of discipline and government is committed to His ministers, proportionable to their dignities and places in the church in a most harmonious way, for the beauty, order, government, and establishment of the same, and consisteth in the exercise and execution of the censors, or rod of correction, he hath appointed therein, for the purgation or pruning of the same, in order to present scandals and offenses, both public and private. And in case of personal and private trespasses between party and party, that the member so offended, tell his offense to his brother, between them alone; and if he shall not hear him, to take one or two more; if he will not hear him then, to tell it unto the church: And the ministers of Christ ought to rebuke them sharply, that sin before them in the church; and in case there be any wicked, public, and scandalous sinners or obstinate heretics, that then the church ought speedily to convene such her members and labor to convict them of their sin and heresy, schism, and profaneness, whatsoever it be; and after such regular suspension and due admonition, if such sinners repent not; that then for the honor of God and preserving the credit of religion and in order to save the sinner's soul, and good of the church, in obedience to God's law, to proceed and excommunicate the sinner, by a judicial sentence in the name of Christ and His church, tendering an admonition of repentance to him, with gravity, love, and authority, and all this without hypocrisy or partiality, praying for the sinner, that his soul may be saved in the day of the Lord; and under this second degree, of withdrawing or excommunication to account him as a heathen or publican that he may be ashamed. But upon the third and highest act of excommunication, it being a most dreadful thunderclap of God's judgment, it is most difficult for any church now to proceed in, it being difficult to know when any man hath sinned the unpardonable sin, and so to incur a total cutting off from the church.

Article 35

Of Communion of Saints and Giving to the Poor

All Christians that have been baptized into one faith and united in one true visible way of worshipping the true God, by

Christ Jesus our Lord, should keep the unity of the Spirit, in the bond of peace, seeing there is but one mystical body of Christ and should have fellowship and communion in each other's sufferings, or afflictions, for if one member suffer, all are pained with it. Hence it is also they partake of each other's gifts in great variety, which make the harmony of dependency on each other, seeing a need of every member, for the public use and common profit of the whole, both in the private as well as more public and solemn worship of God's house; as also an interest in each other's goods and possessions, so far as comports with necessity and charity, according to the charter privileges, or law of their king; and though no equality or property be pleaded for; yet the works of charity and mercy must be minded as a duty to lend to the Lord and pity and relieve the Lord's poor, weekly laying out for them as God hath prospered us, according to our ability in freedom, liberality, and charity, according to our brethren's necessity, whether sick or in prison, to visit and relieve them, and not only within the church, but to all as we have opportunity and ability to be doing good.

Article 36

Of Perseverance

Those that are effectually called, according to God's eternal purpose, being justified by faith, do receive such a measure of the holy unction from the Holy Spirit, by which they shall certainly persevere unto eternal life.

Article 37

Of the Sacred Scripture

The authority of the Holy Scripture dependeth not upon the authority of any man, but only upon the authority of God, who hath delivered and revealed His mind therein unto us, and containeth all things necessary for salvation; so that whatsoever is not read therein, nor may be proved thereby, is not to be required of any man, that it should be believed as an article of the Christian faith or be thought requisite to salvation. Neither ought we, since we have the Scriptures delivered to us now, to depend upon, hearken to, or regard the pretended immediate inspirations, dreams, or prophetical predictions, by or from any person whatsoever, lest we be deluded by them. Nor yet do we believe that the works of creation nor the law written in the heart (natural religion, as some call it, or the light within man, as such) is sufficient to inform man of Christ the Mediator or of the way to salvation or eternal life by Him; but the Holy Scriptures are necessary to instruct all men into the way of salvation and eternal life. And we do believe that all people ought to have them in their mother tongue and diligently and constantly to read them in their particular places and families for their edification and comfort; and endeavor to frame their lives, according to the direction of God's Word, both in faith and practice, the Holy Scriptures being of no private interpretation, but ought to be interpreted according to the analogy of faith and is the best interpreter of itself and is sole judge in controversy. And no decrees of popes or councils or writings of any person whatsoever are of equal authority with the sacred Scriptures. And by the Holy Scriptures we understand the canonical books of the Old and New Testament, as they are now translated into our English mother-tongue, of which there hath never been any doubt of their verity and authority in the protestant churches of Christ to this day. All which are given by the inspiration of God, to be the rule of faith and life.

Article 38

Of the Three Creeds

The three creeds (Nicene Creed, Athanasius's creed, and the Apostles Creed, as they are commonly called) ought thoroughly to be received and believed. For we believe they may be proved by most undoubted authority of Holy Scripture and are necessary to be understood of all Christians; and to be instructed in the knowledge of them by the ministers of Christ, according to the analogy of faith, recorded in sacred Scriptures, upon which these creeds are grounded and catechistically opened and expounded in all Christian families, for the edification of young and old which might be a means to prevent heresy in doctrine and practice these creeds containing all things in a brief manner that are necessary to be known, fundamentally, in order to our salvation; to which end they may be considered and better understood of all men, we have here printed them under their several titles as followeth:

The Apostles Creed:

I believe in God the Father Almighty, Creator of heaven and earth; And in Jesus Christ, His only Son, our Lord, who was conceived by the Holy Spirit, born of the Virgin Mary, suffered under Pontius Pilate, was crucified, dead and buried. He descended to hell, on the third day rose again from the dead, ascended to heaven, sits at the right hand of God the Father Almighty, thence He will come to judge the living and the dead; I believe in the Holy Spirit, the holy catholic Church, the communion of saints, the forgiveness of sins, the resurrection of the body, and the life everlasting. Amen.

The Nicene Creed:

I believe in one God, the Father Almighty; maker of heaven and earth, and of all things visible and invisible.

And in one Lord Jesus Christ, the only-begotten Son of God, begotten of the Father before all worlds, God of God, Light of Light, very God of very God, begotten, not made, being of one substance with the Father; by whom all things were made; who, for us men and for our salvation, came down from heaven, and was incarnate by the Holy Ghost of the Virgin Mary, and was made man; and was crucified also for us under Pontius Pilate; He suffered and was buried; and the third day He rose again, according to the Scriptures; and ascended into heaven, and sitteth on the right hand of the Father; and He shall come again, with glory, to judge both the quick and the dead; whose kingdom shall have no end.

And I believe in the Holy Ghost, the Lord and Giver of Life; who proceedeth from the Father and the Son; who with the Father and the Son together is worshiped and glorified; who spake by the prophets. And I believe one holy catholic and apostolic Church. I acknowledge one baptism for the remission of sins; and I look for the resurrection of the dead, and the life of the world to come. Amen.

Athanasius His Creed:

And the Catholic Faith is this: That we worship one God in Trinity, and Trinity in Unity, neither confounding the Persons, nor dividing the Substance.

For there is one Person of the Father, another of the Son, and another of the Holy Ghost.

But the Godhead of the Father, of the Son, and of the Holy Ghost, is all one, the Glory equal, the Majesty co-eternal.

Such as the Father is, such is the Son, and such is the Holy Ghost.

The Father uncreate, the Son uncreate, and the Holy Ghost uncreate.

The Father incomprehensible, the Son incomprehensible, and the Holy Ghost incomprehensible.

The Father eternal, the Son eternal, and the Holy Ghost eternal.

And yet there are not three eternals, but one eternal.

As also there are not three incomprehensibles, nor three uncreated, but one uncreated, and one incomprehensible.

So likewise the Father is Almighty, the Son Almighty, and the Holy Ghost Almighty.

And yet they are not three Almighties, but one Almighty.

So the Father is God, the Son is God, and the Holy Ghost is God.

And yet there are not three Gods, but one God.

So likewise the Father is Lord, the Son Lord, and the Holy Ghost Lord.

And yet not three Lords, but one Lord.

For like as we are compelled by the Christian verity to acknowledge every Person by himself to be both God and Lord,

So we are forbidden by the Catholic Religion, to say, There be three Gods, or three Lords,

The Father is made of none, neither created, nor begotten.

The Son is of the Father alone, not made, nor created, but begotten.

The Holy Ghost is of the Father and of the Son, neither made, nor created, nor begotten, but proceeding.

So there is one Father, not three Fathers; one Son, not three Sons; one Holy Ghost, not three Holy Ghosts.

And in this Trinity none is afore, or after other; none is greater, or less than another;

But the whole three Persons are co-eternal together and co-equal.

So that in all things, as is aforesaid, the Unity in Trinity and the Trinity in Unity is to be worshipped.

He therefore that will be saved must thus think of the Trinity.

Furthermore, it is necessary to everlasting salvation that he also believe rightly the Incarnation of our Lord Jesus Christ.

For the right Faith is, that we believe and confess, that our Lord Jesus Christ, the Son of God, is God and Man;

God, of the Substance of the Father, begotten before the worlds; and Man, of the Substance of his Mother, born in the world;

Perfect God and perfect Man, of a reasonable soul and human flesh subsisting;

Equal to the Father, as touching his Godhead; and inferior to the Father, as touching his Manhood.

Who although he be God and Man, yet he is not two, but one Christ;

One, not by conversion of the Godhead into flesh, but by taking of the Manhood in God;

One altogether; not by confusion of Substance, but by unity of Person.

For as the reasonable soul and flesh is one man, so God and Man is one Christ;

Who suffered for our salvation, descended into hell, rose again the third day from the dead.

He ascended into heaven, he sitteth on the right hand of the
Father, God Almighty, from whence he shall come to judge
the quick and the dead.

At whose coming all men shall rise again with their bodies and
shall give account for their own works.

And they that have done good shall go into life everlasting; and
they that have done evil into everlasting fire.

Article 39

Of General Councils or Assemblies

General councils or assemblies consisting of bishops, elders,
and brethren of the several churches of Christ, and being legally
convened and met together out of all the church, and the
churches appearing there by their representatives, make but one
church and have lawful right and suffrage in this general meeting or assembly to act in the name of Christ; it being of divine
authority and is the best means under heaven to preserve unity,
to prevent heresy, and superintendency among, or in any congregation whatsoever within its own limits or jurisdiction. And
to such a meeting or assembly, appeals ought to be made in case
any injustice be done, or heresy and schism countenanced in any
particular congregation of Christ, and the decisive voice in such
general assemblies is the major part, and such general assemblies
have lawful power to hear and determine, as also to excommunicate.

Article 40

Of Religious Worship and the Sabbath Day

The light of nature shows there is a God who hath a sovereignty over all, but the Holy Scripture hath fully revealed it; as
also that all men should worship Him according to God's own
institution and appointment. And hath limited us by His own
revealed will, that He may not be worshipped according to the
imaginations and devices of men or the suggestions of Satan

under any visible representations whatsoever, or any other way not prescribed in the Holy Scriptures; and all religious worship is to be given to the Father, Son, and Holy Ghost, and to God alone, not to angels, saints, or any other creature, and since the fall, not without a mediator, nor in the mediation of any other but Christ alone; nor is this worshipping of God now under the Gospel, tied to any place or made more acceptable by one place than another. Yet the assembly of the church ought not to be neglected by any. And in order to His being worshipped and served, God hath instituted one day in seven for His sabbath to be kept holy unto Him, which from the resurrection of Christ, is the first day of the week, which is called the Lord's Day, and is to be observed and continued to the end of the world as a Christian sabbath, the last day of the week being abolished. And this Christian sabbath is to be kept after a due and reverent manner, in preparing of our hearts and ordering of affairs so beforehand, that we may rest that day from worldly and carnal employments and frequent the solemn assemblies of the church and in all public and private duties of religion as hearing, meditating, and conferring, and reading in, or of the Holy Scriptures, to gather with prayer, public and private, and in the duties of necessity, charity, and mercy, and not in any vain or worldly discourse or idle recreations whatsoever.

Article 41

Of Public and Private Prayer

Prayer is an holy, religious, and sacred ordinance of God, and the duty of all men to perform, by the law of God; and to God alone, and no other, whether saint or angel, and in the name of Christ the Mediator, and in His name alone, and no other, whether saint or angel, or any other creature. And that for all men living, except they have sinned the unpardonable sin, both high and low; especially for ministers and magistrates. And not for dead saints, nor infernal spirits. And prayer is to be made in a tongue understood by the people: And we ought to pray for all things necessary according to the will of God in Christ Jesus, in a solemn and reverent manner, every way suitable and agreeable to the platform, or manner of prayer, which Christ taught His disciples, and us in His Holy Gospel, which is the only perfect rule of all prayers; and by the assistance of the Holy Spirit of God, without which we cannot pray aright. And this religious worship all men are bound and required to serve God in, both public and private, at least two times a day, in all Christian families, by prayers and supplications, intercessions and giving of thanks to God the Father, in the name and mediation of Christ Jesus our Lord.

Article 42

Of Public Humiliation, by Fasting and Prayer

Public humiliation, by fasting and prayer, is an ordinance of God, appointed for His church and people. And it being an extraordinary duty, especially as it hath respect to the church generally, or the nation as such, and therefore we must have due regard to the grounds, ends, and manner of its being performed; confessing of and reforming from sin, both in public as well as private fasts. Abstaining from our pleasures, as also our common food, in a sensible and real afflicting of our souls before the Lord; or to seek to God by prayer and fasting for some spiritual or temporal good, that God hath promised us or that we stand in need of having due regard to God's Word and glory, in this solemn or divine ordinance.

Article 44

Of Children Dying in Infancy

We do believe that all little children dying in their infancy (before they are capable to choose either good or evil) whether born of believing parents or unbelieving parents shall be saved by the grace of God and merit of Christ their Redeemer, and work of the Holy Ghost, and so being made members of the invisible church, shall enjoy life everlasting; for our Lord Jesus saith of such belongs the kingdom of heaven. Ergo, we conclude, that that opinion is false which saith that those little infants dying before baptism are damned.

Article 45

Of the Civil Magistrate

The supreme Lord and King of all the world hath ordained civil magistrates to be under Him, over the people for His own glory and the public good. And the office of a magistrate may be accepted of and executed by Christians, when lawfully called thereunto; and God hath given the power of the sword into the hands of all lawful magistrates for the defense and encouragement of them that do well and for the punishment of evil doers and for the maintenance of justice and peace, according to the wholesome laws of each kingdom and commonwealth, and they may wage war upon just and necessary occasions. And subjection in the Lord ought to be yielded to the magistrates in all lawful things commanded by them for conscience sake, with prayers for them, for a blessing upon them, paying all lawful and reasonable custom and tribute to them for the assisting of them against foreign, domestical, and potent enemies.

Article 46

Of Liberty of Conscience

The Lord Jesus Christ, who is King of kings and Lord of all by purchase and is judge of quick and dead, is only Lord of conscience; having a peculiar right so to be. He having died for that end, to take away the guilt and to destroy the filth of sin that keeps the consciences of all men in thraldom and bondage till they are set free by His special grace. And therefore He would not have the consciences of men in bondage to, or imposed upon, by any usurpation, tyranny, or command whatsoever, contrary to His revealed will in His Word, which is the only rule He hath left for the consciences of all men to be rule and regulated, and guided by, through the assistance of His Spirit. And therefore the obedience to any command or decree, that is not revealed in or consonant to His Word in the Holy oracles of Scripture, is a betraying of the true liberty of conscience. And the requiring of an implicit faith and an absolute blind obedience, destroys liberty of conscience, and reason also, it being repugnant to both and that no pretended good end whatsoever by any man, can make that action, obedience, or practice, lawful and good, that is not grounded in or upon the authority of Holy Scripture or right reason agreeable thereunto.

Article 47

Of Marriage

Marriage is to be between one man and one woman; neither is it lawful for any man to have more than one wife, nor for any woman to have more than one husband at the same time. And it is lawful for all sorts of people to marry, who are able of judgment to give their consent. But marriage must not be within the degree of consanguinity or affinity, forbidden in the Word, nor can any such incestuous marriages ever be made lawful by any law of man or consent of parties to live together as man and wife. And it is the duty of Christians to marry in the Lord, and therefore those that profess the true religion ought not to marry with infidels or idolaters, nor profane wicked persons in their life nor yet with any that maintain damnable heresies.

Article 48

Of the Lawfulness of an Oath

A lawful oath is a part of religious worship, wherein the person swearing in truth, righteousness, and judgment, solemnly called God to witness what he sweareth, and to judge him according to the truth or falseness thereof. And we are to swear by no other name, but by the name of God only when we are called before a lawful magistrate, upon a lawful matter, warranted by God's Holy Word; and an oath is to be taken in the plain and common sense of the words, without equivocation or mental reservation, in a solemn and reverent using of God's Holy name; and such an oath, we believe all Christians, when lawfully called thereunto by the magistrate, may take. But the foolish monastical vows of papists, and all idle and vain swearing, is an abominable and wicked profaning of the Holy name of God.

Article 49

Of the State of Man after Death, and of the Resurrection of the Dead

The bodies of men after death return to dust and see corruption; but their souls or spirits, which neither die nor sleep, having an immortal subsistence, immediately return to God who gave them; the souls of the righteous being then made perfect in holiness, are received into paradise where they are with Christ and behold the face of God in light and glory, waiting for the full redemption of their bodies and the souls of the wicked are cast into hell, where they remain in torment and utter darkness, reserved to the judgment of the great day. And besides these two places for souls separated from their bodies, the Holy Scripture mentions none. And at the last day, such of the saints as shall be found alive, shall not sleep, but be changed, and all the dead shall be raised up with the self-same bodies and none other, although with different qualities, which shall be united to their souls forever and ever, but the bodies of the unjust shall by the power of Christ, as a severe and just judge, be raised to dishonor; and the bodies of the just and righteous, by His Spirit, as He is Head of the catholic church, unto honor, and be made conformable with His glorious body, and shall enjoy everlasting life; in singing perpetual praises and hallelujahs to God forever and ever. Amen.

Article 50

And lastly, we believe God hath appointed a day wherein He will judge the world in righteousness by Jesus Christ to whom all power and judgment is given of the Father; in which day, not only the apostate angels shall be judged, but likewise all persons that have lived upon the earth, shall appear before the tribunal of Christ to give an account of their thoughts, words and deeds and shall receive a just sentence, according to what they have done in their bodies, whether good or evil, when God, according to His purpose, will manifest the glory of His mercy in the salvation of His elect and of His justice in the eternal damnation of the wicked and disobedient; for then shall the righteous go into everlasting life and receive the fullness of joy and glory, but the wicked, who know not God, nor obey the Gospel offered them in Christ, shall be cast into eternal torments and punished with everlasting destruction from the presence of the Lord and from the glory of His power. Amen.

CHAPTER EIGHT

The New Hampshire Confession (1833)

1. Of the Scriptures

We believe the Holy Bible was written by men divinely inspired, and is a perfect treasure of heavenly instruction; that it has God for its author, salvation for its end, and truth, without any mixture of error, for its matter; that it reveals the principles by which God will judge us; and therefore is, and shall remain to the end of the world, the true center of Christian union, and the supreme standard by which all human conduct, creeds, and opinions should be tried.

2. Of the True God

That there is one, and only one, living and true God, whose name is JEHOVAH, the Maker and Supreme Ruler of heaven and earth; inexpressibly glorious in holiness; worthy of all possible honor, confidence, and love; revealed under the personal and relative distinctions of the Father, the Son, and the Holy Spirit; equal in every divine perfection, and executing distinct but harmonious offices in the great work of redemption.

3. Of the Fall of Man

That man was created in a state of holiness, under the law of his Maker; but by voluntary transgression fell from that holy and happy state; in consequence of which all mankind are now sinners, not by constraint but choice, being by nature utterly void of that holiness required by the law of God, wholly given to the gratification of the world, of Satan, and of their own sinful passions, therefore under just condemnation to eternal ruin, without defense or excuse.

4. Of the Way Of Salvation

That the salvation of sinners is wholly of grace; through the mediatorial offices of the Son of God, who took upon Him our nature, yet without sin; honored the law by His personal obedience, and made atonement for our sins by His death; being risen from the dead He is now enthroned in heaven; and uniting in His wonderful person the tenderest sympathies with divine perfections, is every way qualified to be a suitable, a compassionate, and an all-sufficient Savior.

5. Of Justification

That the great gospel blessing which Christ in His fullness bestows on such as believe in Him, is justification; that justification consists in the pardon of sin and the promise of eternal life, on principles of righteousness; that it is bestowed not in consideration of any works of righteousness which we have done, but solely through His own redemption and righteousness, that it brings us into a state of most blessed peace and favor with God, and secures every other blessing needful for time and eternity.

6. Of the Freeness of Salvation

That the blessings of salvation are made free to all by the gospel; that it is the immediate duty of all to accept them by a cordial, and obedient faith; and that nothing prevents the salvation of the greatest sinner on earth except his own voluntary refusal to submit to the Lord Jesus Christ, which refusal will subject him to an aggravated condemnation.

7. Of Grace in Regeneration

That in order to be saved, we must be regenerated or born again; that regeneration consists in giving a holy disposition to the mind; and is effected in a manner above our comprehension or calculation, by the power of the Holy spirit, so as to secure our voluntary obedience to the gospel; and that its proper evidence is found in the holy fruit which we bring forth to the glory of God.

8. Of God's Purpose of Grace

That election is the gracious purpose of God, according to which He regenerates, sanctifies, and saves sinners; that being perfectly consistent with the free agency of man, it comprehends all the means in connection with the end; that it is a most glorious display of God's sovereign goodness, being infinitely wise, holy, and unchangeable; that it utterly excludes boasting, and promotes humility, prayer, praise, trust in God, and active imitation of His free mercy; that it encourages the use of means in the highest degree; that it is ascertained by its effects in all who believe the gospel; is the foundation of Christian assurance; and that to ascertain it with regard to ourselves, demands and deserves our utmost diligence.

9. Of the Perseverance of Saints

That such only are real believers as endure unto the end; that their persevering attachment to Christ is the grand mark which distinguishes them from mere professors; that a special providence watches over their welfare; and they are kept by the power of God through faith unto salvation.

10. Harmony of the Law and the Gospel

That the law of God is the eternal and unchangeable rule of His moral government; that it is holy, just, and good; and that the inability which the Scriptures ascribe to fallen men to fulfill its precepts, arises entirely from their love of sin; to deliver them from which, and to restore them through a mediator to unfeigned obedience to the holy law, is one great end of the gospel, and of the means of grace connected with the establishment of the visible Church.

11. Of a Gospel Church

That a visible Church of Christ is a congregation of baptized believers, associated by covenant in the faith and fellowship of the gospel; observing the ordinances of Christ; governed by His laws; and exercising the gifts, rights, and privileges invested in them by His Word; that its only proper officers are bishops or pastors, and deacons, whose qualifications, claims, and duties are defined in the epistles to Timothy and Titus.

12. Of Baptism and the Lord's Supper

That Christian baptism is the immersion of a believer in water, in the name of the Father, Son, and Spirit, to show forth in a solemn and beautiful emblem, our faith in a crucified, buried, and risen Savior, with its purifying power; that it is prerequisite to the privileges of a church relation; and to the Lord's Supper, in which the members of the church, by the use of bread and wine, are to commemorate together the dying love of Christ; preceded always by solemn self-examination.

13. Of the Christian Sabbath

That the first day of the week is the Lord's day, or Christian Sabbath; and is to be kept sacred to religious purposes, by abstaining from all secular labor and recreations; by the devout observance of all the means of grace, both private and public; and by preparation for that rest which remaineth for the people of God.

14. Of Civil Government

That civil government is of divine appointment, for the interests and good order of human society; and that magistrates are to be prayed for, conscientiously honored, and obeyed, except in things opposed to the will of our Lord Jesus Christ, who is the only Lord of the conscience, and the Prince of the kings of the earth.

15. Of the Righteous and the Wicked

That there is a radical and essential difference between the righteous and the wicked; that such only as through faith are justified in the name of the Lord Jesus, and sanctified by the Spirit of our God, are truly righteous in His esteem; while all such as continue in impenitence and unbelief are in His sight wicked, and under the curse; and this distinction holds among men both in and after death.

16. Of the World to Come.

That the end of this world is approaching: that at the last day, Christ will descend from heaven, and raise the dead from the grave to final retribution; that a solemn separation will then take place; that the wicked will be adjudged to endless punishment, and the righteous to endless joy; and that this judgment will fix forever the final state of men in heaven or hell, on principles of righteousness.

CHAPTER NINE

The Baptist Faith and Message (1963)

Report of Committee on Baptist Faith and Message

(Adopted by the Southern Baptist Convention, May 9, 1963)

The 1962 session of the Southern Baptist Convention, meeting in San Francisco, California, adopted the following motion.

"Since the report of the Committee on Statement of Baptist Faith and Message was adopted in 1925, there have been various statements from time to time which have been made, but no overall statement which might be helpful at this time as suggested in Section 2 of that report, or introductory statement which might be used as an interpretation of the 1925 Statement.

"We recommend, therefore, that the president of this Convention be requested to call a meeting of the men now serving as presidents of the various state Conventions that would qualify as a member of the Southern Baptist Convention committee under Bylaw 18 to present to the Convention in Kansas City some similar statement which shall serve as information to the churches, and which may serve as guidelines to the various agencies of the Southern Baptist Convention. It is understood that any group or individuals may approach this committee to be of service. The expenses of this committee shall be borne by the Convention Operating Budget."

Your committee thus constituted begs leave to present its report as follows:

Throughout its work your committee has been conscious of the contribution made by the statement of "The Baptist Faith and Message" adopted by the Southern Baptist Convention in 1925. It quotes with approval its affirmation that "Christianity is supernatural in its origin and history. We repudiate every theory of religion which denies the supernatural elements in our faith."

Furthermore, it concurs in the introductory "statement of the historic Baptist conception of the nature and function of confessions of faith in our religious and denominational life." It is, therefore, quoted in full as part of this report to the Convention.

"1. That they constitute a consensus of opinion of some Baptist body, large or small, for the general instruction and guidance of our own people and others concerning those articles of the Christian faith which are most surely held among us. They are not intended to add anything to the simple conditions of salvation revealed in the New Testament, viz., repentance towards God and faith in Jesus Christ as Saviour and Lord.

"2. That we do not regard them as complete statements of our faith, having any quality of finality or infallibility. As in the past so in the future Baptists should hold themselves free to revise their statements of faith as may seem to them wise and expedient at any time.

"3. That any group of Baptists, large or small, have the inherent right to draw up for themselves and publish to the world a confession of their faith whenever they may think it advisable to do so.

"4. That the sole authority for faith and practice among Baptists is the Scriptures of the Old and New Testaments. Confessions are only guides in interpretation, having no authority over the conscience.

"5. That they are statements of religious convictions, drawn from the Scriptures, and are not to be used to hamper freedom of thought or investigation in other realms of life."

The 1925 Statement recommended "the New Hampshire Confession of Faith, revised at certain points, and with some additional articles growing out of certain needs . . ." Your present committee has adopted the same pattern. It has sought to build upon the structure of the 1925 Statement, keeping in mind the "certain needs" of our generation. At times it has reproduced sections of the Statement without change. In other instances it has substituted words for clarity or added sentences for emphasis. At certain points it has combined articles, with minor changes in wording, to endeavor to relate certain doctrines to each other. In still others—e.g., "God" and "Salvation"—it has sought to bring together certain truths contained throughout the 1925 Statement in order to relate them more clearly and concisely. In no case has it sought to delete from or to add to the basic contents of the 1925 Statement.

Baptists are a people who profess a living faith. This faith is rooted and grounded in Jesus Christ who is "the same yesterday, and today, and for ever." Therefore, the sole authority for faith and practice among Baptists is Jesus Christ whose will is revealed in the Holy Scriptures.

A living faith must experience a growing understanding of truth and must be continually interpreted and related to the needs of each new generation. Throughout their history Baptist bodies, both large and small, have issued statements of faith which comprise a consensus of their beliefs. Such statements have never been regarded as complete, infallible statements of faith, nor as official creeds carrying mandatory authority. Thus this generation of Southern Baptists is in historic succession of intent and purpose as it endeavors to state for its time and theological climate those articles of the Christian faith which are most surely held among us.

Baptists emphasize the soul's competency before God, freedom in religion, and the priesthood of the believer. However, this emphasis should not be interpreted to mean that there is an absence of certain definite doctrines that Baptists believe, cherish, and with which they have been and are now closely identified.

It is the purpose of this statement of faith and message to set forth certain teachings which we believe.

The Baptist Faith and Message

I. The Scriptures

The Holy Bible was written by men divinely inspired and is the record of God's revelation of Himself to man. It is a perfect treasure of divine instruction. It has God for its author, salvation for its end, and truth, without any mixture of error, for its matter. It reveals the principles by which God judges us; and therefore is, and will remain to the end of the world, the true center of Christian union, and the supreme standard by which all human conduct, creeds, and religious opinions should be tried. The criterion by which the Bible is to be interpreted is Jesus Christ.

II. God

There is one and only one living and true God. He is an intelligent, spiritual, and personal Being, the Creator, Redeemer, Preserver, and Ruler of the universe. God is infinite in holiness and all other perfections. To Him we owe the highest love, reverence, and obedience. The eternal God reveals Himself to us as Father, Son, and Holy Spirit, with distinct personal attributes, but without division of nature, essence, or being.

A. God the Father. God as Father reigns with providential care over His universe, His creatures, and the flow of the stream of human history according to the purpose of His grace. He is all powerful, all loving, and all wise. God is Father in truth to those who become children of God through faith in Jesus Christ. He is fatherly in His attitude toward all men.

B. God the Son. Christ is the eternal Son of God. In His incarnation as Jesus Christ he was conceived of the Holy Spirit and born of the virgin Mary. Jesus perfectly revealed and did the will of God, taking upon Himself the demands and necessities of human nature and identifying Himself completely with mankind yet without sin. He honored the divine law by His personal obedience, and in His death on the cross He made provision for the redemption of men from sin. He was raised from the dead with a glorified body and appeared to His disciples as the person who was with them before His crucifixion. He ascended into heaven and is now exalted at the right hand of God where He is the One Mediator, partaking of the nature of God and of man, and in whose Person is effected the reconciliation between God and man. He will return in power and glory to judge the world and to consummate His redemptive mission. He now dwells in all believers as the living and ever present Lord.

C. God the Holy Spirit. The Holy Spirit is the Spirit of God. He inspired holy men of old to write the Scriptures. Through illumination He enables men to understand truth. He exalts Christ. He convicts of sin, of righteousness, and of judgment. He calls men to the Saviour, and effects regeneration. He cultivates Christian character, comforts believers, and bestows the spiritual gifts by which they serve God through His church. He seals the believer unto the day of final redemption. His presence in the Christian is the assurance of God to bring the believer into the fullness of the stature of Christ. He enlightens and empowers the believer and the church in worship, evangelism, and service.

III. Man

Man was created in the special act of God, in His own image, and is the crowning work of His creation. In the beginning man was innocent of sin and was endowed by his Creator with freedom of choice. By his free choice man sinned against God and brought sin into the human race. Through the temptation of

Satan man transgressed the command of God, and fell from his original innocence; whereby his posterity inherit a nature and an environment inclined toward sin, and as soon as they are capable of moral action become transgressors and are under condemnation. Only the grace of God can bring man into His holy fellowship and enable man to fulfill the creative purpose of God. The sacredness of human personality is evident in that God created man in His own image, and in that Christ died for man; therefore every man possesses dignity and is worthy of respect and Christian love.

IV. Salvation

Salvation involves the redemption of the whole man, and is offered freely to all who accept Jesus Christ as Lord and Saviour, who by His own blood obtained eternal redemption for the believer. In its broadest sense salvation includes regeneration, sanctification, and glorification.

A. Regeneration. Regeneration, or the new birth, is a work of God's grace whereby believers become new creatures in Christ Jesus. It is a change of heart wrought by the Holy Spirit through conviction of sin, to which the sinner responds in repentance toward God and faith in the Lord Jesus Christ.

Repentance and faith are inseparable experiences of grace. Repentance is a genuine turning from sin toward God. Faith is the acceptance of Jesus Christ and commitment of the entire personality to Him as Lord and Saviour. Justification is God's gracious and full acquittal upon principles of His righteousness of all sinners who repent and believe in Christ. Justification brings the believer into a relationship of peace and favor with God.

B. Sanctification. Sanctification is the experience, beginning in regeneration, by which the believer is set apart to God's purposes, and is enabled to progress toward moral and spiritual perfection through the presence and power of the Holy Spirit dwelling in him. Growth in grace should continue throughout the regenerate person's life.

C. Glorification. Glorification is the culmination of salvation and is the final blessed and abiding state of the redeemed.

V. God's Purpose of Grace

Election is the gracious purpose of God, according to which He regenerates, sanctifies, and glorifies sinners. It is consistent with the free agency of man, and comprehends all the means in connection with the end. It is a glorious display of God's sovereign goodness, and is infinitely wise, holy, and unchangeable. It excludes boasting and promotes humility.

All true believers endure to the end. Those whom God has accepted in Christ, and sanctified by His Spirit, will never fall away from the state of grace, but shall persevere to the end. Believers may fall into sin through neglect and temptation, whereby they grieve the Spirit, impair their graces and comforts, bring reproach on the cause of Christ, and temporal judgments on themselves, yet they shall be kept by the power of God through faith unto salvation.

VI. The Church

A New Testament church of the Lord Jesus Christ is a local body of baptized believers who are associated by covenant in the faith and fellowship of the gospel, observing the two ordinances of Christ, committed to His teachings, exercising the gifts, rights, and privileges invested in them by His Word, and seeking to extend the gospel to the ends of the earth.

This church is an autonomous body, operating through democratic processes under the Lordship of Jesus Christ. In such a congregation members are equally responsible. Its Scriptural officers are pastors and deacons.

The New Testament speaks also of the church as the body of Christ which includes all of the redeemed of all the ages.

VII. Baptism and the Lord's Supper

Christian baptism is the immersion of a believer in water in the name of the Father, the Son, and the Holy Spirit. It is an act of obedience symbolizing the believer's faith in a crucified, buried, and risen Saviour, the believer's death to sin, the burial of the old life, and the resurrection to walk in newness of life in Christ Jesus. It is a testimony to his faith in the final resurrection of the dead. Being a church ordinance, it is prerequisite to the privileges of church membership and to the Lord's Supper.

The Lord's Supper is a symbolic act of obedience whereby members of the church, through partaking of the bread and the fruit of the vine, memorialize the death of the Redeemer and anticipate His second coming.

VIII. The Lord's Day

The first day of the week is the Lord's Day. It is a Christian institution for regular observance. It commemorates the resurrection of Christ from the dead and should be employed in exercises of worship and spiritual devotion, both public and private, and by refraining from worldly amusements, and resting from secular employments, work of necessity and mercy only being excepted.

IX. The Kingdom

The Kingdom of God includes both His general sovereignty over the universe and His particular kingship over men who willfully acknowledge Him as King. Particularly the Kingdom is the realm of salvation into which men enter by trustful, childlike commitment to Jesus Christ. Christians ought to pray and to labor that the Kingdom may come and God's will be done on earth. The full consummation of the Kingdom awaits the return of Jesus Christ and the end of this age.

X. Last Things

God, in His own time and in His own way, will bring the world to its appropriate end. According to His promise, Jesus Christ will return personally and visibly in glory to the earth; the dead will be raised; and Christ will judge all men in righteousness. The unrighteous will be consigned to Hell, the place of everlasting punishment. The righteous in their resurrected and glorified bodies will receive their reward and will dwell forever in Heaven with the Lord.

XI. Evangelism and Missions

It is the duty and privilege of every follower of Christ and of every church of the Lord Jesus Christ to endeavor to make disciples of all nations. The new birth of man's spirit by God's Holy Spirit means the birth of love for others. Missionary effort on the part of all rests thus upon a spiritual necessity of the regenerate life, and is expressly and repeatedly commanded in the teachings of Christ. It is the duty of every child of God to seek constantly to win the lost to Christ by personal effort and by all other methods in harmony with the gospel of Christ.

XII. Education

The cause of education in the Kingdom of Christ is co-ordinate with the causes of missions and general benevolence, and should receive along with these the liberal support of the churches. An adequate system of Christian schools is necessary to a complete spiritual program for Christ's people.

In Christian education there should be a proper balance between academic freedom and academic responsibility. Freedom in any orderly relationship of human life is always limited and never absolute. The freedom of a teacher in a Christian school, college, or seminary is limited by the pre-eminence of Jesus Christ, by the authoritative nature of the Scriptures, and by the distinct purpose for which the school exists.

XIII. Stewardship

God is the source of all blessings, temporal and spiritual; all that we have and are we owe to Him. Christians have a spiritual debtorship to the whole world, a holy trusteeship in the gospel, and a binding stewardship in their possessions. They are therefore under obligation to serve Him with their time, talents, and material possessions; and should recognize all these as entrusted to them to use for the glory of God and for helping others. According to the Scriptures, Christians should contribute of their means cheerfully, regularly, systematically, proportionately, and liberally for the advancement of the Redeemer's cause on earth.

XIV. Cooperation

Christ's people should, as occasion requires, organize such associations and conventions as may best secure cooperation for the great objects of the Kingdom of God. Such organizations have no authority over one another or over the churches. They are voluntary and advisory bodies designed to elicit, combine, and direct the energies of our people in the most effective manner. Members of New Testament churches should cooperate with one another in carrying forward the missionary, educational, and benevolent ministries for the extension of Christ's Kingdom. Christian unity in the New Testament sense is spiritual harmony and voluntary cooperation for common ends by various groups of Christ's people. Cooperation is desirable between the various Christian denominations, when the end to be attained is itself justified, and when such cooperation involves no violation of conscience or compromise of loyalty to Christ and His Word as revealed in the New Testament.

XV. The Christian and the Social Order

Every Christian is under obligation to seek to make the will of Christ supreme in his own life and in human society. Means and methods used for the improvement of society and the establishment of righteousness among men can be truly and permanently helpful only when they are rooted in the regeneration of the individual by the saving grace of God in Christ Jesus. The Christian should oppose in the spirit of Christ every form of greed, selfishness, and vice. He should work to provide for the orphaned, the needy, the aged, the helpless, and the sick. Every Christian should seek to bring industry, government, and society as a whole under the sway of the principles of righteousness, truth, and brotherly love. In order to promote these ends Christians should be ready to work with all men of good will in any good cause, always being careful to act in the spirit of love without compromising their loyalty to Christ and His truth.

XVI. Peace and War

It is the duty of Christians to seek peace with all men on principles of righteousness. In accordance with the spirit and teachings of Christ they should do all in their power to put an end to war.

The true remedy for the war spirit is the gospel of our Lord. The supreme need of the world is the acceptance of His teachings in all the affairs of men and nations, and the practical application of His law of love.

XVII. Religious Liberty

God alone is Lord of the conscience, and He has left it free from the doctrines and commandments of men which are contrary to His Word or not contained in it. Church and state should be separate. The state owes to every church protection and full freedom in the pursuit of its spiritual ends. In providing for such freedom no ecclesiastical group or denomination should be favored by the state more than others. Civil government being ordained of God, it is the duty of Christians to render loyal obedience thereto in all things not contrary to the revealed will of God. The church should not resort to the civil power to carry on its work. The gospel of Christ contemplates spiritual means alone for the pursuit of its ends. The state has no right to impose penalties for religious opinions of any kind. The state has no right to impose taxes for the support of any form of religion. A free church in a free state is the Christian ideal, and this implies the right of free and unhindered access to God on the part of all men, and the right to form and propagate opinions in the sphere of religion without interference by the civil power.

CHAPTER TEN

Report of the Presidential Theological Study Committee (1994)

Note: The Theological Study Committee was appointed by Southern Baptist Convention President H. Edwin Young in 1992 and submitted its report in the spring of the following year. The purpose of this study group was to examine those biblical truths which are most surely held among the people of God called Southern Baptists and, on this basis, to reaffirm our common commitment to Jesus Christ, the Holy Scriptures and the evangelical heritage of the Christian church. In light of the pressing need for a positive biblical witness on basic Christian beliefs, this report is published, not as a new confession of faith, but rather as a reaffirmation of major doctrinal concerns set forth in the Baptist Faith and Message of 1963.

(Those serving on the Presidential Theological Study Committee: Timothy F. George, Co-chairman; Roy L. Honeycutt, Co-chairman; William E. Bell; J. Walter Carpenter, Jr.; Mark T. Coppenger; Stephen D. C. Corts; Carl F. H. Henry; Herschel H. Hobbs; Richard D. Land; R. Albert Mohler, Jr.; William B. Tolar; and H. Edwin Young, president of the Southern Baptist Convention.)

Part 1

In every generation, the people of God face the decision either to reaffirm "the faith which was once delivered unto the saints" (Jude 3) or to lapse into theological unbelief. Precisely such a challenge now confronts the people of God called Southern Baptists.

As we approach the 150th anniversary of the founding of the Southern Baptist Convention, we are presented with unprecedented opportunities for missionary outreach and evangelistic witness at home and abroad. We must bear a faithful gospel witness to a culture in decline; we must be the salt and light in a society which has lost its moral compass. We must also pass on to the rising generation the fundamentals of the Christian faith and a vital sense of our Baptist heritage. To meet these goals, we seek to move beyond the denominational conflict of recent years toward a new consensus rooted in theological substance and doctrinal fidelity. We pray that our effort will lead to healing and reconciliation throughout the Southern Baptist Convention and, God willing, to a renewed commitment to our founding purpose of "eliciting, combining, and directing the energies of the whole denomination in one sacred effort, for the propagation of the gospel."

Baptists are a people of firm conviction and free confession. Southern Baptists have expressed and affirmed these convictions through THE BAPTIST FAITH AND MESSAGE confessional statements of 1925 and 1963.

This committee affirms and honors THE BAPTIST FAITH AND MESSAGE, as overwhelmingly adopted by the 1963 Convention, embraced by millions of faithful Southern Baptists and their churches, affirmed by successive convention sessions and adopted by Southern Baptist Convention agencies, as the normative expression of Southern Baptist belief. Therefore, this committee declines to recommend any new confession or revision of that statement.

However, each generation of Southern Baptists faces unique and pressing challenges to faithfulness which demand attention and test the integrity of our conviction. This report addresses several issues of contemporary urgency in a spirit of pastoral concern and a commitment to the unity of our Baptist fellowship as well as the integrity of our doctrinal confession. These emphases are intended to illuminate articles of THE BAPTIST FAITH AND MESSAGE, consistent with its intention and content, and are thus commended to the Convention, its agencies, its churches, and the millions of Bible-believing cooperating Southern Baptists who freely join this Convention in its sacred work. We seek to clarify our historic Baptist commitment to Holy Scripture, the doctrine of God, the person and work of Jesus Christ, the nature and mission of the church, and biblical teaching on last things. We reaffirm our commitment to these great theological tenets since they are assailed, in various ways, by subtle compromise, blatant concession, and malign negligence.

We also affirm the historic Baptist conception of the nature and function of confessional statements in our religious and denominational life. Baptists approve and circulate confessions of faith with the following understandings:

1. *As an expression of our religious liberty.* Any group of Baptists, large or small, has the inherent right to draw up for itself and to publish to the world a confession of faith whenever it wishes. As a corollary of this principle, we reject state-imposed religious creeds and attendant civil sanctions.

2. *As a statement of our religious convictions.* We affirm the priesthood of all believers and the autonomy of each local congregation. However, doctrinal minimalism and theological revision, left unchecked, compromises a commitment to the gospel itself. Being Baptist means faith as well as freedom. Christian liberty should not become a license for the masking of unbelief.

3. *As a witness to our confidence in divine revelation.* The sole authority for faith and practice among Baptists is the Bible, God's Holy Word. It is the supreme standard by which all creeds, conduct and religious opinions should be tried. As in the past so in the future, Baptists should hold themselves free to revise their statements of faith in the light of an unchanging Holy Scripture.

None of these principles, sacred to Baptists through the ages, is violated by voluntary, conscientious adherence to an explicit doctrinal standard. Holy living and sound doctrine are indispensable elements of true revival and genuine reconciliation among any body of Christian believers. Desiring this end with all our hearts, we commend the following report to the people of God called Southern Baptists.

Part 2

Article One: Holy Scripture

Southern Baptists have affirmed repeatedly and decisively an unswerving commitment to the divine inspiration and truthfulness of Holy Scripture, the Word of God revealed in written form. We believe that what the Bible says, God says. What the Bible says happened really happened. Every miracle, every event, in every one of the 66 books of the Old and New Testaments is true and trustworthy. In 1900, James M. Frost, first president of the Baptist Sunday School Board, declared: "We accept the Scriptures as an all-sufficient and infallible rule of faith and practice, and insist upon the absolute inerrancy and sole authority of the Word of God. We recognize at this point no room for division either, of practice or belief, or even sentiment. More and more we must come to feel as the deepest and mightiest power of our conviction that a 'thus saith the Lord' is the end of all controversy."

THE BAPTIST FAITH AND MESSAGE affirms this high view of Scripture by declaring that the Bible "has God for its author, salvation for its end, and truth without any mixture of error, for its matter." The chairman of the committee who drafted this statement, Herschel Hobbs, explained this phrase by reference to 2 Timothy 3:16 which says, "all Scripture is given by inspiration of God." He explained: "The Greek New Testament reads 'all'—without the definite article and that means every single part of the whole is God-breathed. And a God of truth does not breathe error."

Recent developments in Southern Baptist life have underscored the importance of a renewed commitment to biblical authority in every area of our denominational life.

In 1986 the presidents of the six southern Baptist Convention seminaries issued the GLORIETA STATEMENT which affirmed the "infallible power and binding authority" of the Bible, declaring it to be "not errant in any area of reality." The miracles of the Old and New Testaments were described as "historical evidences of God's judgment, love and redemption."

In 1987 the Southern Baptist Convention Peace Committee called upon Southern Baptist institutions to recruit faculty and staff who clearly reflect the dominant convictions and beliefs of Southern Baptists concerning the factual character and historicity of the Bible in such matters as

1. The direct creation of humankind including Adam and Eve as real persons;

2. The actual authorship of biblical writings as attributed by Scripture itself;

3. The supernatural character of the biblical miracles which occurred as factual events in space and time;

4. The historical accuracy of biblical narratives which occurred precisely as the text of Scripture indicates.

In 1991 the Baptist Sunday School Board published the first volume of the NEW AMERICAN COMMENTARY, a projected 40-volume series of theological expositions on every book of the Bible. The commentary was intended to reflect a "commitment to the inerrancy of Scripture" and "the classic Christian tradition." THE CHICAGO STATEMENT ON BIBLICAL INERRANCY was adopted as a guideline more fully expressing for writers the intent of Article I of THE BAPTIST FAITH AND MESSAGE.

In light of these historical commitments, we call upon all Southern Baptists:

1. To foster a deep reverence and genuine love for the Word of God in personal, congregation and denomination life;

2. To use the Scriptures in personal evangelistic witnessing, since they are "able to make one wise unto salvation;"

3. To read the Bible faithfully and to study it systematically; and

4. To encourage the translation and dissemination of the Bible throughout the world.

We commend to all Baptist educational institutions and agencies the REPORT OF THE PEACE COMMITTEE (1987), the CHICAGO STATEMENT ON BIBLICAL INERRANCY (1978), and the CHICAGO STATEMENT ON BIBLICAL HERMENEUTICS (1982) as biblically grounded and sound guides worthy of respect in setting forth a high view of Scripture. We encourage them to cultivate a biblical world view in all disciplines of learning and to pursue a reverent, believing approach to biblical scholarship that is both exegetically honest and theologically sound. There need be no contradiction between "firm faith and free research" as long as both are exercised under the Lordship of Jesus Christ and in full confidence of the truthfulness of His Word.

Article Two: The Doctrine of God

The God revealed in Holy Scripture is the sovereign God who created the world and all therein, the God who called Israel out from the nations as a witness to His name, the God who spoke from a burning bush, and the God who decisively and definitively revealed Himself through His Son, Jesus Christ, through whom He brought redemption and reconciliation.

Baptists, and all evangelical Christians, recognize the centrality of biblical theism. We honor and worship the one true God and our first act of worship is to acknowledge Him even as He has revealed Himself.

This means that we affirm God's nature as revealed in Holy Scripture. He alone has the right to define Himself, and He has done so by revealing His power and His grace, seen in His absolute holiness and love.

The biblical doctrine of God has been compromised in recent years as efforts to redefine God have rejected clear biblical teachings in the face of modern challenges. Southern Baptists cannot follow this course. As a fellowship of evangelical Christians we must recommit ourselves to the eternal truths concerning God, even as He has freely, graciously, and definitively revealed Himself. As Norvell Robertson, one of our earliest Southern Baptist theologians, wrote: "The Word of God is truth. What He says of Himself is true . . . He alone knows Himself."

Thus, we must submit ourselves to the knowledge God has imparted concerning Himself and His divine nature.

First, Baptists affirm that God is limitless in power, knowledge, wisdom, love, and holiness. He suffers no limitations upon His power or His personality. He is not constrained by any external force or internal contradiction. We reject any effort to redefine God as a limited deity.

Second, Baptists affirm that God, the Father of our Lord Jesus Christ, is none other than the God of Abraham, Isaac, and Jacob, or Sarah, and Rachel, and Ruth. God's self-revelation in Scripture is progressive, but fully consistent. He is the universal Creator and thus deserves universal recognition and worship as the one true God.

Third, Baptists affirm that God is one, and that He has revealed Himself as a Trinity of three eternally co-existent persons, Father, Son, and Holy Spirit. We acknowledge the Trinity as essential and central to our Christian confession, and we reject any attempt to minimize or compromise this aspect of God's self-disclosure.

Fourth, Baptists affirm that God has revealed Himself as the Father of the redeemed. Jesus characteristically addressed God as His Father, and instructed His disciples to do the same. We have no right to reject God's own name for Himself, not to employ impersonal or feminine names in order to placate modern sensitivities. We honor the integrity of God's name, and acknowledge His sole right to name Himself even as we affirm that no human words can exhaust the divine majesty. But God has accommodated Himself to us by naming Himself in human words.

Fifth, Baptists affirm that God is the sovereign Creator of the universe, who called all things into being by the power of His Word, and who created the worlds out of nothing. His creative acts were free and unconstrained by any other creative force.

Sixth, Baptists affirm that God is sovereign over history, nature, time, and space, and that His loving and gracious providence sustains and orders the world.

These statements, based upon Scripture and undergirded by historic Baptist confessions, force our attention to contemporary compromises which threaten the fidelity and integrity of our faith.

We call upon the Southern Baptist Convention, its churches and its institutions, to beware lest revisionist views of God such as those popularly modelled in process and feminist theologies, as well as the esoteric doctrines of the New Age movement, compromise our faithful commitment to biblical truth.

Article Three: The Person and Work of Christ

Jesus Christ is the center and circumference of the Christian faith. The God of heaven and earth has revealed Himself supremely and definitively in the Son, and the most fundamental truth of Christianity is that "God was in Christ, reconciling the world unto Himself" (2 Cor. 5:19)

Jesus Christ is the sole and sufficient Savior of the redeemed throughout the world and of all ages. He is the divine Word by which the worlds were created; He is also the unique and solitary Savior in whom alone there is redemption and forgiveness of sin. From beginning to end the Bible proclaims salvation through Jesus Christ and no other. The Church is commanded to teach and preach no other gospel.

In His incarnation—an event in historical space and time—Jesus Christ was the perfect union of the human and the divine. He was truly God and truly man, born of a virgin and without sin, remaining sinless throughout His earthly incarnation. He was crucified, died, and was buried. On the third day, he rose from the dead, the first fruits of the redeemed. He ascended to the Father and now rules as King and Judge. He will consummate the age by His physical return to earth as Lord and King.

Scripture bears faithful witness to Jesus Christ. The words and deeds of Christ set forth in the New Testament are an accurate record of what He said and did, even as the Old Testament prophetically revealed His identity and His purpose of redemption. The miracles of Jesus as revealed to us in Scripture were historical events which demonstrated Christ's identity and His power over sin, earth and Satan.

All human beings, marked by original sin and their own individual sins, are utterly helpless before God and without excuse, deserving of eternal punishment and separation from God. Nevertheless, in Jesus Christ and His cross, God revealed both the extent of our lostness and the depth of His redemptive love. All human beings—in all places and of all ages—are lost but for salvation through Jesus Christ. He is the only hope of salvation and the only Savior.

Christ's redemption was wrought by His atonement which was both penal and substitutionary. Christ died in our place, bearing in His body the penalty for our sin and purchasing our redemption by His blood.

The cross of Christ is thus the apex of God's plan of redemption, revealing God's absolute holiness and infinite love. The gospel of that cross is the only message which can and does save.

The redeemed are justified before God by grace through faith in Jesus Christ, trusting in Him alone for their salvation and acknowledging Him as Savior and Lord.

Therefore, Baptists must reject any effort to deny the true nature and identity of Jesus Christ or to minimize or to redefine His redemptive work. Baptists must reject any and all forms of universalism and bear faithful witness to salvation in Jesus Christ, and in Him alone. Furthermore, Baptists must join with all true

Christians in affirming the substitutionary nature of Christ's atonement and reject calls—ancient and modern—for redefining Christ's reconciling work as merely subjective and illustrative.

Article Four: The Church

We acknowledge Jesus Christ not only as personal Savior and Lord, but also as the head, foundation, lawgiver, and Teacher of the church which is His building, body, and bride. The person who despises the church despises Christ, for "Christ . . . loved the church, and gave Himself for it" (Eph. 5:25).

In the New Testament the word "church" sometimes refers to all of the redeemed of all ages but, more often, to a local assembly of baptized believers. Until Jesus comes again the local church is a "colony of heaven" (Phil. 3:20), a "sounding board" of the gospel (1 Thess. 1:8), and a fellowship through which God's people carry out the Great Commission of their Lord. The central purpose of the church is to honor and glorify God; the central task of the church is to bear witness to the gospel of Jesus Christ through evangelism and missions.

In light of this mandate, we call upon all Southern Baptists to reaffirm our commitment to these distinctive principles of our Baptist heritage.

The Priesthood of All Believers

Every Christian has direct access to God through Jesus Christ, our great High Priest, the sole mediator between God and human beings. However, the priesthood of all believers is exercised within a committed community of fellow believers—priests who share a like precious faith. The priesthood of all believers should not be reduced to modern individualism, not used as a cover for theological relativism. It is a spiritual standing which leads to ministry, service, and a coherent witness in the world for which Christ died.

The Autonomy of the Local Church

A New Testament church is a gathered congregation of baptized believers who have entered into covenant with Christ and with one another to fulfil, according to the Scriptures, their mutual obligations. Under the Lordship of Christ, such a body is free to order its own internal life without interference from any external group. This same freedom applies to all general Baptist bodies, such as associations and state and national conventions. Historically, Baptist churches have freely cooperated in matters of common interest without compromise of beliefs. We affirm the wisdom of convictional cooperation in carrying out our witness to the world and decry all efforts to weaken our denomination and its cooperative ministries.

A Free Church in a Free State

Throughout our history Baptists have not wavered in our belief that God intends for a free church to function in a free state. Since God alone is Lord of the conscience, the temporal realm has no authority to coerce religious commitments. However, the doctrine of religious liberty, far from implying doctrinal laxity or unconcern, guarantees the ability of every congregation and general Baptist body to determine (on the basis of the Word of God) its own doctrinal and disciplinary parameters.

We declare our fervent commitment to these distinctive convictions of the Baptist tradition. We also call for a renewed emphasis on the faithful proclamation of God's Word, believers' baptism by immersion, and the celebration of the Lord's Supper as central elements of corporate worship.

Article Five: Last Things

With all true Christians everywhere, Baptists confess that "Christ has died, Christ is risen, Christ will come again." The God who has acted in the past, and is acting even now, will continue to act, bringing to final consummation His eternal purpose in Jesus Christ. Our faith rests in the confidence that the future is in His hands.

While detailed interpretations of the end times should not be made a test of fellowship among Southern Baptists, we affirm with confidence the clear teaching of Holy Scripture on these essential doctrinal truths:

The Return of Jesus Christ in Glory

Christians await with certainty and expectancy the "blessed hope" of the outward, literal, visible and personal return of Jesus Christ to consummate history in victory and judgment. As E. Y. Mullins put it, "He will come again in person, the same Jesus who ascended from the Mount of Olives."

The Resurrection of the Body

In His glorious resurrection, Jesus Christ broke the bonds of death, establishing His authority over it, and one day He will assert that authority on our behalf and raise us. The righteous dead will be raised unto life everlasting. The unrighteous dead will be cast into hell which is the second death (Rev. 20:14–15).

Eternal Punishment and Eternal Bliss

Following the resurrection and judgment, the redeemed shall be forever with the Lord in heaven, a place of light and glory beyond description, and the lost shall be forever with the devil in hell, a place of utter darkness and inexpressible anguish. Nowhere does the Bible teach the annihilation of the soul or a temporary purgatory for those who die without hope in Christ.

The second coming of Christ is the blessed, comforting, and purifying hope of the church. We call upon all Southern Baptists to claim this precious promise in every area of our life and witness, and thus "to live holy and godly lives as we look forward to the day of God and speed its coming" (2 Pet. 3:11).

The Chicago Statement on Biblical Inerrancy

(The International Conference on Biblical Inerrancy
[ICBI], Chicago, October 1978.)

1. God, who is Himself Truth and speaks truth only, has inspired Holy Scripture in order thereby to reveal Himself to lost mankind through Jesus Christ as Creator and Lord, Redeemer and Judge. Holy Scripture is God's witness to Himself.

2. Holy Scripture, being God's own Word, written by men prepared and superintended by His Spirit, is of infallible divine authority in all matters upon which it touches; it is to be believed, as God's instruction, in all that it affirms; obeyed, as God's command, in all that it requires; embraced, as God's pledge, in all that it promises.

3. The Holy spirit, Scripture's divine Author, both authenticates it to us by His inward witness and opens our minds to understand its meaning.

4. Being wholly and verbally God-given, Scripture is without error or fault in all its teaching, no less in what it states about God's acts in creation, about the events of world history, and about its own literary origins under God, than in its witness to God's saving grace in individual lives.

5. The authority of Scripture is inescapably impaired if this total divine inerrancy is in any way limited or disregarded, or made relative to a view of truth contrary to the Bible's own; and such lapses being serious loss to both the individual and the Church.

Articles of Affirmation and Denial

Article 1

We affirm that the Holy Scriptures are to be received as the authoritative Word of God.

We deny that Scriptures receive their authority from the Church, tradition, or any other human source.

Article 2

We affirm that the Scriptures are the supreme written norm by which God binds the conscience, and that the authority of the Church is subordinate to that of Scripture.

We deny that Church creeds, councils, or declarations have authority greater than or equal to the authority of the Bible.

Article 3

We affirm that the written Word in its entirety is revelation given by God.

We deny that the Bible is merely a witness to revelation, or only becomes revelation in encounter, or depends on the responses of men for its validity.

Article 4

We affirm that God who made mankind in His image has used language as a means of revelation.

We deny that human language is so limited by our creatureliness that it is rendered inadequate as a vehicle for divine revelation. We further deny that the corruption of human culture and language through sin has thwarted God's work of inspiration.

Article 5

We affirm that God's revelation in the Holy Scriptures was progressive.

We deny that later revelation, which may fulfill earlier revelation, never corrects or contradicts it. We further deny that any normative revelation has been given since the completion of the New Testament writings.

Article 6

We affirm that the whole of Scripture and all its parts, down to the very words of the original, were given by divine inspiration.

We deny that the inspiration of Scripture can rightly be affirmed of the whole without the parts, or of some parts but not the whole.

Article 7

We affirm that inspiration was the work in which God by His Spirit, through human writers, gave us His Word. The origin of Scripture is divine. The mode of divine inspiration remains largely a mystery to us.

We deny that inspiration can be reduced to human insight, or to heightened states of consciousness of any kind.

Article 8

We affirm that God in His Work of inspiration utilized the distinctive personalities and literary styles of the writers whom He had chosen and prepared.

Article 9

We affirm that inspiration, though not conferring omniscience, guaranteed true and trustworthy utterance on all matters of which the biblical authors were moved to speak and write.

We deny that the finitude or fallenness of these writers, by necessity or otherwise, introduced distortion or falsehood into God's Word.

Article 10

We affirm that inspiration, strictly speaking, applies only to the autographic text of Scripture, which in the providence of God can be ascertained from available manuscripts with great accuracy. We further affirm that copies and translations of Scriptures are the Word of God to the extent that they faithfully represent the original.

We deny that any essential element of the Christian faith is affected by the absence of the autographs. We further deny that this absence renders the assertion of biblical inerrancy invalid or irrelevant.

Article 11

We affirm that Scripture, having been given by divine inspiration, is infallible, so that, far from misleading us, it is true and reliable in all the matters it addresses.

We deny that it is possible for the Bible to be at the same time infallible and errant in its assertions. Infallibility and inerrancy may be distinguished, but not separated.

Article 12

We affirm that Scripture in its entirety is inerrant, being free from all falsehood, fraud, or deceit.

We deny that biblical infallibility and inerrancy are limited to spiritual, religious, or redemptive themes, exclusive of assertions in the fields of history and science. We further deny that scientific hypotheses about earth history may properly be used to overturn the teaching of Scripture on creation and the flood.

Article 13

We affirm the propriety of using inerrancy as a theological term with reference to the complete truthfulness of Scripture.

We deny that it is proper to evaluate Scripture according to standards of truth and error that are alien to its usage or purpose. We further deny that inerrancy is negated by biblical phenomena such as a lack of modern technical precision, irregularities of grammar or spelling, observational descriptions of nature, the reporting of falsehoods, the use of hyperbole and round numbers, the topical arrangement of material, variant selections of material in parallel accounts, or the use of free citations.

Article 14

We affirm the unity and internal consistency of Scripture.

We deny that alleged errors and discrepancies that have not yet been resolved vitiate the truth claims of the Bible.

Article 15

We affirm that the doctrine of inerrancy is grounded in the teaching of the Bible about inspiration.

We deny that Jesus' teaching about Scripture may be dismissed by appeals to accommodation or to any natural limitation of His humanity.

Article 16

We affirm that the doctrine of inerrancy has been integral to the Church's faith throughout its history.

We deny that inerrancy is a doctrine invented by Scholastic Protestantism, or is a reactionary position postulated in response to negative higher criticism.

Article 17

We affirm that the Holy Spirit bears witness to the Scriptures, assuring believers of the truthfulness of God's written Word.

We deny that this witness of the Holy Spirit operates in isolation from or against Scripture.

Article 18

We affirm that the text of Scripture is to be interpreted by grammatico-historical exegesis, taking into account of its literary forms and devices, and that Scripture is to interpret Scripture.

We deny the legitimacy of any treatment of the text or quest for sources lying behind it that leads to relativizing, dehistoricizing, or discounting its teaching, or rejecting its claims to authorship.

Article 19

We affirm that a confession of the full authority, infallibility, and inerrancy of Scripture is vital to a sound understanding of the whole of the Christian faith. We further affirm that such confession should lead to increasing conformity to the image of Christ.

We deny that such confession is necessary for salvation. However, we further deny that inerrancy can be rejected without grave consequences, both to the individual and to the Church.

The Chicago Statement on Biblical Hermeneutics

(The International Conference on Biblical Inerrancy [ICBI], Chicago, November 1982.)

Articles of Affirmation and Denial

Article 1

We affirm that the normative authority of Holy Scripture is the authority of God Himself, and is attested by Jesus Christ, the Lord of the Church.

Article 2

We affirm that as Christ is God and Man in one Person, so Scripture is, indivisibly, God's Word in human language.

We deny that the humble, human form of Scripture entails errancy any more than the humanity of Christ, even in His humiliation, entails sin.

Article 3

We affirm that the Person and work of Jesus Christ are the central focus of the entire Bible.

We deny that any method of interpretation which rejects or obscures the Christ-centeredness of Scripture is correct.

Article 4

We affirm that the Holy Spirit who inspired Scripture acts through it today to work faith in its message.

We deny that the Holy Spirit ever teaches to any one anything which is contrary to the teaching of Scripture.

Article 5

We affirm that the Holy Spirit enables believers to appropriate and apply Scripture to their lives.

We deny that the natural man is able to discern spiritually the message apart from the Holy Spirit.

Article 6

We affirm that the Bible expresses God's truth in propositional statements, and we declare that biblical truth is both objective and absolute. We further affirm that a statement is true if it represents matters as they actually are, but is an error if it misrepresents the facts.

We deny that, while Scripture is able to make one wise unto salvation, biblical truth should be defined in terms of this function. We further deny that error should be defined as that which willfully deceives.

Article 7

We affirm that the meaning expressed in each biblical text is single, definite, and fixed.

We deny that the recognition of this single meaning eliminates the variety of its application.

Article 8

We affirm that the Bible contains teachings and mandates which apply to all cultural and situational contexts and other mandates which the Bible itself shows apply only to particular situations.

We deny that the distinction between the universal and particular mandates of Scripture can be determined by cultural and situational factors. We further deny that universal mandates may ever be treated as culturally or situationally relative.

Article 9

We affirm that the term hermeneutics, which historically signified the rules of exegesis, may properly be extended to cover all that is involved in the process of perceiving what the biblical revelation means and how it bears on our lives.

We deny that the message of Scripture derives from, or is dictated by, the interpreter's understanding. Thus we deny that the "horizons" of the biblical writer and the interpreter may rightly "fuse" in such a way that what the text communicates to the interpreter is not ultimately controlled by the expressed meaning of the Scripture.

Article 10

We affirm that Scripture communicates God's truth to us through a wide variety of literary forms.

We deny that any of the limits of human language render Scripture inadequate to convey God's message.

Article 11

We affirm that translations of the text of Scripture can communicate knowledge of God across all temporal and cultural boundaries.

We deny that the meaning of biblical texts is so tied to the culture out of which they came that understanding of the same meaning in other cultures is impossible.

Article 12

We affirm that in the task of translating the Bible and teaching it in the context of each culture, only those functional equivalents which are faithful to the content of biblical teaching should be employed.

We deny the legitimacy of methods which either are insensitive to the demands of cross-cultural communication or distort biblical meaning in the process.

Article 13

We affirm that awareness of the literary categories, formal and stylistic, of the various parts of Scripture is essential for proper exegesis, and hence we value genre criticism as one of the many disciplines of biblical study.

We deny that generic categories which negate historicity may rightly be imposed on biblical narratives which present themselves as factual.

Article 14

We affirm that the biblical record of events, discourses and sayings, though presented in a variety of appropriate literary forms, corresponds to historical fact.

We deny that any event, discourse, or saying reported in Scripture was invented by the biblical writers or by the traditions they incorporated.

Article 15

We affirm the necessity of interpreting the Bible according to its literal, or normal, sense. The literal sense is the grammatical-historical sense, that is, the meaning which the writer expressed. Interpretation according to the literal sense will take account of all figures of speech and literary forms found in the text.

We deny the legitimacy of any approach to Scripture that attributes to it meaning which the literal sense does not support.

Article 16

We affirm that legitimate critical techniques should be used in determining the canonical text and its meaning.

We deny the legitimacy of allowing any method of biblical criticism to question the truth or integrity of the writer's expressed meaning, or of any other scriptural teaching.

Article 17

We affirm the unity, harmony, and consistency of Scripture and declare that it is its own best interpreter.

We deny that Scripture may be interpreted in such a way as to suggest that one passage corrects or militates against another. We deny that later writers of Scripture misinterpreted earlier passages of Scripture when quoting from or referring to them.

Article 18

We affirm that the Bible's own interpretation of itself is always correct, never deviating from, but rather elucidating, the single meaning of the inspired text. The single meaning of a prophet's words includes, but is not restricted to, the understanding of those words by the prophet and necessarily involves the intention of God evidenced in the fulfillment of those words.

We deny that the writers of Scripture always understood the full implications of their own words.

Article 19

We affirm that any preunderstandings which the interpreter brings to Scripture should be in harmony with scriptural teaching and subject to correction by it.

We deny that Scripture should be required to fit alien preunderstandings, inconsistent with itself, such as naturalism, evolutionism, scientism, secular humanism, and relativism.

Article 20

We affirm that since God is the author of all truth, all truths, biblical and extrabiblical, are consistent and cohere, and that the Bible speaks truth when it touches on matters pertaining to nature, history, or anything less. We further affirm that in some cases extrabiblical dates have value for clarifying what Scripture teaches, and for prompting correction of faulty interpretations.

We deny that extrabibilical views ever disprove the teaching of Scripture or hold priority over it.

Article 21

We affirm the harmony of special with general revelation and therefore of biblical teaching with the facts of nature.

We deny that any genuine scientific facts are inconsistent with the true meaning of any passage of Scripture.

Article 22

We affirm that Genesis 1–11 is factual, as is the rest of the book.

We deny that the teachings of Genesis 1–11 are mythical and that scientific hypotheses about earth history or the origin of humanity may be invoked to overthrow what Scripture teaches about creation.

Article 23

We affirm the clarity of Scripture and specifically of its message about salvation from sin.

We deny that all passages of Scripture are equally clear or have equal bearing on the message of redemption.

Article 24

We affirm that a person is not dependent for understanding of Scripture on the expertise of biblical scholars.

We deny that a person should ignore the fruits of the technical study of Scripture by biblical scholars.

Article 25

We affirm that the only type of preaching which sufficiently conveys the divine revelation and its proper application to life is that which faithfully expounds the text of Scripture as the Word of God.

We deny that the preacher has any message from God apart from the text of Scripture.

PART II

Covenants

CHAPTER ELEVEN

Covenant Of Broadmead Baptist Church
BRISTOL, ENGLAND (1640)

So that in the year of our forever blessed Redeemer, the Lord Jesus, one thousand six hundred and forty (1640), those five persons, namely Goodman Atkins of Stapleton, Goodman Cole, a butcher of Lawford's Gate, Richard Moone, a farrier in Wine Street, and Mr. Bacon, a young minister, with Mrs. Hazzard at Mrs. Hazard's house at the upper end of Broad Street in Bristol, they met together and came to a holy resolution to separate from the worship of the world and times they lived in, and that they would go no more to it, and with godly purpose of heart joined themselves together in the Lord; and only thus covenanting, that they would, in the strength and assistance of the Lord, come forth of the world and worship the Lord more purely, persevering therein to their end.

CHAPTER TWELVE

Covenant Of The Baptist Church

IN LEOMINSTER, HEREFORDSHIRE, ENGLAND (1656)

The 25th of the 7th month, 1656, the Church of Christ meeting at Brother Joseph Patshall's House in Leominster was constituted and the persons undernamed did after solemn seeking of God by prayer, give up themselves to the Lord and to each other to walk together in all the ordinances of Jesus Christ according to His appointments, which was done in the presence of our Brother Daniel King and other brethren.

CHAPTER THIRTEEN

Covenant of Benjamin and Elias Keach (1697)

We who desire to walk together in the fear of the Lord do, through the assistance of His Holy Spirit, profess our deep and serious humiliation for all our transgressions. And we do also solemnly, in the presence of God, of each other, in the sense of our own unworthiness, give up ourselves to the Lord, in a church state according to the apostolical constitution that He may be our God and we may be His people through the everlasting covenant of His free grace in which alone we hope to be accepted by Him through His blessed Son, Jesus Christ, whom we take to be our high Priest, to justify and sanctify us, and our prophet to teach us and to subject to Him as our Law-giver, and the King of saints; and to conform to all His holy laws and ordinances for our growth, establishment, and consolation that we may be as a holy spouse unto Him and serve Him in our generation and wait for His second appearance as our glorious Bridegroom.

Being fully satisfied in the way of church communion, and the truth of grace in some good measure upon one another's spirits, we do solemnly join ourselves together in a holy union and fellowship, humbly submitting to the discipline of the gospel and all holy duties required of a people in such a spiritual relation.

1. We do promise and engage to walk in all holiness, godliness, humility, and brotherly love, as much as in us lieth to render our communion delightful to God, comfortable to ourselves, and lovely to the rest of the Lord's people.

2. We do promise to watch over each other's conversations, and not to suffer sin upon one another, so far as God shall discover it to us, or any of us; and to stir up another to love and good works; to warn, rebuke, and admonish one another with meekness, according to the rules left to us of Christ in that behalf.

3. We do promise in an especial manner to pray for one another and for the glory and increase of this church and for the presence of God in it, and the pouring forth of His Spirit on it, and His protection over it to His glory.

4. We do promise to bear one another's burdens, to cleave to one another, and to have a fellow-feeling with one another, in all conditions both outward and inward as God in His providence shall cast any of us into.

5. We do promise to bear with one another's weaknesses, failings, and infirmities with much tenderness, not discovering to any without the church, nor any within, unless according to Christ's rule and the order of the gospel provided in that case.

6. We do promise to strive together for the truths of the gospel and purity of God's ways and ordinances, to avoid causes and causers of division, endeavoring to keep the unity of the Spirit in the bond of peace (Eph. 4:3).

7. We do promise to meet together on the Lord's Days, and at other times, as the Lord shall give us opportunities to serve and

glorify God in the way of His worship, to edify one another, and to contrive the good of His church.

8. We do promise according to our ability (or as God shall bless us with the good things of this world) to communicate to our pastor or minister, God having ordained that they that preach the gospel should live of the gospel. (And now can anything lay a greater obligation upon the conscience than this covenant, what then is the sin of such who violate it?)

These and all other gospel duties we humbly submit unto, promising and purposing to perform, not in our own strength, being conscious of our own weaknesses, but in the power and strength of the blessed God, whose we are and whom we desire to serve. To whom be glory now and forevermore.

CHAPTER FOURTEEN

Covenant of Great Ellingham Baptist Church

NORFOLK, ENGLAND (1699)

We, a little handful of the meanest, both of the children of men and of the children of God, being called by the grace of God out of the iron furnace of the land of Egypt, judge it our duty to enquire by what methods we may glorify our Redeemer in the highest form the saints are capable of attaining to in this life. After a diligent inquiry into the mind of God in this great concern, we are satisfied by Holy Writ, that a church state is next to a state of grace, and in order to a state of glory, the most conducive to the saints' happiness here below, and forasmuch as the Lord hath showed us the form of His house and the fashion thereof, we judge it our privilege as well as our duty, to be waiting at the place of wisdom's doors; for it is better to be door-keeper in the house of the Lord than to dwell in the tents of wickedness. Besides we find the way which God chose to lead His people in, both in the Old Testament's days, and also in the primitive times of the gospel, He had His church in the wilderness then, and He hath His churches in the wilderness now. And we esteem it a more honorable thing to follow Christ in a more solitary path than to enjoy the pleasures of sin, which are but for a season.

We likewise find in Holy Writ, that an explicit covenanting with, and giving up ourselves to the Lord and one another, is the formal cause of particular visible gospel church. We likewise desiring to be added to the Lord, do make a sure covenant, according to the example of the church in Nehemiah's time; who made a sure covenant and wrote it; and we do hereby engage ourselves (as the Lord shall assist us) to walk with one another to the glory of God and the edification of each other in love, for the bearing of one another's burdens, for the strengthening of one another's faith, for the improving of each other's gifts, and the watching over one another's souls: and we do hereby further engage ourselves as the Lord shall assist us, to keep close to the ordinances of our Lord Jesus Christ, as they are delivered to us in the Holy gospel, without any mixture of human inventions.

We do likewise covenant and agree together to separate ourselves wholly from the worship of the world, and the religion of the times we are fallen into, that we may (through the strength of Christ) keep our garments unspotted from the world. And we likewise engage ourselves to walk circumspectly in God's house, not forsaking the assembling ourselves together, but to worship God in public, and so oft as may be in private, one with another. We also engage ourselves so far as we are, or shall be able, to keep up the ministry of the Word, and ordinances of Christ, among ourselves, that our souls may be edified and the church multiplied, and increased with the increase of God.

And this covenant engagement of ours, we [word omitted] through the strength of Christ to pursue, so long as we can walk together to the glory of God, and the comfort and edification of our own souls. And this, so far as we have learned from the

Word, is that covenant which the son of the stranger and the eunuch, viz. The Gentiles are to take hold of that they may have a name and a place in God's house, and within His walls, even a better name than of sons and of daughters, and this is implied in giving ourselves to the Lord and therein to one another by the will of God, thereby to be visibly added to the Lord and one another.

CHAPTER FIFTEEN

Covenant of the Baptist Church

AT CAERLEON, WALES (1770)

In the name and fear of the Lord and according to the golden rule of His Word and the dictates of our own consciences, we will endeavor, and it is our firm resolution, to fulfil and live under the influence of the following articles:

1. We believe there is one God and He has authority over all His creatures; therefore it is the duty of all reasonable creatures to obey Him in the whole of His revealed will.

2. In solemn and religious manner we give ourselves unto the Lord, bodies and souls, to be His in life or death; likewise our time and talents (as far as we think it our duty) to the glory of His name and the support of His interests.

3. We give ourselves to one another according to the will of God to be a part of the visible church of Christ here upon earth,

accounting it to our privilege and greatest honor to establish a church to God in a place where it never was before.

4. We desire and it is our unfeigned intention, in the name of fear and strength of Jehovah, to strive together for the faith of the gospel: that is to say the doctrines of grace in their several branches, as far as we can see them in the Word of God and other useful books, particularly the Confession of Faith as it was published by our baptized brethren in the year 1689.

5. Moreover in the same strength we will endeavor to support and practice the ordinances of the gospel in their apostolic purity, taking the Word of God as our chief rule in this and all other things.

6. Besides we earnestly desire and pray and firmly resolve to walk in love with one another as far as possible without offense towards those without, and in the practice of every other duty to God and man though it has not been mentioned here.

7. Desire we do, and endeavor we will, to spread and adorn the interest of the Lord and Savior Jesus Christ with fervent and constant prayers for the influence of His Spirit, and rich communications of His grace to assist us herein.

We do in the presence of the ever blessed Trinity, the angels of heaven and this congregation sincerely, uprightly and religiously give the right hand of fellowship to one another, and set our names to the above articles saying, so help us God, Amen.

CHAPTER SIXTEEN

Covenant of the Baptist Church

IN HORSE FAIR, STONY STRATFORD, BUCKS, ENGLAND (1790)

We whose names are underwritten do now declare that we embrace the Word of God as our only guide in matters of religion, and acknowledge no other authority whatever as binding upon the conscience. Having, we hope, found mercy at the hands of God, in delivering us from the power of darkness, and translating us into the Kingdom of His dear Son, we think and feel ourselves bound to walk in obedience to His divine commands. On looking into the sacred Scripture, we find it was common in the first ages of Christianity for such as professed repentance towards God and faith in our Lord Jesus Christ, voluntarily to unite together in Christian societies called in the New Testament, churches. Their ends in so doing were to honor God and promote their own spiritual edification. Having searched the written Word, we trust, with a degree of diligence, in order that we may know how to act, as well as what to believe, and sought unto God by prayer for divine direction, we heartily approve of, and mean to follow their example. With a view to this, we now solemnly, in the presence of the all-seeing and heart-searching God, do mutually covenant and agree, in manner and form following.

1. To maintain and hold fast the important and fundamental truths of revelation. These we apprehend to be such as respect the natural and moral character of Jehovah, and the various relations He stands in to His rational creatures; the original purity but present depravity of human nature; the total moral inability and yet absolute inexcusableness of man as a guilty sinner before God; the perpetuity of a divine law, and the equity of its awful sanction; the infinite dignity of the Son of God in His original character as a divine Person, possessed of all the perfections of Deity, and His all-sufficiency for the office of Mediator between God and man, in consequence of the union of the divine and human natures in one person; the acceptance of our persons with, and the enjoyment of all good from God, through His mediation; the proper divinity and blessed agency of the Holy Spirit in our regeneration, sanctification, and consolation; in one word, that our full salvation, from its first cause to its final consummation, is a display of sovereign goodness accomplishing the gracious purposes of Him, who worketh all things according to the counsel of His own will, and known unto whom is the end from the beginning.

2. To seek by all proper means the good of the church with which we stand connected. To this end we engage to attend regularly, as far as we have opportunity, all seasons of public worship, church meetings, and meetings of prayer appointed by the church. When we are absent we will be ready to give an account why we were so, if required. We will diligently watch for the appearances of God's work in our congregation; and if we see any setting their faces Zion-ward, we will endeavor to instruct and encourage; and having hopeful evidence of the reality of God's work upon their souls, will lay before them the privileges

they have a right unto, and the duties they ought to be found in, of following Christ in His ordinances and institutions. If called to the painful work of executing the penalties of Christ upon the breakers of the laws of His house, we will endeavor to exercise it in the spirit of the gospel, without respect of persons. In all questions that shall be debated at our church meetings, the brethren shall speak but one at a time, and if a difference in sentiment should take place, we will endeavor in brotherly love to weigh the matter fully and deliberately, and then put it to the vote in order that it may be determined by the majority. Also we engage that according to our ability, we will contribute our share towards defraying all necessary expenses attending the worship of God. We likewise promise to keep the secrets of the church and not to expose its concerns to the world around.

3. To esteem our pastor highly in love for his work's sake, this we will endeavor to manifest by frequently and fervently praying for him; diligently attending on his ministry; encouraging his heart and strengthening his hands to the utmost of our power in the work of the Lord; freely consulting him as we have occasion and opportunity, respecting our spiritual affairs; treating him affectionately when present, and speaking respectfully of him when absent. As he is a man of like passions with others, we will endeavor to conceal and cover with a mantle of love, his weaknesses and imperfections; also to communicate unto him of our temporal good things, knowing that the Lord hath ordained that they that preach the gospel should live of the gospel.

4. To walk in love toward those with whom we stand connected in bonds of Christian fellowship. As the effect of this, we will pray much for one another. As we have opportunity, we will associate together for religious purposes. Those of us who are in more comfortable situations in life than some of our brethren, with regard to the good things of providence, will administer as we have ability and see occasion, to their necessities. We will bear one another's burdens, sympathize with the afflicted in body and mind, so far as we know their case, under their trials; and as we see occasion, advise, caution, and encourage one another. We will watch over one another for good. We will stu-

diously avoid giving or taking offenses. Thus we will make it our study to fulfil the law of Christ.

5. To be particularly attentive to our station in life, and the peculiar duties incumbent on us in that situation. We who are husbands or wives will conscientiously discharge relative duties towards our respective yoke-fellows. We who are heads of families will maintain the daily worship of God in our houses, and endeavor to instruct those under our care, both by our words and actions. We who are children will be obedient to our parents in the Lord. We who are masters will [render] unto our servants that which is just and equal. We who are servants engage to be diligent and faithful, not acting with eye-service as men-pleasers, but with singleness of heart as unto God, knowing we have a Master in heaven. We will in our different places of abode, inquire what we can do for the good of the church to which we belong, and as far as we have ability, we will open or encourage the opening of a door wherever we can, for the preaching of the Word, remembering that we ought to be as the salt of the earth.

6. To walk in a way and manner becoming the gospel, before them that are without, that we may by well-doing put to silence the ignorance of gainsayers. We will practice the strictest honesty in our dealings, and faithfulness in fulfilling all our promises. It shall be our study to represent a fair picture of religion before the eyes of the world in the whole of our conduct and conversation. We will abstain from all vain amusements and diversions, by which time would be foolishly spent, money wasted, our minds carnalized, and we exposed to many dangerous temptations. We engage in a special manner to sanctify the Lord's Day. In fine it shall be our study to keep our garments unspotted by the flesh, and walk as becometh saints.

7. To receive such, and only such, into communion with us as in a judgment of charity we think are born again; have been baptized according to the primitive mode of administering that ordinance, and profess their hearty approbation of, and subjection to, this our solemn church covenant.

These things, and whatever else may appear enjoined by the Word of God, we promise in the strength of divine grace to observe and practice. But knowing our insufficiency for anything that is spiritually good, in and of ourselves, we look up to Him who giveth power to the faint, rejoicing that in the Lord we have not only righteousness but strength. Hold thou us up, O Lord, and we shall be safe! Amen.

CHAPTER SEVENTEEN

Covenant of Swansea Baptist Church

REHOBOTH, MASSACHUSETTS (1663)

Swansea in New England. A true copy of the Holy Covenant the first founders of Swansea entered into at the first beginning, and all the members thereof for divers years.

Whereas, we poor creatures are, through the exceeding riches of God's infinite grace, mercifully snatched out of the kingdom of darkness, and by His infinite power translated into the kingdom of His dear Son, there to be partakers with all the saints of all those privileges which Christ by the shedding of His precious blood hath purchased for us, and that we do find our souls in some good measure wrought on by divine grace to desire to be conformable to Christ in all things, being also constrained by the matchless love and wonderful distinguishing mercies that we abundantly enjoy from His most free grace to serve Him according to our utmost capacities, and that we also know that it is our most bounden duty to walk in visible communion with Christ and each other according to the prescript rule of His most Holy Word, and also that it is our undoubted right through Christ to enjoy all the privileges of God's house which our souls for a long time panted after, and finding no other way at present by the all-working providence of our only wise God and gracious Father to us opened for the enjoying of the same, we do therefore, after often and solemn seeking to the Lord for help and direction in the fear of His holy name, and with hands lifted up to Him, the most High God, humble and freely offer up ourselves this day a living sacrifice unto Him, who is our God in covenant through Christ our Lord and only Savior, to walk together according to His revealed Word in the visible gospel relation both to Christ, our only Head, and to each other as fellow-members and brethren of the same household of faith.

And we do humble pray that through His strength we will henceforth endeavor to perform all our respective duties towards God and each other, and to practice all the ordinances of Christ according to what is or shall be revealed to us in our respective place, to exercise, practice and submit to the government of Christ in this His church, viz: further protesting against all rending or dividing principles or practices from any of the people of God as being most abominable and loathsome to our souls and utterly inconsistent with that Christian charity which declares men to be Christ's disciples. Indeed, further declaring in that as union in Christ is the sole ground of our communion, each with other, so we are ready to accept of, receive to and hold communion with all such by judgment of charity we conceive to be fellow-members with us in our Head, Christ Jesus, though differing from us in such controversial points as are not absolutely and essentially necessary to salvation.

We also hope that though of ourselves we are altogether unworthy and unfit thus to offer up ourselves to God or to do Him a favor, to expect any favor with, or mercy from Him, He will graciously accept of this our freewill offering in and through the merit and mediation of our dear Redeemer, and that He will employ and improve us in this service to His praise, to whom be all glory, honor, now and forever. Amen.

CHAPTER EIGHTEEN

Covenant of First Baptist Church

NEWPORT, RHODE ISLAND (1727)

We who desire to walk together in the fear of the Lord do by the help and assistance of the Holy Ghost profess our deep sense of sin and humiliation therefore and do now solemnly in the presence of the great God, the elect angels, and one another, having a sense of our unworthiness, considered of ourselves and looking wholly and alone to the Lord Jesus Christ for worthiness and acceptance give up ourselves to the Lord in a church state that He may be our God and we His people through the everlasting covenant of His free grace desiring to submit to Jesus Christ as the King and Head of His church, embracing Him as the Prophet, Priest, and King of our salvation and to conform to all His holy laws and ordinances for our growth, establishment, and consolation that we may be a holy spouse unto Him; being fully satisfied in the way of church communion and of the truth of grace on each other's soul in some good measure we do now solemnly in the name and fear of God, join ourselves together in a holy union and fellowship humbly submitting to the discipline of the gospel and all holy duties which our spiritual relation enjoys and requires we promise by the help of divine grace without which we can do nothing to walk in all godliness, humility, and brotherly love so that our communion may be delightful to God and comfortable to ourselves and the rest of the Lord's people to watch over each other's conversation and not suffer sin upon one another as God shall discover it to us or any of us and to stir up each other to love and good works, and if any fall into sin to warn and admonish them according to the nature of the offense with a spirit of meekness as the gospel requires.

We promise and engage to pray with and for one another as God shall enable us from time to time for the glory of this church that the presence of God may be in it and His Spirit rest upon it and His protection over it that it may be increased with the increase of God we do promise to bear one another's burdens, weaknesses, short comings, and infirmities, and not to acquaint any without the garden of Christ of them but to observe the rule of Christ in such cases we do promise to strive together for the truth of the gospel and purity of God's ordinances and endeavor to pass a Christian construction upon these that in some lesser and extra fundamental points differ from us; endeavoring to keep the unity of the Spirit in the bond of peace with all that hold the Head, Jesus Christ, both their Lord and ours, and that we will not retain a pharisaical Spirit to withdraw in the time of prayer, but will join with all such as in the ground of charity as true believers and churches of Jesus Christ.

We promise to observe the public worship of God on Lord's Days and at other times, as God may afford opportunity and strive what in us lies for each other's edification, each and every of these things we humbly submit to in the name and fear of God promising and purposing to perform not in our own strength, being conscious of our own weakness, but in the power and strength of the blessed God whose redeemed ones we trust we are and whom we sincerely desire to serve—to whom be glory in all the churches now and evermore. Amen.

Signed by us in the name and behalf of the whole church at a church meeting this 4th day of May in the year 1727.

CHAPTER NINETEEN

Covenant of Middleborough Baptist Church

MIDDLEBOROUGH, MASSACHUSETTS (1756)

We do now in the presence of the great all seeing and most glorious God; and before angels and men, give up ourselves to the Lord Jehovah, Father, Son, and Holy Ghost, and account Him this day to be our God, our Father, our Savior, and our Leader, and receive Him as our portion forever. We give up ourselves unto the Lord Jesus Christ and adhere to Him as the Head of His people in the covenant of grace, and rely on Him as our Prophet, Priest, and King to bring us to eternal blessedness. We acknowledge our everlasting and indispensable obligation to glorify our God by living a holy, righteous, and godly life in this present world, in all our several places and relations; and we do engage by the assistance of the divine Spirit to improve all our time and strength, talents and advantages for His glory and the good of our fellow men: promising by divine help to walk in our houses with a perfect heart and to train up those under our care in the ways of God.

And we also give up ourselves to one another in covenant, promising to act towards each other as brethren in Christ; watching over one another in the love of God; and to watch not only against them that are reckoned more gross evils, but also against all foolish talking and jesting which is not convenient; vain disputing about words and things which gender strife; disregarding promises and not fulfilling of engagements; vain and unnecessary worldly conversation on Lord's Days, and whatsoever else that is contrary to sound doctrine according to the glorious gospel of Christ.

Promising to hold communion together in the worship of God, and in the ordinances and discipline of His church according as we are or shall be guided by the Spirit of God in His world; expecting that He will yet further and more gloriously open His Word and the mysteries of His kingdom, flying to the blood of the everlasting covenant for the pardon of our many errors and praying that the Lord would prepare and strengthen us for every good work to do His will, working in us that which is well pleasing in His sight through Jesus Christ, to whom be glory forever and ever. Amen.

CHAPTER TWENTY

Covenant of Grassy Creek Baptist Church

GRASSY CREEK, NORTH CAROLINA (1757)

Holding believers' baptism, the laying on of hands; particular election of grace by the predestination of God in Christ; effectual calling by the Holy Ghost; free justification through the imputed righteousness of Christ; progressive sanctification through God's grace and truth; the final perseverance, or continuance of the saints in grace; the resurrection of these bodies after death, at that day which God has appointed to judge the quick and dead by Jesus Christ, by the power of God, and by the resurrection of Christ; and life everlasting. Amen.

1. We do, as in the presence of the great and everlasting God, who knows the secrets of all hearts, and in the presence of angels and men, acknowledge ourselves to be under the most solemn

covenant with the Lord, to live for Him and no other. We take the only living and true God to be our God, one God in three persons, Father, Son, and Holy Ghost.

2. We receive the Holy Scriptures of the Old and New Testament to be the revealed mind and will of God, believing them to contain a perfect rule for our faith and practice, and promise through the assistance of the Holy Spirit, to make them the rule of our life and practice, in all church discipline, acknowledging ourselves by nature children of wrath, and our hope of mercy with God, to be only through the righteousness of Jesus Christ, apprehended by faith.

3. We do promise to bear with one another's infirmities and weaknesses, with much tenderness, not discovering them to any in the church, but by gospel rule and order, which is laid down in Matthew 18:15,16,17.

4. We do believe that God has ordained that they who preach the gospel shall live of the gospel; and we call heaven and earth to witness that we without the lease reserve, give up ourselves, through the help and aiding grace of God's Spirit, our souls and bodies and all that we have to this one God, to be entirely at His disposal, both ourselves, our names and estates, as God shall see best for His own glory; and that we will faithfully do, by the help of God's Spirit, whatsoever our consciences, influenced by the Word and Spirit of God, shall direct to be our duty, both to God and man; and we do, by the assistance of divine grace, unitedly give up ourselves to one another in covenant, promising by the grace of God to act towards one another as brethren in Christ, watching over one another in the love of God, especially to watch against all jesting, light and foolish talking which are not convenient (Eph. 5:4). Everything that does not become the followers of the Holy Lamb of God; and that we will seek the good of each other, and the church universally, for God's glory; and hold communion together in the worship of God, in the ordinances and discipline of this church of God, according to Christ's visible kingdom, so far as the providence of God admits of the same: "Not forsaking the assembling of ourselves together, as the manner of some is," but submitting ourselves

unto the discipline of the church, as a part of Christ's mystical body, according as we shall be guided by the Word and Spirit of God, and by the help of divine grace, still looking for more light from God, as contained in the Holy Scriptures, believing that there are greater mysteries to be unfolded and shine in the church, beyond what she has ever enjoyed: looking and waiting for the great power, and "have dominion also from sea to sea, and from the river unto the ends of the earth."

This covenant we make with full and free consent of our minds, believing that through free and boundless grace, it is owned of God and ratified in heaven, before the throne of God and the Lamb. Amen. Even so, come, Lord Jesus. Amen, and amen.

CHAPTER TWENTY-ONE

Covenant of Kiokee Baptist Church

KIOKEE, GEORGIA (1771; REVISED, 1826)

1. According to God's appointment in His Word, we do hereby in His name and strength covenant and promise to keep up and defend all the articles of faith, according to God's Word, such as the great doctrine of election, effectual calling, particular redemption, justification by the imputed righteousness of Christ alone, sanctification by the spirit of God, believers' baptism by immersion, the saints' absolute final perseverance in grace, the resurrection of the dead, future rewards and punishments, etc., all according to Scripture which we take as the rule of our faith and practice, with some other doctrines herein not mentioned, as are commanded and supported by that blessed Book: denying the Arian, Socinian, and Arminian errors, and every other prin-

ciple contrary to the Word of God. Now yet since we are exhorted to prove all things, orderly ministers of any denomination may when invited, preach in our meeting house.

2. We believe that believers should attend to the celebration of the Lord's Supper, and should any neglect or refuse to attend, they may be required to give a reason of their conduct, this article forbids any of our members from communing with any who do not practice believers' baptism by immersion.

3. We do promise by the grace of God helping us, to bear with each other as brethren, and to manifest love by not receiving evil reports against each other without undeniable evidences: not to speak railingly of one another, but according to Matthew 18, admonish each other with a prudent and Godly fear, not to look on sin with the least allowance in any of the brethren, we also promise to manifest love to each other by Godly encouragement, waiting for all opportunity to do all kind offices to each other, as become saints, such as bearing with the weak in love, sympathizing with the afflicted and tempted, administering both godly admonitions and all such relief to them as Christian charity demands, promising also each for him, or herself to submit to all such admonitions, exhortations, and reproofs administered to us by any prudent member or church.

4. We do also promise as much as in our power to give all due attendance to the public worship of God on the Lord's Days, and all other days, as we may have opportunity, also on such days as are appointed to transact the business of the church, and when met calmly and faithfully give our opinions, avoiding clamorous disputations and whispering during discussion, and to do all in our power to maintain peace and good order among us—and whoever fails attending our regular meetings, three times in succession without sending or rendering a sufficient excuse, the church shall appoint some person or persons to cite and require such delinquent person to attend, and should he or she neglect or refuse yet to attend, he shall be dealt with as a disorderly member and for the better observance of this rule, the clerk shall be required at the conclusion of each conference to note down, and call for such absentees who shall be required at

the next conference to give the reason of absence, the minutes of the last conference shall be read at the commencement of the next when thought necessary.

5. We promise to contribute according to our abilities for the support of our minister and poor of the flock, also for the Lord's table, and the keeping, opening, shutting, and cleansing our meeting house and spring; also to encourage promising gifts in our own church, traveling ministers who are orderly and in fellowship in their own church and such other persons as shall appear conformable to the rule of love and charity—no disorderly minister shall preach in our meeting house, and if any suspicious stranger attempts it, the deacons and minister of this church is hereby privileged to examine and call on him for his license or credentials, to be satisfied.

6. We promise to strive together for the faith once delivered to the saints, to avoid all just cause of offense either amongst ourselves or those that are without, to keep good order in our families, not to go to law with each other, if avoidable, or which the church shall judge—

7. All persons desiring to become members of this church shall be received into our fellowship only by the unanimous agreement of this church present, and they shall be kept in only by unanimous consent—this regards the taking in or turning out of members.

8. We promise to make us of our endeavors to adorn our holy profession with a holy life and conversation that God in all things may be glorified through Jesus Christ our Lord, this and all other possible duties, we do humbly submit by promising to perform them, not in our own strength but in the power and strength of the everlasting and ever blessed God, whose we are in Him we desire to serve. To whom be glory and dominion forever and ever. Amen.

CHAPTER TWENTY-TWO

Covenant of Meherrin Baptist Church

LUNENBURG COUNTY, VIRGINIA (1779)

Whereas in the providence of God we, a part of the Baptist Church of Christ residing and being in Meherrin, Virginia, known by the name of Meherrin Church are now settled upon the waters of the Yadkin, very remote from the seat of constitution and it being inexpedient in the present circumstance of affairs for us to join any neighboring church and that we did not fully intend or expect when we removed having our former pastor or minister of Meherrin with us, and being privileged if we thought expedient to embody as a church; we therefore taking the matter into our serious and deliberate consideration, with fasting and prayer to God, believe it will be for the glory of God so to do. We therefore solemnly in the presence of God, covenant to and with each other under an humble sense of our own unworthiness and give up ourselves to the Lord and to each other in a church state, according to the primitive mode and custom of constitutions, praying that God may be with us and enable us to conform to all His desired laws and ordinances, that we may be a spiritual house built up together by His divine grace, that we be enabled to serve and glorify Him and at last be received into the mansions of eternal glory.

1. We agree solemnly in the presence of God to give up ourselves to God and to each other in a spiritual union and fellowship, humbly submitting to the gospel discipline and to engage in all religious duties required of the people to each other in such a spiritual connection, and to stir up each other to love and good works, to warn, reprove, rebuke, exhort and admonish each other in meekness, according as the various circumstances occur or require, and as the Word of God shall direct in particular cases.

2. We agree and do promise, God assisting, to strive together for the faith of the gospel and purity of godliness and endeavor to keep the unity of the Spirit in the bond of peace and that we shall bear one another's burdens, weaknesses and infirmities, with much tenderness and conduct ourselves in such cases as to divulging or secreting agreeable to the plain rule given us in Matthew 18:15,16,17.

3. We agree and do promise, God assisting, to meet together on the Lord's Day and at other times, as the Lord shall give opportunity (agreeable to the divine injunction, Hebrews 24 and 25) to receive instruction from the Word preached, to comfort and edify each other, to promote godliness and do service to the church of Christ.

4. We agree and do promise, God assisting, to do all the good we possibly can to all men both in a spiritual and temporal sense, but especially to the household of faith, agreeable to Galatians 6 and 10, and that we will do all the duties required of us in God's Word, to our own minister or succeeding minister, but God in His providence has or may later set over us to watch for our souls.

5. Whereas there has been and as yet in many parts of these states of Virginia and North Carolina certain bars of communion kept up and maintained between what is called Regular and Separate Baptists, much to the grief and mortification of many pious people and very prejudicial to the interest and establishment of Christ's Kingdom, which bars were taken down in full church meeting in Meherrin Church in December, 1774, and a free and open communion kept up with all orderly Baptists without distinction with regard to the terms Regular and Separate—we therefore agree not to restrict our communion to any people baptized upon profession of their faith where we have sufficient ground to believe that gospel order and piety are maintained by and among them.

6. And lasting, Meherrin Church, at the time of their constitution, January 1772, did fully adopt and receive a confession of faith by the delegates and ministers of upward of one hundred congregations in England and Wales met in London in July, 1689, and since adopted by the Philadelphia Baptist Association met in Philadelphia, September, 1742, and now well known by the name of the Philadelphia Confession of Faith. We therefore do hereby testify that that is yet a brief summary of our faith and principles (with some few exceptions not essential to salvation or church communion). We therefore adopt it as good human composition in the general, which we agree to observe both in principle and church government as long as we shall believe it agreeable to God's Word—no longer, as we believe the Scriptures of the Old and New Testament is the only standard of truth by which the church is to conduct herself (whatever respect she may have to good human composition) for that we believe the church of Christ will now grow and make more discovery of light into the glorious treasure of God's Word while she continues her militant state, and so consequently it would be presumption before God and forming chains to fetter our consciences with to bind ourselves unalterably and unchangeably to any set of principles whatever, except what is written and contained in the glorious unchangeable Word of God, which liveth

and abideth forever. We pray for grace to enable us to understand and walk agreeable thereto.

The above is a true copy of the covenant received and signed by the aforesaid members of the day and the year above written.

CHAPTER TWENTY-THREE

Covenant of Cherokee Creek Baptist Church

WASHINGTON COUNTY, NORTH CAROLINA (now Jonesboro, Tennessee) (1783)

As the professors of Christianity are so divided their principles and practice that they cannot hold communion together and passing by the several classes of pedobaptists. There are several classes of Antepedobaptists, with which we cannot agree. Namely, the Seven Day Baptists, the non-Sabbath Baptists, and those that dip three times in baptism, with all of which we cannot agree. Therefore think it expedient to covenant or agree together in matters of faith and order, yet so as not to reject those Christians as only differ from us in contra essential matters. But as a distinct society do embody ourselves and the following rules references and articles to our several names are annex. Yet as we do not look upon ourselves infallible we still

213

look to be further taught by the Word and Spirit of God into those ministries contained in the Holy Scriptures.

The solemn covenant of the Baptist Church on Cherokee Creek and the waters adjacent in the county of Washington and state of North Carolina entered into the first Saturday in September 1783. Holding believers' baptism by immersion the laying on of hands particular, election of grace by the predestination of God in Christ, effectual calling by the Holy Ghost, free justification by the righteousness of Christ imputed to us and apprehended by faith, progression sanctification through God's grace and truth, and final perseverance of the saints in grace and holiness, the resurrection of the body and life everlasting . . . and now we do in the presence of the great and eternal God who knoweth the secrets of all hearts unitedly, give ourselves to the Lord to be at His disposal, taking this one God to be our God, one God and three Persons, and to one another in covenant promising by the grace of God to act towards each other as brethren in Christ.

1. To attend our respective meetings and especially church meetings unless providentially hindered and the reason to be given to the church if called for.

2. To hold communion together in the worship of God, in the celebration of His ordinances;

3. To bear with each others infirmities with tenderness, not to discover them out of the community where it may be avoided, nor in the community, but by the gospel rule and order as we shall be directed by the Word and Spirit of God;

4. To bear reproof and admonition from each other patiently, to reprove and admonish each other faithfully, yet tenderly, in Christian charity and brotherly love;

5. To live orderly in our families in keeping up the worship of God, in being faith to instruct to admonish and to cease from vice according to our several abilities and respective opportunities;

6. To use reasonable industry for temporal sustenance,

7. To be liberal according to our several abilities in communicating to the support of the worship of God in money;

8. Not to remove our abode out of the bounds of this church without informing and consulting the church.

9. Not to take any in our particular membership that will not sign this covenant, that disputes may be avoided and concord maintained. And if any shall preach, profess, or practice contrary to these articles of this covenant of principals referred to therein, he, she or they shall be liable to the censure of the church. And in case of obstinate continuance shall be excluded our communion, nevertheless when the case calls for it they may and ought to excommunicate instantly.

And in testimony of our sincerity and that we have no reserve, we have hereunto set out hands. Amen.

CHAPTER TWENTY-FOUR

VERSE EDITION:
Covenant of Peter
Philanthropos Roots
(1806)

1. Our solemn covenant now we make,
O may we never this covenant break,
May God and men and angels see,
And witness our sincerity.

2. The Father, Son, and Spirit now,
Our God and portion we avow:
We'll love His name, obey His laws,
And seek to build the Christian cause.

3. The Scriptures we will daily read,
And to this light give earnest heed;
Our children in the righteous way
We'll strive to teach, and with them pray.

4. No frothy wit, nor tattling vile,
Shall waste our time, our hearts beguile;
In conversation we will try
Those who us hear to edify.

5. To one another we'll be kind,
Each other's good will daily mind;
To all men we'll be just and true,
Nor hold from them their proper due.

6. The church appointments we'll attend,
The Lord's Day too in worship spend;
To discipline we will submit.
O may we never these vows forget.

7. Revengeful anger we'll suppress,
'Tis very wrong we do confess;
In love and peace to all we'll speak.
O may we never this covenant break.

Conclusion

New rules we do not mean to make,
The Bible rules we only take,
And show by this our Scriptural creed,
In Bible truth we are agreed.

CHAPTER TWENTY-FIVE

Covenant of the New Hampshire Baptist Convention (1833)

Having been, as we trust, brought by divine grace to embrace the Lord Jesus Christ, and to give up ourselves wholly to Him; we do now solemnly and joyfully covenant with each other, to walk together in Him with brotherly love, to His glory as our common Lord. We do, therefore, in His strength engage,

That we will exercise a mutual care as members one of another to promote the growth of the whole body in Christian knowledge, holiness, and comfort; to the end that we may stand perfect and complete in all the will of God.

That to promote and secure this object, we will uphold the public worship of God and the ordinances of His house; and hold constant communion with each other therein; that we will cheerfully contribute of our property for the support of the poor, and for the maintenance of a faithful ministry of the gospel among us.

That we will not omit closet and family religion at home; nor allow ourselves in the too common neglect of the great duty of religiously training up our children, and those under our care, with a view to the service of Christ, and the enjoyment of heaven.

That we walk circumspectly in the world, that we may win their souls; remembering that God hath not given us the spirit of fear, but of power and of love and of a sound mind; that we are the light of the world and the salt of the earth, and that a city set on a hill cannot be hid.

That we will frequently exhort, and if occasion shall require, admonish one another, according to Matthew 18th, in the spirit of meekness; considering ourselves lest we also be tempted, and that as in baptism we have been buried with Christ and raised again; so there is on us a special obligation henceforth to walk in newness of life.

And may the God of peace, who brought again from the dead our Lord Jesus, that great Shepherd of the sheep, through the blood of the everlasting covenant, make us perfect in every good work to do His will; working in us that which is well-pleasing in His sight through Jesus Christ: to whom be glory forever and ever. Amen.

CHAPTER TWENTY-SIX

Covenant of James Allen, Avery Briggs, And E. C. Messinger
(MASSACHUSETTS, 1838)

In the presence of God, His holy angels, and this assembly, you do now solemnly avouch the Lord Jehovah, Father, Son, and Holy Ghost, to be your God; the object of your supreme affection, and your portion forever. You cordially acknowledge the Lord Jesus Christ in all His mediatorial offices, Prophet, Priest, and King, as your only Savior, and the Holy Spirit as your Sanctifier, Comforter, and Guide. You humbly and cheerfully devote yourselves to God in the everlasting covenant of His grace; you consecrate all your powers and faculties to His service and glory; and you promise, that through the assistance of His Spirit, you will cleave to Him as your chief good; that you will give diligent attendance to His Word and ordinances, that you will seek the honor and interest of His kingdom; and that henceforth, denying all ungodliness, and every worldly lust, you will live soberly, righteously, and godly in the world.

You do now cordially join yourselves to this church of Christ, engaging to strive earnestly for its peace, edification, and purity, and to walk with its members in love, faithfulness, circumspection, meekness, and sobriety, and contribute your proportion as God shall prosper you, toward the pecuniary support of the gospel ministry. This you severally profess and engage.

In consequence of these professions and engagements, we, the members of this church, affectionately receive you to our communion, and in the name of Christ declare you entitled to all its privileges. We welcome you to this fellowship with us in the blessings of the Gospel, and on our part engage to watch over you and seek your edification as long as you shall continue with us. And hereafter you can never withdraw from the watch and communion of saints, without a breach of covenant.

And now, beloved in the Lord, let it be impressed on your minds that you have entered into solemn obligations from which you can never escape. Wherever you go, these vows will be upon you; they will follow you to the bar of God, and will abide upon you to eternity. You can never be as you have been. You have unalterably committed yourselves, and henceforth you must be the servants of God. Hereafter the eyes of the world will be upon you, and as you demean yourself, so religion will be honored or dishonored; if you walk worthily of your profession you will be a credit and comfort to us, but if otherwise, it will be an occasion of grief and reproach. But, beloved, we are persuaded better things of you, and things which accompany salvation, though we thus speak. May the Lord guide and preserve you till death, and at last receive you and us to that blessed world where our love and joy shall be forever perfect. Amen.

CHAPTER TWENTY-SEVEN

Covenant of J. Newton Brown's *The Baptist Church Manual (1853)*

Having been led, as we believe, by the Spirit of God to receive the Lord Jesus Christ as our Savior; and, on the profession of our faith, having been baptized in the name of the Father and of the Son and of the Holy Ghost, we do now, in the presence of God, angels, and this assembly, most solemnly and joyfully enter into covenant with one another, as one body in Christ.

We engage, therefore, by the aid of the Holy Spirit, to walk together in Christian love; to strive for the advancement of this church, in knowledge, holiness, and comfort; to promote its prosperity and spirituality; to sustain its worship, ordinances, discipline, and doctrines; to contribute cheerfully and regularly to the support of the ministry, the expenses of the church, the relief of the poor, and the spread of the gospel through all nations.

We also engage to maintain family and secret devotion; to religiously educate our children; to seek the salvation of our kindred and acquaintances; to walk circumspectly in the world; to be just in our dealings, faithful in our engagements, and exemplary in our deportment; to avoid all tattling, backbiting, and excessive anger; to abstain from the sale and use of intoxicating drinks as a beverage, and to be zealous in our efforts to advance the kingdom of our Savior.

We further engage to watch over one another in brotherly love, to remember each other in prayer, to aid each other in sickness and distress; to cultivate Christian sympathy in feeling and courtesy in speech; to be slow to take offense, but always ready for reconciliation, and mindful of the rules of our Savior, to secure it without delay.

We moreover engage, that when we remove from this place, we will as soon as possible unite with some other church, where we can carry out the spirit of this covenant, and the principles of God's Word.

Prayer: Now the God of peace, who brought again from the dead our Lord Jesus, that Great Shepherd of the sheep, through the blood of the everlasting covenant, make you perfect in every good work, to do His will; working in you that which is well-pleasing in His sight, through Jesus Christ, to whom be glory forever and ever. Amen.

PART III

Catechisms

CHAPTER TWENTY-EIGHT

A Catechism for Babes, or, Little Ones

(Suitable To Their Capacity More Than Others Have Been Formerly.) BY H. JESSEY, A SERVANT OF JESUS CHRIST (1652)

Prov. 22:6: Catechize or begin the child in his way, according to his capacity, and when he is old, he will not depart from it.

2 Tim. 3:15: From infancy thou hast known the Holy Scriptures, which are able to make thee wise unto salvation.

To All Parents, Schoolmasters, Or Others . . .

*That are to train up young weaned children, and need direction;
the leader into all truth direct you.*

Knowing what account is to be given by all that profess themselves Christians, (Abraham's seed), if they endeavor not to instruct such as they have charge of, to know and fear the Lord, and keep His ways (Gen. 18:9; 2 Tim. 1:5, 3:14; Deut. 6:5, 6; Pro. 22:6, 31:1–2.) And rejoicing much, that good use hath been made of the catechisms by Mr. Perkins, Mr. Elton, Mr. Egerton, Mr. Ball, Mr. Dan Rogers, and others, for help to youths and elder people.

Yet it clearly appearing that in very many (if not in the most) of the answers, are some things like Latin, or Greek to the younger, not being suited to their understandings, as it were to be wished: I much desired to see one so plain and easy in the expressions, as that the very babes that can speak but stammeringly, and are of very weak capacities, might understand what they say: and might have some help in prayer and thanksgiving to be with their understandings; and not as in a strange tongue, 1 Cor. 14:9, 15, 19.

And not finding any such, I being desired to it, make an essay above twelve years ago: and the Lord giving aid, and good success therein: and more copies of it being desired than my time would permit to write over and over again, having added and enlarged some passages, I have yielded to the desires of some that it might be printed for a more general good to many, that are very easily convinced of the great want of such little ones generally by such a plain, easy, familiar catechism: stammering (as it were) to their capacities, as the Lord is pleased ofttimes to do to ours. And I have added herein, in a less letter at this mark until this what may before-born at first by the youngest children, and may be learned by them afterwards.

If it be asked why the answers are not put in . . . black letter called English letter? I answer: At first I had so intended: but for the child's far greater profit, and more ease, and for preventing the more toil in reading the Testament, Bible, and any usual book, it's put in our most usual letter; that English letter being very seldom now in use, may be learned with more ease afterwards.

A Catechism for Babies, or Little Ones

Q. Who made you?

A. God made me. (Ps. 100:3: "Know that the Lord is God, He made us, and not we.")

Q. When did God make you?

A. God made me before I was born. (Ps. 139:13, 16.)

Q. Where did God make you?

A. God made me in my mother's womb. (Job 31:15. "Did not He that made me in the womb, make him?")

Q. Wherefore did God make you?

A. God made me that I should serve Him. (Ps. 100:3. "Serve the Lord, He made us." Luke 1:74.)

Q. Must you not then learn to know God, that so you may rightly serve Him?"

A. Yea I must learn to know God. (1 Chron. 28:9: "Know the God of thy fathers.")

Q. When must you learn to know God?

A. I must learn to know God now, when I am but a child. (2 Tim. 3:14, 15; Eccles. 12:1, 2; Prov. 22:6. "Remember now thy Creator.")

Q. How may you learn to know God?

A. I may learn to know God by His Word, and by His works. (Deut. 17:19; Ps. 91:7, 11:1; 1 John 39:40; Rom. 1:19, 20. "He shall read it all the days of his life, that he may learn to fear the Lord his God." "The heavens declare the glory of God." Ps. 19:1.)

Q. What do we call the Word of God?

A. The Bible, the Holy Scripture, is the Word of God. (Matt. 1:1; 2 Tim. 3:15, 16; Acts 13:5, 15. "Almost the whole city came to hear the Word of God," with 44, 45, 48, 49, with Acts 26:22, 23.)

Q. What's the first book of the Bible called, and what's the last book?

A. Genesis is the first book of the Bible, and the Revelation is the last book. (Rev. 22:18, 19; Acts 3:23.)

Q. What doth the Scripture say that God is?

A. The Scriptures say that God is a Spirit; a good God; a wise God; a holy God; a mighty God; a merciful God; a righteous Judge of all men. (1 John 4:22; Ps. 34:8; 1 Tim. 1:17, Josh. 24:19; Isa. 6:3; Gen. 17:1; Rev. 15:3; Exod. 34:6; Gen. 18:25.)

Q. How may gods are there?

A. There is but one Jehovah, one God the Father, of whom are all things; and one Lord and Saviour Jesus Christ, by whom are all things, and there is one Comforter, which is the Holy Spirit; and these are one. (Deut. 6:4; "Jehovah is one." 1 Cor. 8:6; Eph. 4:5, 6, 1 Tim. 2:5; John 14:16, 17, 26; Eph. 44; 1 John 5:7.)

Q. What works hath God made?

A. God made heavens and earth and waters and all things in them. (Gen. 1:1; Ex. 20:11.)

Q. Of what did God make all things?

A. God made all things at first of nothing. (Heb. 11:3.)

Q. How can this be?

A. Nothing is impossible to God Almighty. (Mark 10:27; Luke 1:37; Luke 18:27.) Nothing is too hard to God. (Jer. 37:17, 27; 1 Cor. 15:35, 36.)

Q. Why must we believe that God made all of nothing?

A. We must believe it, because God hath said it; and God cannot lie. (Heb. 11:3; Heb. 6:18; Titus 1:2.)

Q. How did God make all things?

A. God made all by His Almighty power; God said, Let them be made, [or, they shall be made] and they were all made by His Word. (Gen. 1:3, 6, 9, 11, 14; Ps. 33:6; Rev. 4:11; Jer. 32:17.)

Q. In how may days did God make all things in the beginning?

A. God made all things in six days. (Gen. 2:1, 2, 3.)

Q. What did the Lord God on the seventh day?

A. God rested on the seventh day, and God blessed the seventh day and sanctified it. (Gen. 2:2, 3; Exod. 20:10, 11.)

Q. What must we and you do on the Lord's Sabbath day?

A. We must not work, nor prate, nor play, on the Sabbath day. (Isa. 58:13.)

Q. Whether did God make all things good or bad?

A. God is a good God, and God made all things very good. (Ps. 119:68. "Thou art good, and dost good." Gen. 1:4, 31.)

Q. What other works doth God, besides His making of all things?

A. God upholds and preserves all; and God governs and orders all things. (Isa. 40:26, 29; Ps. 135:6; Ps. 36:6; Matt. 10:29, 30; Eph. 1:11.)

Q. *Why doth the Lord uphold, preserve, and govern all things in heaven and earth?*

A. God doth all for His own glory, and for His people's good. (Rom. 11:36; Gen. 1:26, 28; Rom. 8:28.)

Q. *Whereas God made all very good. How then came in naughtiness and death and all pains?*

A. Death and all pains came by the first Adam's sin and fall: for we sinned and lost our goodness and our happiness in Him. (Rom. 5:12, 18.)

Q. *How came Adam to sin and fall?*

A. Eve his wife was tempted by that old serpent the devil; and they both did eat of the fruit that God forbade. (2 Cor. 11:3; Rev. 12:9; Gen. 3:1, 2–4.)

Q. *What hurt came to them and to us by that sin?*

A. By this sin came the loss of the life and glory of God. By this came sin and death. (Eph. 4:17; Rom. 3:23; Rom. 5:12; Rom. 6:23.)

Q. *What is sin?*

A. Sin is any naughtiness against any of God's ten commands. (1 John 3:4.)

Q. *What do we deserve by any sin or naughtiness?*

A. By any sin or naughtiness, we deserve death, and God's curse. (Rom. 6:23; Gal. 3:12.)

Q. *How then can you avoid God's curse?*

A. I am guilty and I cannot avoid God's curse by any deeds that I can do. (Rom. 3:19, 20; Rom. 11:6; 2 Cor. 3:5.)

Q. *But yet God is wonderful, good, and merciful; what hath God done for redeeming these naughty ones?*

A. God so loved the world that He gave His only Son, Jesus Christ, God-man, to be our surety, to redeem us, and to procure all good to us. (John 3:16; Matt. 1:21, 23; Heb. 7:22, 25; Gal. 3:13; 1 Cor. 1:30; Col. 9:10.)

Q. *What did and what doth this surety for us?*

A. Christ was made a curse for us; and Christ died for our naughtiness and was laid in the grave; and God was fully satisfied and released Him from that prison and took Him up to heaven and set Him on His right hand. (Gal. 3:13; 1 Cor. 15:3, 4; Isa. 42:1; Matt. 12:18; 17:5; Phil. 2:7, 8; 1 Cor. 15:4; Isa. 53:8, 11; Acts 1:2, 9; Rom. 8:34; Heb. 1:3, 13.)

Q. *For what end was all this done?*

A. All this was done that God might be honored in thus forgiving, humbling, renewing, making holy, and happy forever such naughty ones as we are. (Rom. 5:20; Titus 2:11, 12, 14; Eph. 1:3, 4, 6, 7, 12.)

Q. *Who comes to reap these benefits by Jesus Christ?*

A. They reap these benefits, that by the Spirit are convinced of sin, of righteousness, and of judgment, and that receive Jesus Christ as their Prophet, Priest, and King. (John 16:9; Rom. 8:9, 13; John 1:11, 12; col. 2:6.)

Q. *What assurance have we that God will do so great thing for naughty ones?*

A. God hath given assurance of this by giving us His own Son, and making Him our surety; and by making a new covenant, and by confirming it by His Son's death for us; and by raising Him from death, to be a Prince and a Saviour, to give repentance and pardon to Israel, to serve Him all our days. (Rom. 8:31, 32, 33; Heb. 7:22, 25; Heb. 8:10; Gal. 3:13, 15; 1 Cor. 11:25; Acts 5:30, 31; Ps. 68:18.)

Q. *How must the Lord God be served?*

A. We must serve God as He commands us in the Law and Gospel. (Num. 15:39; Jer. 7:31; Matt. 28:20; John 14:15.)

Q. *How many commandments are there in the Law?*

A. There are ten commandments in the Law. (Exod. 34:28; Deut. 10:4.)

Q. *Must you not hearken to God's Word and to God's counsel, and pray for all this?*

A. Yea I must hearken, that my soul may live; and I must pray, that Jesus Christ would draw me to Him, and turn me that I may be turned. (Isa. 55:2, 3; Ezek. 36:25, 26, 37; Acts 8:21; Jer. 31:18; Prov. 2:1–4.)

Q. Wherefore did God give the Law?

A. The Law entered that sin might abound; that His grace, to such undone sinners, by giving Christ to die for their sins, might the more abound. (Rom. 5:20.)

Q. How do they live and how must they live, that hope to be saved by Jesus Christ?

A. Everyone that hath this hope will labor to be good in heart, word, and deed. (1 John 3:2, 3; 2 Cor. 5:17, 18.)

Q. Must we always live here?

A. No: God hath appointed that we must once die. (Heb. 9:27.)

Q. What must be after our death?

A. After death must be the great day of judgment. (Heb. 9:27.)

Q. What will become of all naughty people at that day of judgment after death?

A. All must come to judgment: naughty men and naughty women, naughty children, must be in hell torments forever. (2 Cor. 10:5; Rom. 14:10; Matt. 25:41, 46; Mark 9:44, 45.)

Q. What will then be done to all good men, and to good women, and to good children?

A. Good men and good women and good children shall go to heaven and everlasting happiness. (Matt. 25:34, 46; 1 Thess. 4:15.)

The Chief Heads of This Catechism Fitted for Children's Capacity

The God that made all, learn to know,
His Word and works as they Him shew.
Scriptures begin with Genesis;
With Revelation the ending is.
Heaven, earth and waters, all therein,
God made in six days, everything.
God rests and holdeth Sabbath day,
That we must not prate nor play.

By sin God's curse, we all should have,
Christ was a curse, died, rose to save
And ransomed us from all distress,

And be our wisdom, righteousness;
As He's to all that him receive,
Who self-deny in Him believe.

For all this love that God hath done,
In giving us His only Son.
We not our own, but His must be,
His will, not ours, obey must we.
In love keep His commandments,
In Him enjoying all contents.

The Sum of the Two Tables of the Law.

With all thy heart love God above,
Thy neighbor as thyself so love.

The Ten Commandments, the Sum of Each

The First Table

1. Jehovah alone thy God have thou.

2. No idol make, nor to it bow.

3. The name of God take not in vain.

4. Do not the Sabbath day profane.

The Second Table

5. Honor thy father and mother too.

6. Thou shalt not any murder do.

7. Do not commit adultery.

8. Steal not, by any injury.

9. False witness see thou do not bear.

10. Thy neighbors state do not desire.

Why the Law Was Given

The Law was given to show our sin. And wrath that's due thereby. That we to Christ for righteousness, and life, might always flee.

(Rom. 5:20, 21, 13; Rom. 4:15; Rom. 10:4, 9,10; Gal. 3:13, 18; John 3:15, 15, 17, 36; John 10:10, 28.)

God made, upholds and governs all.
God is a Spirit eternal.
Most holy, wise, great good, and just.
Before Him all to judgment (must)
Then naughty ones to Hell are cast.
Good go to Heaven, where joys do last.

The Conclusion

O happy child, if this I know.
And love and learn in life to show.
Here happy, in adversity:
And happy to eternity.

Another Short

(Suited to the capacity of the youngest learners.)

Of the four conditions of every man; namely, what it (1) was; (2) is; (3) may be; (4) must be, to all eternity: And how this last may be known in this life.

Of the four conditions of every man.

The First Catechism

1. *Q. What was our condition at first, when God made all things very good?*

A. Our condition at first was very good: it was holy and happy. (Gen. 1:26, 27, 31. God created man in His own image very good.)

2. *Q. What is our condition now by Adam's sin and naughtiness in eating the fruit that God forbade him?*

A. Our condition by nature is very bad: it is sinful and cursed. (Eph. 2:1–3. Dead in sins. Rom. 5:12, 18; Gal. 3:12. Cursed is everyone that sinneth.)

3. *Q. What may be our condition by the grace of our Lord Jesus Christ (who is the second Adam) and by the love of God, and by the communion of the Holy Spirit? (2 Cor. 13:14.)*

A. Our condition may be very good again, in the good way of happiness, if that grace be received; but if it be neglected, it will be very bad in the naughty way of woe, forevermore. (Matt. 7:13-14. Enter in at the strait gate. Rom. 2:7, 10; Heb. 2:1-3; 2 Cor. 6:1-2.)

4. *Q. What must be our condition after death, when God sends Jesus Christ to judgment?*

A. Naughty ones, in the naughty way, for their naughtiness, must be in hell forever. Good ones, in the good way, by the grace of our Lord Jesus Christ, must be in heaven forever. (Matt. 25:46.) These shall go away into everlasting punishment. But the righteous into life everlasting. (Rom. 6:23.) Sin's wages is death: but the gift of God is eternal life through Jesus Christ our Lord.

These four conditions are more fully unfolded in the second Catechism.

The Second Catechism of the Four Conditions of Every Man

1. Of Man's First Condition

1. *Q. What was man's condition at first, when God made all the world and was man then bad or good?*

A. God made all good, God made man life Himself, good; for God is good. (Gen. 1:31, 26, 27. Ps. 34:8; Ps. 119:68. Thou art good and doest good.)

Q. What goodness or excellency is in God, wherein man was like to God?

A. God is wise, and God is holy, and God is righteous, and God is perfect. (1 Tim. 1:17; Ps. 145:17; Ps. 129:4; Ps. 7:9; Is. 40:26-28.)

Q. What more excellency is in God?

A. God is the Lord and Ruler of all the world; God is happy; God hath no naughtiness, nor misery. (Ps. 24:1; 1 Tim. 1:11; James 1:13, 17; Job 34:16; Ps. 36:8-9.)

Q. How then was man at first like to God?

A. Man at first was like to God, thus: At first, man was wise, man was holy, and man was righteous, and man was perfect. (Col. 3:10; Eph. 4:24; Eccles. 7:29.)

Q. Wherein besides, was man at first like to God?

A. Man was lord and ruler of all the world, and man was happy; man had no naughtiness nor misery. (Gen. 1:26, 28. Ps. 65:4; Gen. 1:27, 31; Rom. 5:12.)

2. Of Man's Second Condition

2. *Q. When Adam the first man had sinned by doing naughtily, against what God bade him, yielding to Eve his wife, and to the devil, more than to God: What was Adam's condition then? And what is now the condition of every child, of every man, and of every woman by nature?*

A. By the sin and naughtiness of Adam our father, both Adam and we became not like to God, but like the devil. (Gen. 3:12; John 8:44.)

Q. How is this condition of all now like the devil?

A. The devil is sinful, naughty; and he is miserable: So every man, every woman, and child, is by nature very naughty and miserable. (John 8:44; Eph. 2:2–3; Acts 26:18.)

3. Of Man's Third Condition

3. *Q. Man's condition was good at first by creation: now 'tis bad by corruption: what may be your condition here in this world by regeneration?*

A. Man's condition may be in the good way of blessedness; or may remain in the bad way of woe and cursedness forever. (Deut. 30:19. Choose life.)

Q. How may man's condition be brought here into that good way of blessedness?

A. Man's condition here may be brought into that good way of blessedness by the grace of our Lord Jesus Christ who is Abraham's blessed seed. (2 Cor. 8:9; 13:14; Gal. 3:18, 16.)

Q. And how else?

A. By the love of God the Father. (John 3:16.)

Q. And how else?

A. By the communion of the Holy Spirit. (2 Cor. 13:14; John 16:9.)

Q. How may man's condition and your own condition be in the bad way of woe and of cursedness forever?

A. My condition and other's condition, may be in that bad way; if we despise or neglect that grace of our Lord Jesus Christ; and that love of God the Father; and that communion of the Holy Spirit. (Heb. 2:1–3; 4:1–2, 11; 10:26; 2 Cor. 6:1–2.)

4. Of Man's Fourth Condition

4. *Q. Man's condition at first was holy and happy; now it is sinful and woeful; it may be here in this life, in the good way of happiness, or in the bad way of woe forever. What must be all men's condition at the day of judgment after death?*

A. All that are dead shall be raised out of their graves. And we all must come before the judgment seat of Christ. (Heb. 9:27; John 5:28; 2 Cor. 5:10; Rom. 14:10.)

Q. What shall then be done to all naughty people that died in the bad way?

A. To naughty people that died in the bad way, Christ will say, Depart ye cursed into everlasting fire prepared for the devil and his angels; and they must be cursed in hell fire forever. (Matt. 25:31, 41, 46.)

Q. What shall then be done to all good people and good children?

A. To good people and good children that died in that good way, Christ will say, Come ye blessed of my Father, inherit ye the kingdom prepared for you from the foundation of the world, and they must be blessed in heaven forever. (Matt. 25:34–46.)

1. Wast! 2. Art! 3. Maist be! 4. Must be!

Oh that thou wouldst remember these four conditions! That wherein thou instruct the child, that God made all very good, and that all the good we have, or shall have, is from God. And therefore, that we should be thankful to Him for all the good we have, by day or by night. And we should pray to God for all the good we would have. (Eccl. 12:1; Prov. 22:6; 3:6; Ps. 119:68; 145:9; Rom. 1:21; Acts 8:21-23; 1 Thess. 5:18; Luke 18:1; 1 Thes. 5:17; Deut. 6:5–7; Ex. 20:7.)

Prayers

In the Morning Give Thanks and pray

Blessed be God that gave me sleep; and makes me see, and hear, and speak: God Almighty bless me, and keep me from ill all this day, for Jesus Christ's sake. Amen. (Eph. 1:3; Ps. 127:2; Ex. 4:11; Gen. 28:3, 20; Ps. 121:7; John 14:12.)

Before Meat

Blessed be God that gives me meat. God Almighty bless me and my meat. Amen. (Ps. 104:27–28; 136:2.)

After Meat

Blessed be God, that hath given me meat, and fed me; God Almighty bless me, that I may serve Him. Amen. (Gen. 48:15; Luke 1:74.)

At Going to Bed

Blessed be God, that kept me from ill this day. God Almighty bless me, and give me sleep, and keep me from ill this night, for Jesus Christ's sake. Amen.

CHAPTER TWENTY-NINE

The Baptism Catechism Commonly Called Keach's Catechism (1693)

1. *Who is the first and chiefest being?*

A. God is the first and chiefest being. (Ps. 97:9)

2. *Ought everyone to believe there is a God?*

A. Everyone ought to believe there is a God; and it is their great sin and folly who do not.

3. *How may we know there is a God?*

A. The light of nature in man and the works of God plainly declare there is a God; but His Word and Spirit only do it fully and effectually for the salvation of sinners.

4. *What is the Word of God?*

A. The Holy Scriptures of the Old and New Testament are the Word of God, and the only certain rule of faith and obedience.

5. May all men make use of the Holy Scriptures?

A. All men are not only permitted, but commanded and exhorted to read, hear, and understand the Holy Scriptures.

6. What things are chiefly contained in the Holy Scriptures?

A. The Holy Scriptures chiefly contain what man ought to believe concerning God, and what duty God requireth of man.

7. What is God?

A. God is a Spirit, infinite, eternal, and unchangeable in His being, wisdom, power, holiness, justice, goodness, and truth.

8. Are there more gods than one?

A. There is but one only, the living and true God.

9. How many persons are there in the Godhead?

A. There are three persons in the Godhead, the Father, the Son, and the Holy Spirit; and these three are one God, the same in essence, equal in power and glory.

10. What are the decrees of God?

A. The decrees of God are His eternal purpose according to the counsel of His will, whereby, for His own glory, He hath forever dained whatsoever comes to pass.

11. How doth God execute His decrees?

A. God executeth His decrees in the works of creation and providence.

12. What is the world of creation?

A. The work of creation is God's making all things of nothing, by the Word of His power, in the space of six days, and all very good.

13. How did God create man?

A. God created man, male and female, after His own image, in knowledge, righteousness, and holiness, with dominion over the creatures.

14. What are God's works of providence?

A. God's works of providence are His most holy, wise, and powerful preserving, and governing all His creatures, and all their actions.

15. What special act of providence did God exercise towards man in the estate wherein he was created?

A. When God had created man, He entered into a covenant of life with him upon condition of perfect obedience: forbidding him to eat of the tree of the knowledge of good and evil, upon pain of death.

16. *Did our first parents continue in the state wherein they were created?*

A. Our first parents being left to the freedom of their own will, fell from the estate wherein they were created, by sinning against God

17. *What is sin?*

A. Sin is any want of conformity unto, or transgression of, the law of God.

18. *What was the sin whereby our first parents fell from the estate wherein they were created?*

A. The sin whereby our parents fell from the estate wherein they were created, was their eating the forbidden fruit.

19. *Did all mankind fall in Adam's first transgression?*

A. The covenant being made with Adam, not only for himself but for his posterity, all mankind descending from him by ordinary generation sinned in him, and fell with him in his first transgression.

20. *Into what estate did the fall bring mankind?*

A. The fall brought mankind into an estate of sin and misery.

21. *Wherein consists the sinfulness of that estate whereinto man fell?*

A. The sinfulness of that estate whereinto man fell, consists in the guilt of Adam's first sin, the want of original righteousness, and the corruption of his whole nature, which is commonly called original sin; together with all actual transgressions which proceed from it.

22. *What is the misery of that estate whereinto man fell?*

A. All mankind by their fall lost communion with God, are under His wrath and curse, and so made liable to all miseries in this life, to death itself, and to the pains of hell forever.

23. *Did God leave all mankind to perish in the estate of sin and misery?*

A. God having out of His mere good pleasure, from all eternity, elected some to everlasting life, did enter into a covenant of grace, to deliver them out of the estate of sin and misery, and to bring them into an estate of salvation by a Redeemer.

24. *Who is the Redeemer of God's elect?*

A. The only Redeemer of God's elect is the Lord Jesus Christ; who, being the eternal Son of God, became man, and so was and continueth to be God and man in two distinct natures, and one person forever.

25. *How did Christ, being the Son of God become man?*

A. Christ the Son of God became man by taking to Himself a true body, and a reasonable soul, being conceived by the power of the Holy spirit in the womb of the Virgin Mary, and born of her, yet without sin.

26. *What offices doth Christ execute as our Redeemer?*

A. Christ as our Redeemer executeth the offices of a prophet, of a priest, and of a king, both in His state of humiliation and exaltation.

27. *How doth Christ execute the office of a prophet?*

A. Christ executeth the office of prophet in revealing to us, by His Word and Spirit, the will of God for our salvation.

28. *How doth Christ execute the office of a priest?*

A. Christ executeth the office of a priest in His once offering up Himself a sacrifice to satisfy divine justice and reconcile us to God, and in making continual intercession for us.

29. *How doth Christ execute the office of a king?*

A. Christ executeth the office of a king, in subduing us to Himself, in ruling, and defending us, and in restraining and conquering all His and our enemies.

30. *Wherein did Christ's humiliation consist?*

A. Christ's humiliation consists in His being born, and that in a low condition; made under the law, undergoing the miseries of this life, the wrath of God, and the cursed death of the cross; in being buried, and continuing under the power of death for a time.

31. *Wherein consisteth Christ's exaltation?*

A. Christ's exaltation consisteth in His rising again from the dead on the third day, in ascending up into heaven, in sitting at the right hand of God the Father, and in coming to judge the world at the last day.

32. *How are we made partakers of the redemption purchased by Christ?*

A. We are made partakers of the redemption purchased by Christ, by the effectual application of it to us by His Holy Spirit.

33. *How doth the Spirit apply to us the redemption purchased by Christ?*

A. The spirit applieth to us the redemption purchased by Christ, by working faith in us, and thereby united us to Christ, in our effectual calling.

34. *What is effectual calling?*

A. Effectual calling is the work of God's Spirit, whereby convincing us of our sin and misery, enlightening our minds in the knowledge of Christ, and renewing our wills, He doth persuade and enable us to embrace Jesus Christ freely offered to us in the gospel.

35. *What benefits do they that are effectually called partake of in this life?*

A. They that are effectually called do in this life partake of justification, sanctification, and the several benefits which in this life do either accompany or flow from them.

36. *What is justification?*

A. Justification is an act of God's free grace, wherein He pardoneth all our sins, and accepteth us as righteous in His sight, only for the righteousness of Christ imputed to us, and received by faith alone.

37. *What is adoption?*

A. Adoption is an act of God's free grace, whereby we are received into the number and have a right to all the privileges of the sons of God.

38. *What is sanctification?*

A. Sanctification is the work of God's free grace, whereby we are renewed in the whole man after the image of God, and are enabled more and more to die unto sin, and live unto righteousness.

39. *What are the benefits which in this life do accompany or flow from justification, adoption, and sanctification?*

A. The benefits which in this life do accompany or flow from justification, adoption, and sanctification, are assurance of God's love, peace of conscience, joy in the Holy spirit, increase of grace, and perseverance therein to the end.

40. *What benefits do believers receive from Christ at their death?*

A. The souls of believers are at their death made perfect in holiness, and do immediately pass into glory; and their bodies being still united to Christ, do rest in their graves, till the resurrection.

41. *What benefits do believers receive from Christ at the resurrection?*

A. At the resurrection believers, being raised up in glory, shall be openly acknowledged, and acquitted in the day of judgment, and made perfectly blessed, both in soul and body, in the full enjoyment of God, to all eternity.

42. *But what shall be done to the wicked at their death?*

A. The souls of the wicked shall, at their death, be cast into the torments of hell, and their bodies lie in their graves, till the resurrection and judgment of the great day.

43. *What shall be done to the wicked at the day of judgment?*

A. At the day of judgment the bodies of the wicked, being raised out of their graves, shall be sentenced, together with their souls, to unspeakable torments with the devil and his angels forever.

44. *What is the duty which God requireth of man?*

A. The duty which God requireth of man is, obedience to His revealed will.

45. *What did God at first reveal to man for the rule of his obedience?*

A. The rule which God at first revealed to man for his obedience, was the moral law.

46. *Where is the moral law summarily comprehended?*

A. The moral law is summarily comprehended in the ten commandments.

47. *What is the sum of the ten commandments?*

A. The sum of the ten commandments is, to love the Lord our God with all our heart, with all our soul, with all our strength, and with all our mind; and our neighbor as ourselves.

48. *What is the preface to the ten commandments?*

A. The preface to the ten commandments is in these words; "I am the Lord thy God which have brought thee out of the land of Egypt, out of the house of bondage."

49. *What doth the preface to the ten commandments teach us?*

A. The preface to the ten commandments teacheth us that because God is the Lord, and our God and Redeemer, therefore we are bound to keep all His commandments.

50. *Which is the first commandment?*

A. The first commandment is, "thou shalt have no other gods before Me."

51. *What is required in the first commandment?*

A. The first commandment requireth us to know and acknowledge God to be the only true God and our God; and to worship and glorify Him accordingly.

52. *What is forbidden in the first commandment?*

A. The first commandment forbiddeth the denying, or not worshipping and glorifying the true God, as God and our God, and the giving that worship and glory to any other, which is due unto Him alone.

53. *What are we especially taught by these word "before Me," in the first commandment?*

A. These words "before Me," in the first commandment, teach us, that God, who seeth all things, taketh notice of and is much displeased with the sin of having any other God.

54. *Which is the second commandment?*

A. The second commandment is, "Thou shall not make unto thee any graven image, or the likeness of anything that is in heaven above, or that is in the earth beneath, or that is in the water under the earth; thou shalt not bow down thyself to them, nor serve them; for I the Lord thy God am a jealous God, visiting the iniquity of the fathers upon the children unto the third and fourth generation of them that hate Me; and shewing mercy unto thousands of them that love Me, and keep my commandments."

55. *What is required in the second commandment?*

A. The second commandment requireth the receiving, observing, and keeping pure and entire all such religious worship and ordinances, as God hath appointed in His Word.

56. *What is forbidden in the second commandment?*

A. The second commandment forbiddeth the worshipping of God by images, or any other way not appointed in His Word.

57. *What are the reasons annexed to the second commandment?*

A. The reasons annexed to the second commandment are, God's sovereignty over us, His propriety in us, and the zeal He hath to His own worship.

58. *Which is the third commandment?*

A. The third commandment is, "thou shalt not take the name of the Lord thy God in vain; for the Lord will not hold him guiltless that taketh His name in vain."

59. *What is required in the third commandment?*

A. The third commandment requireth the holy and reverent use of God's names, attributes, ordinances, Word, and works.

60. *What is forbidden in the third commandment?*

A. The third commandment forbiddeth all profaning and abusing of anything whereby God makes Himself known.

61. *What is the reason annexed to the third commandment?*

A. The reason annexed to the third commandment is, that however the breakers of this commandment may escape punishment from men, yet the Lord our God will not suffer them to escape His righteous judgment.

62. *What is the fourth commandment?*

A. The fourth commandment is, "Remember the sabbath day to keep it holy: six days shalt thou labor and do all thy work; but the seventh day is the sabbath of the Lord thy God, in it thou shalt not do any work, thou, nor thy son, nor thy daughter, thy man-servant nor thy maid-servant, nor thy cattle, nor the stranger that is within thy gates: for in six days the Lord made heaven and earth, the sea, and all that in them is, and rested the seventh day; wherefore the Lord blessed the sabbath day and hallowed it."

63. *What is required in the fourth commandment?*

A. The fourth commandment requireth the keeping holy to God one whole day in seven to be a sabbath to Himself.

64. *Which day of the seven hath God appointed to be the weekly sabbath?*

A. Before the resurrection of Christ, God appointed the seventh day of the week to be the weekly sabbath; and the first day of the week ever since, to continue to the end of the world, which is the Christ sabbath.

65. *How is the sabbath to be sanctified?*

A. The sabbath is to be sanctified by a holy resting all that day, even from such worldly employments and recreations as are lawful on other days; and spending the whole time in the public and private exercises of God's worship, except so much as is to be taken up in the works of necessity and mercy.

66. *What is forbidden in the fourth commandment?*

A. The fourth commandment forbiddeth the omission or careless performance of the duties required, and the profaning the day by idleness, or doing that which is in itself sinful, and the profaning the day of idleness, or doing that which is in itself sinful, or by unnecessary thoughts, words, or works, about worldly employments or recreations.

67. *What are the reasons annexed to the fourth commandment?*

A. The reasons annexed to the fourth commandment, are God's allowing us six days of the week for our own lawful employments, His challenging a special propriety in a seventh, His own example, and His blessing the sabbath day.

68. *Which is the fifth commandment?*

A. The fifth commandment is "Honor thy father and thy mother; that thy days may be long in the land which the Lord thy God giveth thee."

69. *What is required in the fifth commandment?*

A. The fifth commandment requireth the preserving the honour and performing the duties belonging to every one in their several places and relations, as superiors, inferiors, or equals.

70. *What is forbidden in the fifth commandment?*

A. The fifth commandment forbiddeth the neglect of, or doing anything against the honour and duty which belongeth to every one in their several places and relations.

71. *What is the reason annexed to the fifth commandment?*

A. The reason annexed to the fifth commandment is a promise of long life and prosperity (as far as it shall serve for God's glory, and their own good) to all such as keep this commandment.

72. *What is the sixth commandment?*

A. The sixth commandment is, "thou shalt not kill."

73. *What is required in the sixth commandment?*

A. The sixth commandment requireth all lawful endeavors to preserve our own life, and the life of others.

74. *What is forbidden in the sixth commandment?*

A. The sixth commandment absolutely forbiddeth the taking away of our own life, or the life of our neighbor unjustly, or whatsoever tendeth thereunto.

75. *Which is the seventh commandment?*

A. The seventh commandment is "thou shalt not commit adultery."

76. *What is required in the seventh commandment?*

A. The seventh commandment requireth the preservation of our own and our neighbor chastity, in heart, speech, and behavior.

77. *What is forbidden in the seventh commandment?*

A. The seventh commandment forbiddeth all unchaste thoughts, words, and actions.

78. *What is the eighth commandment?*

A. The eighth commandment is, "Thou shalt not steal."

79. *What is required in the eighth commandment?*

A. The eighth commandment requireth the lawful procuring and furthering the wealth and outward estate of ourselves and others.

80. *What is forbidden in the eighth commandment?*

A. The eighth commandment forbiddeth whatsoever or may unjustly hinder our own or our neighbor's wealth or outward estate.

81. *Which is the ninth commandment?*

A. The ninth commandment is, "thou shalt not bear false witness against thy neighbor."

82. *What is required in the ninth commandment?*

A. The ninth commandment requireth the maintaining and promoting of truth between man and man, and of our own neighbor's good name, especially in witness-bearing.

83. *What is forbidden in the ninth commandment?*

A. The ninth commandment forbiddeth whatsoever is prejudicial to the truth, or injurious to our own or our neighbor's good name.

84. *Which is the tenth commandment?*

A. The tenth commandment is, "thou shalt not covet thy neighbor's house, thou shalt not covet thy neighbor's wife, nor his man-servant, nor his maid-servant, nor his ox, nor his ass, nor anything that is thy neighbor's."

85. *What is required in the tenth commandment?*

A. The tenth commandment requireth full contentment with our own condition, with a right and charitable frame of spirit toward our neighbor, and all that is his.

86. *What is forbidden in the tenth commandment?*

A. The tenth commandment forbiddeth all discontentment with our own estate, envying or grieving at the good of our neighbor, and all inordinate motions and affections to anything that is his.

87. *Is any man able perfectly to keep the commandments of God?*

A. No mere man since the fall is able in this life perfectly to keep the commandments of God, but doth daily break them in thought, word, or deed.

88. *Are all transgressions of the law equally heinous?*

A. Some sins in themselves, and by reason of several aggravations, are more heinous in the sight of God than others.

89. *What doth every sin deserve?*

A. Every sin deserveth God's wrath and curse, both in this life and that which is to come.

90. *What doth God require of us that we may escape His wrath and curse, due to us for sin?*

A. To escape the wrath and curse of God due to us for sin, God requireth of us faith in Jesus Christ, repentance unto life, with the diligent use of all the outward means whereby Christ communicateth to us the benefits of redemption.

91. *What is faith in Jesus Christ?*

A. Faith in Jesus Christ is a saving grace, whereby we receive and rest upon Him alone for salvation, as He is offered to us in the gospel.

92. *What is repentance unto life?*

A. Repentance unto life is a saving grace, whereby a sinner, out of a true sense of his sin, and apprehension of the mercy of God in Christ, doth, with grief and hatred of his sin, turn from it unto God, with full purpose of and endeavor after new obedience.

93. *What are the outward means whereby Christ communicateth to us the benefits of redemption?*

A. The outward and ordinary means whereby Christ communicateth to us the benefits of redemption are His ordinances, especially the Word, baptism, the Lord's supper, and prayer; all which means are made effectual to the elect for salvation.

94. *How is the Word made effectual to salvation?*

A. The Spirit of God maketh the reading, but especially the preaching of the Word, an effectual means of convincing and converting sinners, and of building them up in holiness and comfort through faith unto salvation.

95. *How is the Word to be read and heard, that it may become effectual to salvation?*

A. That the Word may become effectual to salvation, we must attend thereunto with diligence, preparation, and prayer; receive it with faith and love, lay it up in our hearts, and practice it in our lives.

96. *How do baptism and the Lord's supper become effectual means of salvation?*

A. Baptism and the Lord's supper become effectual means of salvation, not for any virtue in them, or in him that doth administer them, but only by the blessing of Christ, and the working of the Spirit in those that by faith receive them.

97. *What is baptism?*

A. Baptism is an ordinance of the New Testament instituted by Jesus Christ, to be unto the party baptized a sign of His fellowship with Him, in His death, burial, and resurrection; of His being ingrafted into Him; of remission of sins; and of His giving up Himself unto God through Jesus Christ, to live and walk in newness of life.

98. *To whom is baptism to be administered?*

A. Baptism is to be administered to all those who actually profess repentance towards God, faith in and obedience to our Lord Jesus Christ, and to none other.

99. *Are the infants of such as are professing believers to be baptized?*

A. The infants of such as are professing believers are not to be baptized, because there is neither command or example in the Holy Scriptures, or certain consequence from them to baptize such.

100. *How is baptism rightly administered?*

A. Baptism is rightly administered by immersion, or dipping the whole body of the party in water, into the name of the Father, and of the Son, and of the Holy Spirit, according to Christ's institution, and the practice of the apostles, and not by sprinkling or pouring of water, or dipping some part of the body, after the tradition of men.

101. *What is the duty of such who are rightly baptized?*

A. It is the duty of such who are rightly baptized to give up themselves to some particular and orderly church of Jesus Christ that they may walk in all the commandments and ordinances of the Lord blameless.

102. *What is the Lord's supper?*

A. The Lord's supper is an ordinance of the New Testament, instituted by Jesus Christ; wherein by giving and receiving bread and wine, according to His appointment, His death is shown forth and the worthy receivers are, not after a corporal and carnal manner, but by faith, made partakers of His body and blood, with all His benefits, to their spiritual nourishment and growth in grace.

103. *Who are the proper subjects of this ordinance?*

A. They who have been baptized upon a person profession of the faith in Jesus Christ, and repentance from dead works.

104. *What is required to the worthy receiving of the Lord's supper?*

A. It is required of them that would worthily partake of the Lord's supper, that they examine themselves of their knowledge to discern the Lord's body, of their faith to feed upon Him, of their repentance, love, and new obedience, lest coming unworthily they eat and drink judgment to themselves.

105. *What is prayer?*

A. Prayer is an offering up our desires to God, by the assistance of the Holy Spirit, for things agreeable to His will, in the name of Christ, believing with confession of our sins, and thankful acknowledgments of His mercies.

106. *What rule hath God given for our direction in prayer?*

A. The whole Word of God is of use to direct us in prayer; but the special rule of direction is that prayer which Christ taught His disciples, commonly called the Lord's prayer.

107. *What doth the preface of the Lord's prayer teach us?*

A. The preface of the Lord's prayer, which is "Our Father which art in heaven," teacheth us to draw near to God with all holy reverence and confidence, as children to a father, able and ready to help us; and that we should pray with and for others.

108. *What do we pray for in the first petition?*

A. In the first petition, which is, "Hallowed be Thy name," we pray that God would enable us and others to glorify Him in all that whereby He maketh Himself known, and that He would dispose all things to His own glory.

109. *What do we pray for in the second petition?*

A. In the second petition, which is, "Thy kingdom come," we pray that Satan's kingdom may be destroyed, and that the kingdom of grace may be advanced, ourselves and others brought into it and kept in it, and that the kingdom of glory may be hastened.

110. *What do we pray for in the third petition?*

A. In the third petition, which is, "Thy will be done on earth as it is in heaven," we pray that God by His grace would make us able and willing to know, obey, and submit to His will in all things, as the angels do in heaven.

111. *What do we pray for in the fourth petition?*

A. In the fourth petition, which is, "Give us this day our daily bread," we pray that of God's free gift we may receive a competent portion of the good things of this life, and enjoy His blessing with them.

112. *What do we pray for in the fifth petition?*

A. In the fifth petition, which is, "And forgive us our debts as we forgive our debtors," we pray that God, for Christ's sake, would freely pardon all our sins; which we are rather encouraged to ask because of His grace we are enabled from the heart to forgive others.

113. *What do we pray for in the sixth petition?*

A. In the sixth petition, which is, "And lead us not into temptation, but deliver us from evil," we pray that God would either keep us from being tempted to sin, or support and deliver us when we are tempted.

114. *What doth the conclusion of the Lord's prayer teach?*

A. The conclusion of the Lord's prayer, which is, "For thine is the kingdom, and the power, and the glory, forever. Amen," teacheth us to take our encouragement in prayer from God only, and in our prayers to praise Him, ascribing kingdom, power, and glory, to Him. And in testimony of our desire and assurance to be heard, we say, Amen.

CHAPTER THIRTY

A Catechism Of Bible Teaching (1892)

JOHN A. BROADUS

Lesson 1: God

1. *Who is God?*

A. God is the only Being that has always existed, and He is the Creator and Preserver of all things.

2. *How do we know that God exists?*

A. We know that God exists from the worlds He has made, and from our own sense of right and wrong; and the Bible above all tell us of God.

3. *Have men any reason for denying God's existence?*

A. It is foolish and wicked to say there is no God. (Ps. 14:1; Rom. 1:20)

4. *How may we learn the character of God?*

A. We learn the character of God partly from His works, mainly from His Word.

5. *What does God know?*

A. God knows all things, even the secrets of our hearts; God is omniscient. (Heb. 4:13; Eccles. 12:14)

6. *What power has God?*

A. God has all power; God is omnipotent.

7. *Where is God?*

A. God is everywhere, and all things are present to Him; God is omni-present.

8. *What do we know as to the holiness of God?*

A. God is perfectly holy; the angels praise Him as holy. (Is. 6:3; Rev. 4:8)

9. *Is God just?*

A. God is always perfectly righteous and just. (Ps. 145:17)

10. *Is God loving and good?*

A. God is love, and He is good to all. (1 John 4:8; Ps. 145:9)

11. *Is God all love?*

A. God's justice is as truly a part of His nature as His love. (Rev. 15:3)

12. *How ought we to feel and act toward God?*

A. We ought to love God with all our heart and serve Him with all our powers. (Deut. 6:5; 1 John 5:3)

13. *Is it our duty to fear God?*

A. It is our duty to obey God in filial fear, and to fear His wrath if we sin. (Eccles. 12:13; Heb. 10:31)

Advanced Questions

Q. A. May little children easily recognize that there is a God?

A. Young children often think and speak about God. (Ps. 8:2; Matt. 21:16)

Q. B. How do many persons practically deny that there is a God?

A. People practically deny that there is a God by living as if He did not exist.

Q. C. Why is it wrong to use images of God in worship?

A. Men would soon worship the image instead of God, and so God has positively forbidden such use of images. (Ex. 20:4, 5; Rom. 1:23, 25)

Q. D. Is it possible for God to do wrong?

A. For God to do wrong would be contrary to His very nature; He cannot deny Himself. (2 Tim. 2:13)

Lesson 2: Providence of God

1. What is meant by the providence of God?

A. God cares for all His creatures and provides for their welfare.

2. Does God's providence extend to the wicked?

A. God gives to the wicked, sunshine and rain and all the common blessings of life, thereby calling them to repentance. (Matt. 5:45; Ps. 145:9; Rom. 2:4)

3. Does God exercise any special providence over the righteous?

A. God makes all things work together for good to them that love Him. (Rom. 8:28; Ps. 23:1)

4. Is God's providence confined to great things?

A. God notices and provides for even the least things. (Luke 12:7)

5. Is there really any such thing as chance or luck?

A. There is no such thing as chance or luck; everything is controlled by the providence of God.

6. Does God act according to purposes formed beforehand?

A. God has always intended to do whatever He does. (Eph. 1:11; 1 Pet. 1:20.

7. Do God's purposes destroy our freedom of action?

A. We choose and act freely, and are accountable for all we do. (Josh. 21:15; Rom. 14:12)

8. Does God cause evil?

A. God permits evil, but does not cause it.

9. Does God ever check and overrule evil?

A. God often prevents evil, and often brings good out of evil. (Gen. 45:5; Ps. 76:10)

10. What is the greatest example of God's bringing good out of evil?

A. The crucifixion of Christ is the greatest example of God's bringing good out of evil.

11. *How ought we to think and feel about the providence of God?*

A. We ought always to remember our dependence on God, and to trust His providential guidance. (James 4:15; Jer. 10:23)

12. *When God in His providence sends upon us something painful, how ought we to feel?*

A. When God sends on us something painful we ought to be patient, obedient, and thankful. (1 Sam. 3:18; 1 Thess. 5:18)

Advanced Questions

Q. A. Would it be possible to control great events while disregarding all little things?

A. Great things and little things are inseparable and dependent on each other.

Q. B. If all things take place according to fixed laws, how can it be that God controls them?

A. God created all the forces of nature, and made them without violating the laws.

Q. C. Can God then answer prayer by His providential control without violating the laws of nature?

A. Yes, the Bible assures us that God does answer prayer.

Q. D. What instances can you give of special providence in the story of Joseph?

A. Gen. 37:28; 39:2, 3, 21–23; and Ch. 45.

Q. E. What example of speedy answer to prayer in the story of Hezekiah?

A. 2 Kings 20:1–6.

Q. F. If we cannot explain the relations between divine predestination and human freedom, does that warrant us in rejecting either?

A. Both divine predestination and human freedom must be true from the very nature of God and man, and both are plainly taught in the Bible.

Lesson 3: The Word of God

Part 1: The Books Of The Bible

1. *How many separate books are there in the Bible?*

A. There are thirty-nine books in the Old Testament and twenty-seven in the New Testament.

2. *What are the five books of Moses?*

A. The five books of Moses are Genesis, Exodus, Leviticus, Numbers, Deuteronomy.

3. *What are the other historical books in the Old Testament?*

A. The twelve other historical books in the Old Testament are Joshua, Judges, Ruth, 1 and 2 Samuel, 1 and 2 Kings, 1 and 2 Chronicles, Ezra, Nehemiah, Esther.

4. *What are the five poetical books?*

A. The five poetical books are Job, Psalms, Proverbs, Ecclesiastes, Song of Solomon.

5. *What are the four greater prophets?*

A. The four greater prophets are Isaiah, Jeremiah (with Lamentations), Ezekiel, Daniel.

6. *Which are the twelve lesser prophets?*

A. The twelve lesser prophets are Hosea, Joel, Amos; Obadiah, Jonah, Micah; Nahum, Habakkuk, Zephaniah; Haggai, Zechariah, Malachi.

7. *What are the five historical books of the New Testament?*

A. The five historical books of the New Testament are Matthew, Mark, Luke, John, Acts.

8. *What are the fourteen epistles of Paul?*

A. The fourteen epistles of Paul are Romans, 1 and 2 Corinthians, Galatians; Ephesians, Philippians, Colossians; 1 and 2 Thessalonians; 1 and 2 Timothy, Titus; Philemon; Hebrews.

9. *What are the seven other Epistles?*

A. The seven general epistles are James, 1 and 2 Peter, 1, 2 and 3 John, Jude.

10. *What is the last book in the Bible?*

A. The last book in the Bible is Revelation.

Part 2: Inspiration And Authority Of The Bible

11. *Were the books of the Bible written by men?*

A. The books of the Bible were written by men, but these men were moved and guided by the Holy Spirit. (2 Pet. 1:21; 1 Cor. 14:37)

12. *What special proof have we that the entire Old Testament is inspired?*

A. Christ and His apostles speak of "Scripture" or "the Scriptures," as inspired by God, and we know that they meant exactly what we call the Old Testament. (John 10:35; 2 Tim. 3:16)

13. *Does the Bible contain any errors?*

A. The Bible records some things said by uninspired men that were not true; but it is true and instructive that these men said them.

14. *What authority has the Bible for us?*

A. The Bible is our only and all-sufficient rule of faith and practice.

15. *What things does the Bible teach us?*

A. The Bible teaches all that we need to know about our relation to God, about sin and salvation.

16. *How ought we to study Bible history?*

A. We ought to study the Bible as a history of providence and a history of redemption.

17. *Who is the central figure of the Bible history?*

A. The central figure of the Bible history is Jesus Christ, the hope of Israel, the Saviour of mankind.

18. *What does the Bible do for those who believe in Jesus Christ?*

A. The Bible makes those who believe in Jesus wise unto salvation. (2 Tim. 3:15)

19. *What does the Bible contain besides history?*

A. The Bible contains doctrines, devotional portions, precepts, and promises; it teaches us how to live and how to die.

20. *With what disposition ought we to study the Bible?*

A. We ought to study the Bible with a hearty willingness to believe what it says and to do what it requires. (John 7:17)

21. *What great help must we all seek in studying the Bible?*

A. We must pray that the Holy spirit who inspired the Bible will help us to understand it. (Ps. 119:18; Luke 24:45)

Advanced Questions

Q. A. How do we know that Christ and His apostles meant by "the Scriptures" what we call the Old Testament?

A. We know from Jewish writers and early Christian writers, that those who heard Christ and His apostles would understand them to mean the Old Testament; and therefore they must have meant it so.

Q. B. What promise did our Lord give His apostles as to the Holy Spirit?

A. Our Lord promised His apostles that the Holy Spirit should bring all His teachings to their remembrance, and guide them into all the truth. (John 14:26; 61:13)

Q. C. Did the inspired writers receive everything by direct revelation?

A. The inspired writers learned many things by observation or inquiry, but they were preserved by the Holy Spirit from error, whether in learning or in writing these things.

Q. D. What if inspired writers sometimes appear to disagree in their statements?

A. Most cases of apparent disagreement in the inspired writings have been explained, and we may be sure that all could be explained if we had fuller information.

Q. E. Is this also true when the Bible seems to be in conflict with history or science?

A. Yes, some cases of apparent conflict with history or science have been explained quite recently that were long hard to understand.

Q. F. Has it been proved that the inspired writers stated anything as true that was not true?

A. No; there is no proof that the inspired writers made any mistake of any kind.

Lesson 4: Man

1. How did men begin to exist?

A. God created Adam and Eve, and from them are descended all human beings.

2. *What sort of character had Adam and Eve when created?*

A. Adam and Eve were made in the image of God, and were sinless.

3. *Who tempted Eve to sin against God by eating the forbidden fruit?*

A. Eve was tempted by the devil, or Satan, who is chief of the fallen angels, or demons.

4. *What was the beginning of Eve's sin?*

A. The beginning of Eve's sin was that she believed Satan rather than God. (Gen. 3:4, 5)

5. *What was the first sign that Adam and Eve gave of having fallen into sin?*

A. Adam and Eve showed that they had become sinful by trying to hide from God. (Gen. 3:8)

6. *What was the next sign?*

A. Adam and Eve tried to throw the blame on others. (Gen. 3:12, 13)

7. *How did God punish their wilful disobedience?*

A. God condemned Adam and Eve to death, physical, spiritual, and eternal. (Gen. 2:17; Rom. 6:23; Eph. 2:1)

8. *How does this affect Adam and Eve's descendants?*

A. All human beings are sinful and guilty in God's sight. (Rom. 5:12)

9. *How does this sinfulness show itself?*

A. All human beings actually sin as soon as they are old enough to know right from wrong. (Rom. 3:23)

10. *Will those who die without having known right from wrong be punished hereafter for the sin of Adam and Eve?*

A. Those who die without having known right from wrong are saved in the way God has provided.

11. *Can any human beings be saved through their own merits from the guilt and punishment of sin?*

A. No; the second Adam, the Son of God, is the only Savior of sinners. (Acts 4:12; Gen. 3:15)

Advanced Questions

Q. A. Was man to be idle in the garden of Eden?

A. No, man was to keep the garden and to have dominion over the animals. (Gen. 2:15; 1:26)

Q. B. Is work a curse?

A. Work is not a curse, but anxious and wearing toil is a curse and a fruit of sin. (Gen. 3:17)

Q. C. Does the Bible elsewhere speak of Satan as a serpent?

A. Satan is called a serpent in the book of Revelation. (Rev. 12:9; 20:2)

Q. D. What does the New Testament reveal that corresponds to the effect of Adam's sin upon his descendants?

A. The benefits of Christ's salvation for His people correspond to the effect of Adam's sin upon his descendants.

Q. E. How does the apostle Paul state this parallel?

A. "Through one man sin entered into the world, and through sin, death," so likewise through one man came justification, and through justification, life. (Rom. 5:12–19)

Lesson 5: The Savior

1. *Who is the Savior of men?*

A. Jesus Christ, the Son of God, is the Savior of men.

2. *Was Jesus Himself really a man?*

A. Yes, Jesus Christ was really a man; He was the Son of Mary.

3. *Was Jesus the Son of Joseph?*

A. No, people called Jesus the Son of Joseph, but He was really the Son of God. (Luke 1:35)

4. *Can you give any express statement that Jesus was God?*

A. "The Word was God . . . And the Word became flesh, and dwelt among us, full of grace and truth." (John 1:1, 14)

5. *What then is Jesus Christ?*

A. Jesus Christ is both God and man, the God-man.

6. *How does this fit Jesus to be the Savior of men?*

A. Jesus the God-man can stand between men and God as Mediator.

7. *Can you tell the meaning of the two names, Jesus Christ?*

A. Jesus means Savior, and Christ means Anointed, like the Hebrew word Messiah. (Matt. 1:21; John 4:25)

8. *What did Christ do on earth for us?*

A. Christ taught the highest truths, He lived as a perfect example, and He died and rose again to redeem us.

9. *What is Christ doing for us now?*

A. Christ dwells in His people, intercedes for them, and controls all things for their good. (John 14:23; Heb. 7:25; Matt. 28:18)

10. *What will Christ do hereafter for us?*

A. Christ will come a second time and receive us unto Himself to be with Him forever. (John 14:3; Heb. 9:28)

11. *What must we do to be saved through Jesus Christ?*

A. We must believe in Christ, must turn from our sins to love and obey Him, and must try to be like Him.

Advanced Questions

Q. A. How did Christ take our place?

A. He who knew no sin was made sin for us, that we might become righteous in God's sight through Him. (2 Cor. 5:21)

Q. B. Was Christ's work necessary to make God willing to save men?

A. No, Christ simply made it right that God should save those who trust in Him. (Rom. 3:26)

Q. C. What was the origin of Christ's mission to save?

A. The origin of Christ's mission to men was in God's pitying love for the world. (John 3:16; 1 John 4:10)

Q. D. Does God offer to save all men through Christ?

A. Yes, whosoever will may have salvation without cost. (Rev. 22:17; Is. 55:1)

Q. E. Ought we to make this salvation known to all men?

A. Yes, it is our solemn duty to carry the gospel to all nations. (Luke 24:47)

Q. F. How can we carry the gospel to distant lands?

A. We can go ourselves as missionaries, or help to send others.

Lesson 6: The Holy Spirit and the Trinity

1. *Who is the Holy Spirit?*

A. The Holy Spirit is the Spirit of God, and is called the third person in the Trinity.

2. *What did the Holy Spirit do for the prophets and apostles?*

A. The Holy Spirit inspired the prophets and apostles to teach men their duty to God and to each other.

3. *What did the Holy Spirit do for all the writers of the Bible?*

A. The Holy Spirit inspired them to write just what God wished to be written.

4. *Did the Holy Spirit dwell also in Jesus Christ?*

A. Yes, the Holy Spirit was given to Jesus without measure. (Luke 4:1; John 3:34)

5. *When Jesus ascended to heaven, what did He send the Holy Spirit to do?*

A. Jesus sent the Holy Spirit to take His place and carry on His work among men. (John 14:16, 17)

6. *What does the Holy Spirit do as to the world?*

A. The Holy Spirit convicts the world of its sin and its need of Christ's salvation. (John 16:8)

7. *What work does the Holy Spirit perform in making men Christians?*

A. The Holy Spirit gives men a new heart, to turn from sin and trust in Christ. (John 3:5; Ezek. 36:26)

8. *How does the Holy Spirit continue this work?*

A. The Holy Spirit helps those who trust in Christ to become holy in heart and life. (Gal. 5:22; 1 Cor. 3:16)

9. *Is the Holy Spirit Himself divine?*

A. Yes, the Holy Spirit is God. (Acts 5:3, 4)

10. *If the Father is God, and the Savior is God, and the Holy Spirit is God, are there three Gods?*

A. No, there are not three Gods; God is one. (Deut. 6:4; Mark 12:20)

11. *What then do we mean by the doctrine of the Trinity?*

A. The Bible teaches that the Father is God, and the Son is God, and the Holy Spirit is God, and yet God is one.

12. *Are we able to explain the Trinity?*

A. We cannot explain the Trinity; and need not expect to understand fully the nature of God; we cannot fully understand even our own nature.

13. *How is the Trinity recognized in connection with baptism?*

A. We are told to baptize "in the name of the Father and of the Son and of the Holy Spirit." (Matt. 28:19)

14. *How is the Trinity named in a benediction?*

A. "The grace of the Lord Jesus Christ, and the love of God, and the communion of the Holy Spirit, be with you all." (2 Cor. 13:14)

Advanced Questions

Q. A. Did the Holy Spirit give men the power of working miracles?

A. Yes, the Holy Spirit gave to the apostles and others the power of working miracles. (Acts 2:4; 1 Cor. 12:11)

Q. B. What did the Savior mean when He spoke of blaspheming against the Holy Spirit?

A. Blaspheming against the Holy Spirit was saying that a work of the Holy Spirit was a work of Satan. (Mark 3:29)

Q. C. Is there any other unpardonable sin?

A. The Savior says that every sin may be forgiven except the blasphemy against the Holy Spirit. (Mark 3:23; Matt. 12:31; 1 John 5:16)

Q. D. What is the meaning of the word "Trinity"?

A. The word "Trinity" or "Triunity" means that God is in one sense three and in another sense one.

Lesson 7: The Atonement of Christ

1. *What was Christ's chief work as Savior?*

A. Christ died and rose again for His people. (2 Cor. 5:15; Rom. 4:25)

2. *Did Christ voluntarily allow Himself to be slain?*

A. Yes, Christ laid down His life of Himself. (John 10:17, 18)

3. *Was this Christ's design in coming into the world?*

A. Our Lord says that He came "to give His life a ransom for many." (Mark 10:45)

4. *For what purpose did the loving God give His only Son?*

A. God gave His only Son "that whosoever believeth on Him should not perish, but have eternal life." (John 3:16)

5. *How could Christ's dying give us life?*

A. Christ took our place and died like a sinner, that we might take His place and be righteous in Him. (2 Cor. 5:21)

6. *Was it right that the just should die for the unjust?*

A. The Savior was not compelled, but chose to die for the benefit of others.

7. *Is it right for God to pardon men because the Savior died?*

A. God declares it to be right for Him to pardon men if they seek salvation only through Christ. (Rom. 3:26)

8. *May a man go on in sin and expect to be saved through Christ's atoning death?*

A. No, we must live for Him who died for us. (2 Cor. 5:15)

9. *Is salvation offered to all men through the atonement of Christ?*

A. Yes, salvation is offered to all, and all are saved who really take Christ for their Savior. (Ezek. 18:23; 2 Peter 3:9)

10. *What is Christ now doing for men's salvation?*

A. Christ is interceding for all those who trust in His atonement. (Heb. 7:25; Rom. 8:34)

Advanced Questions

Q. A. Is the atonement of Christ sufficient for all men?

A. The atonement of Christ is sufficient for all, and would actually save all if they would repent and believe. (John 1:29; 3:17; 1 John 2:2; 4:14)

Q. B. Does God desire the salvation of all men?

A. God "wishes all men to be saved, and to come to the knowledge of the truth." (1 Tim. 2:4)

Q. C. If any who hear the gospel are not saved, can they justly complain?

A. No, they cannot justly complain, for if they wished it, and would believe, they might be saved.

Q. D. Are the heathen, who never heard the gospel, condemned for not believing it?

A. No, the heathen are judged by the light they have, and are condemned for violating the law that is written in the hearts. (Rom. 1:20; 2:14)

Q. E. Will God punish those who have not heard the gospel as severely as those who hear and reject it?

A. No, those who have not heard the gospel will be punished for disregarding what they know, or might know, of the true God. (Rom. 2:13; 3:23)

Q. F. Has God commanded His people to proclaim salvation to all men?

A. Yes, God commands His people to proclaim salvation to all men. (Matt. 28:19; Rom. 10:13–15)

Lesson 8: Regeneration

1. What is meant by the word "regeneration"?

A. Regeneration is God's causing a person to be born again.

2. Are such persons literally born a second time?

A. No, the regenerated are inwardly changed as if they were born over again.

3. In what respect are men changed in the new birth?

A. In the new birth men have a new heart, so as to hate sin and desire to be holy servants of God. (Ezek. 11:19, 20)

4. Is this new birth necessary in order to salvation?

A. Without the new birth no one can be saved. (John 3:3)

5. Who produces this great change?

A. The Holy Spirit regenerates. (John 3:5, 6)

6. Are people regenerated through baptism?

A. No, only those whose hearts are already changed ought to be baptized.

7. Are people regenerated through Bible teaching?

A. Yes, people are usually regenerated through the Word of God. (1 Pet. 1:23; James 1:18)

8. Can we understand how men are born again?

A. No, we can only know regeneration by its effects. (John 3:8)

9. Does faith come before the new birth?

A. No, it is the new heart that truly repents and believes.

10. *What is the proof of having a new heart?*

A. The proof of having a new heart is living a new life. (1 John 2:29; 2 Cor. 5:17)

Advanced Questions

Q. A. Why is water mentioned in connection with the new birth?

A. Water is mentioned in connection with the new birth to show that this is a pure birth, leading to a new and pure life. (John 3:5; Titus 3:5; Rom. 6:4)

Q. B. Does God give His renewing Spirit as He sees proper?

A. Yes, God gives His renewing Spirit to those whom He always purposed to save. (Eph. 1:3, 4)

Lesson 9: Repentance and Faith

1. *What is it to repent of sin?*

A. Repenting of sin means that one changes his thoughts and feelings about sin, resolving to forsake sin and live for God.

2. *Does not repenting mean being sorry?*

A. Everyone who truly resolves to quit sinning will be sorry for his past sins, but people are often sorry without quitting.

3. *What is the great reason for repenting of sin?*

A. The great reason for repenting of sin is because sin is wrong, and offensive to God. (Ps. 51:4)

4. *Is repentance necessary to a sinner's salvation?*

A. Those who will not turn from sin must perish. (Luke 13:3; Ezek. 33:11)

5. *What do the Scriptures mean by faith in Christ?*

A. By faith in Christ the Scriptures mean believing Christ to be the divine Savior, and personally trusting in Him for our salvation.

6. *Is faith in Christ necessary to salvation?*

A. No person capable of faith in Christ can be saved without it. (John 3:6; Heb. 11:6)

7. *Can those who die in infancy be saved without faith?*

A. Yes, we feel sure that those who die in infancy are saved for Christ's sake.

8. *Are they saved without regeneration?*

A. Infants are not saved without regeneration, for without holiness none shall see God. (Heb. 12:14; John 3:3)

9. Can we see why persons capable of faith cannot be saved without it?

A. Persons capable of faith must by faith accept God's offered mercy; and His truth cannot become the means of making them holy unless it is believed.

10. Is refusing to believe in Christ a sin?

A. It is fearfully wicked to reject the Savior and insult God who gave His Son in love. (John 3:18; 1 John 5:10)

11. Do faith in Christ and true repentance ever exist separately?

A. No, either faith or repentance will always carry the other with it. (Acts 20:21)

Advanced Questions

Q. A. How is it that some persons say they believe the Bible to be true, and yet are not Christians?

A. Many persons who say they believe the Bible are not willing to forsake sin, and often they do not really believe what the Bible says about Christ. (John 5:46)

Q. B. Is a man responsible for his belief as to the Bible?

A. Yes, a man is responsible for his belief as to the Bible, because it depends partly on whether he is willing to know the truth, willing to forsake sin and serve God. (John 7:17)

Q. C. Were not people in Old Testament times saved without faith in Christ?

A. The truly pious in Old Testament times believed in God's promise of a future provision for salvation, and some of them looked clearly forward to Christ Himself. (Gen. 3:15; John 8:56; Ps. 110:1; Ps. 53:6)

Q. D. How can we explain the statement that Judas repented and killed himself?

A. When it is said that Judas repented, that is another Greek word, which means simply sorrow, and not at all the repentance that leads to salvation. (2 Cor. 7:10)

Lesson 10: Justification and Sanctification

1. *What is meant in the Bible by justification?*

A. God justifies a sinner in treating him as just, for Christ's sake.

2. *Can any person be justified by his own works?*

A. By works of the law shall no flesh be justified. (Rom. 3:20)

3. *How are we justified by faith?*

A. Believing in Christ our Savior, we ask and receive justification for His sake alone. (Rom. 3:24; 5:1)

4. *Has this faith that justifies any connection with our works?*

A. The faith that justifies will be sure to produce good works. (Gal. 5:6; James 2:17)

5. *What is meant by sanctification?*

A. To sanctify is to make holy in heart and life.

6. *What connection is there between sanctification and regeneration?*

A. The new birth is the beginning of a new and holy life.

7. *Is justification complete at once?*

A. Yes, the moment a sinner really believes in Christ he is completely justified.

8. *Is sanctification complete at once?*

A. No, sanctification is gradual, and ought to go on increasing to the end of the earthly life. (Phil. 3:13; 14)

9. *Is it certain that a true believer in Christ will be finally saved?*

A. Yes, God will preserve a true believer in Christ to the end. (John 10:28; Phil. 1:6)

10. *What is the sure proof of being a true believer?*

A. The only sure proof of being a true believer is growing in holiness and in usefulness, even to the end. (2 Pet. 1:10)

11. *To what will justification and sanctification lead at last?*

A. Justification and sanctification will lead at last to glorification in heaven. (Rom. 5:2; 8:30; Matt. 25:21)

Advanced Questions

Q. A. How can it be right for God to treat a believing sinner as just, when he has only begun a holy life?

A. God treats a believing sinner as just for Christ's sake, and God will be sure to make him completely holy in the end. (Rom. 3:26)

Q. B. Does faith in Christ procure justification by deserving it?

A. No, faith does not deserve justification; it only brings us into union with Christ, for whose sake we are justified. (Rom. 8:1)

Lesson 11: Baptism and the Lord's Supper

1. *Who ought to be baptized?*

A. Every believer in Christ ought to be baptized.

2. *Why ought every believer in Christ to be baptized?*

A. Because Christ has commanded us to declare our faith in Him by being baptized. (Matt. 28:19; Acts 8:12; 10:48)

3. *What is the action performed in Christian baptism?*

A. The action performed in Christian baptism is immersion in water. (Mark 1:9, 10; Acts 8:39)

4. *What does this signify?*

A. The water signifies purification from sin, and the immersion signifies that we are dead to sin, and like Christ have been buried and risen again. (Acts 22:16; Rom. 6:4)

5. *Does baptism procure forgiveness or the new birth?*

A. No, baptism only represents regeneration and forgiveness like a picture. (John 3:15; Acts 2:38)

6. *What is meant by our being baptized "in the name of the Father and of the Son and of the Holy Spirit"?*

A. It means that we take God the Father, the Son, and the Spirit as our Sovereign and Savior. (Matt. 28:19)

7. *What is the solemn duty of all who have been baptized?*

A. It is the duty of all who have been baptized to live that new life of purity and obedience which their baptism signifies. (Rom. 6:4)

8. *What is the Lord's Supper?*

A. A church observes the Lord's Supper by eating bread and drinking wine to represent the body and blood of our Savior. (1 Cor. 11:20, 26)

9. *Why ought the bread and wine to be thus taken?*

A. Because Christ has commanded us to eat bread and drink wine in remembrance of Him. (Luke 22:19)

10. *Who ought to partake of the Lord's Supper?*

A. Those ought to partake of the Lord's Supper who have believed in Christ, and have been baptized, and are trying to live in obedience of Christ's commands.

Advanced Questions

Q. A. Can there be Christian baptism without immersion?

A. No. Christ was immersed, and commanded us to be immersed, and sprinkling or pouring water will not represent burial and rising again. (Rom. 6:4; Col. 2:12)

Q. B. If the person were very ill or the water could not be had, would not something else than immersion suffice?

A. In cases of extreme illness or scarcity of water it is not a duty to be baptized.

Q. C. When we insist that nothing ought to be substituted for immersion, what is the principle involved?

A. The principle we insist upon is that of strict obedience to the Word of God.

Q. D. Ought the bread and wine to be taken by one person alone?

A. No, all the instances in the New Testament are of a church together taking the bread and wine.

Q. E. Does not the joint participation become a bond of fellowship?

A. Yes, our partaking together promotes Christian fellowship, but the word "communion" means simply the partaking. (1 Cor. 10:16)

Q. F. Why ought Baptists not to take the Lord's Supper with believers of other denominations?

A. Because we think they have not been baptized, or are not walking orderly as to church connection.

Lesson 12: The Lord's Day

1. *What does the word Sabbath mean?*
A. The word Sabbath means rest.
2. *Why was the Sabbath at first appointed?*

A. The Sabbath was at first appointed to represent the rest of God after finishing the creation. (Gen. 2:3)

3. *What says the fourth commandment given through Moses at Mount Sinai?*

A. Remember the Sabbath day to keep it holy. (Exod. 20:8, 11)

4. *What does this show?*

A. The fourth commandment shows that the children of Israel knew about the Sabbath, but were apt to neglect it.

5. *When the Savior was charged with breaking the Sabbath, what did He teach about it?*

A. The Savior taught that it was not breaking the Sabbath to heal the sick, to provide food for the hungry, or to do any work of necessity or mercy. (Matt. 12:3; Mark 3:4; Luke 13:15, 16)

6. *What change was gradually made under the direction of the apostles as to the day to be observed?*

A. The day to be observed was changed from the seventh day to the first day of the week, the day on which the Lord Jesus rose from the dead. (John 20:1, 19, 26)

7. *What is this day called?*

A. The first day of the week is called the Lord's day. (Rev. 1:10)

8. *What do we find the first Christians doing on the Lord's day?*

A. They met for public worship, heard preaching, took the Lord's Supper, and gave money for religious objects. (1 Cor. 16:2; Acts 20:7)

9. *Ought we to keep the Lord's day as the Sabbath?*

A. Yes, we ought to keep the Lord's day as a day of rest and holy employments.

10. *Ought we to keep the Lord's day as the first Christians did?*

A. Yes, we ought to keep the Lord's day as a day for public worship, with Bible study and preaching, for religious gifts and ordinances, and for doing good in every way.

Advanced Questions

Q. A. Does the New Testament say that the Sabbath was changed to the first day of the week?

A. No, the New Testament speaks of religious exercises on the first day of the week as something that everybody understood. (1 Cor. 16:1, 2; Acts 20:7; Rev. 1:10)

Q. B. What explanation have we of these statements?

A. Several Christian writers just after the apostles speak of worship on the first day of the week is such language as to show plainly what the New Testament references meant.

Lesson 13: Some Duties of the Christian Life

1. *What is our duty as to speaking the truth?*

A. We must always speak truth and never lie. (Eph. 4:25; Exod. 20:16; Rev. 21:8)

2. *Is it possible to act a lie without speaking it?*

A. Yes, to act a lie may be one of the worst forms of falsehood. (Acts 5:3)

3. *What is our duty as to speaking evil of others?*

A. We must never speak so as to wrong any person. (James 4:11)

4. *What is meant by profane speech?*

A. Profane speech is cursing or swearing, or speaking in an irreverent way of God, or of the Bible, or of anything sacred.

5. *What does the Bible say about stealing?*

A. "Thou shalt not steal." (Exod. 20:15; Eph. 4:28)

6. *Can you tell some things which this forbids?*

A. The commandment forbids all unfair buying and selling, and any failure to pay promised wages or perform promised work.

7. *Is it wrong even to wish to take away another person's property?*

A. Yes, the Bible says we must not covet what belongs to another. (Exod. 20:17)

8. *May we properly strive to do better than others?*

A. Yes, we may strive to excel others, but we must not envy others nor try to pull them back. (1 Pet. 2:1)

9. *May we revenge ourselves on those who have wronged us?*

A. No, revenge is very wicked, and we must leave punishment of those who have wronged us with God. (Rom. 12:19)

10. *Ought we to love our enemies just as we love our friends?*

A. We ought to love our enemies as God loves His enemies, and so be ready always to do them a kindness. (Matt. 5:44, 45)

11. *What is our duty as to purity?*

A. We must avoid all impure actions and words, thoughts and feelings.

12. *How many Christians hope to perform these and all duties of the Christian life?*

A. Christians may hope to perform their duties by watchful effort and constant prayer for the help of the Holy Spirit. (Matt. 26:41; Luke 11:13)

Advanced Questions

Q. A. Does truthfulness require us to tell everything we know or think?

A. No, we may keep to ourselves what others have no claim to know, when we are not professing to tell everything. (1 Sam. 16:2)

Q. B. When may we say things that will damage others?

A. We may say things that will damage others when the things said are true, and it is needful that they should be known to prevent wrong.

Q. C. What may we do for the punishment of one who has injured us?

A. If a person has injured us we may help to secure his punishment according to law, not for private revenge, but for public good.

Q. D. Is it ever right to take an oath?

A. It is right to take an oath only in a court of justice or on some other important occasion, and always in a very solemn way. (Matt. 26:63, 64; 2 cor. 1:23)

Q. E. Ought we to be careful about the examples we set to others?

A. Yes, it is the duty of Christians to be the salt of the earth, and the light of the world. (Matt. 5:13, 14)

Lesson 14: Imitation of Christ

1. *Did the Savior live a real human life?*

A. Yes, the Savior lived a real human life, but without sin of any kind.

2. *Was He tempted to sin?*

A. He was tempted in all points just as we are, but He always overcame the temptation. (Heb. 4:15)

3. *Is it the duty of Christians to imitate Christ?*

A. Yes, Christ has left us a beautiful and perfect example, which we ought to imitate. (1 Pet. 2:21; 1 Cor. 11:1)

4. *How may we hope to imitate Christ?*

A. We may hope to imitate Christ by the help of the Holy Spirit. (Luke 4:1)

5. *What example did the Savior set as to obeying parents?*

A. The Savior did as His parents directed, and "was subject unto them." (Luke 2:51)

6. *What example did He set as to the Scriptures?*

A. The Savior attended a Bible Class, and had great knowledge of the Scriptures even when a child. (Luke 2:46, 47)

7. *Did He use the Bible when tempted or suffering?*

A. Yes, the Savior quoted the Bible three times against the tempter, and twice while on the cross.

8. *What is His example as to public worship?*

A. Our Lord's custom was to go into the synagogue on the Sabbath day and worship. (Luke 4:16)

9. *What example did Christ set as to private praying?*

A. Christ prayed often and much, sometimes through a whole night.

10. *What example in doing good to men?*

A. Jesus all the time "went about doing good."

11. *What example as to the love of enemies?*

A. Jesus prayed for the men who were crucifying Him, "Father, forgive them, for they know not what they do." (Luke 23:34)

12. *What example as to loving Christians?*

A. Christ laid down His life for us, and we ought to lay down our lives for the brethren. (1 John 3:16; John 13:34)

13. *What is our highest hope for the future life?*

A. "We shall be like Him." (1 John 3:2)

Advanced Questions

Q. A. Which books of the Old Testament did the Savior quote when tempted or suffering?

A. In the great temptation Christ three times quoted Deut. 8:3; 6:13, 16, and on the cross He twice quoted the Psalms 22:1; 31:5.

Q. B. Did He use the Old Testament Scriptures on other occasions?

A. Yes, Christ often quoted Scripture to convince the Jews and to instruct His disciples.

Q. C. Can you mention some special occasions on which Jesus prayed?

A. (Luke 3:21; 6:12; 9:29; 11:1; John 17:1; Matt. 26:39, 42, 44)

Lesson 15: The Future Life

1. Do men everywhere believe in a future life?

A. In all nations and races men have generally believed in a future and endless life.

2. Does the Bible confirm this belief?

A. The Bible leaves no room to doubt that every human being will always continue to exist.

3. What becomes of the soul at death?

A. The soul is undying, and passes at once into blessedness or suffering. (2 Cor. 5:8; Luke 16:23, 28)

4. What becomes of the body after death?

A. The body returns to dust, but it will rise again. (Gen. 3:19; Eccles. 12:7; Acts 24:15)

5. Will the same body live again?

A. Yes, the very same body will live again, but greatly changed as to its condition and mode of life. (1 Cor. 15:42–44)

6. What is meant by the day of judgment?

A. The day of judgment means a great and awful day, on which the living and the dead will stand before Christ to be judged. (Acts 17:31; Matt. 25:31, 32; 2 Cor. 5:10)

7. To what will Christ condemn the wicked?

A. Christ will send the wicked away to everlasting punishment in hell. (Matt. 25:41, 46)

8. To what will Christ welcome the righteous?

A. Christ will welcome the righteous to everlasting blessedness with Him in heaven. (Matt. 25:34, 46)

9. *Will there be different degrees of punishment?*

A. The future punishment will be greater according to the degrees of sin, and the knowledge men had of God's will and of the way of salvation through Christ. (Luke 12:47, 48; Mark 12:40)

10. *How is hell described in the Bible?*

A. Hell is a place of darkness and torment, of endless sin and endless suffering.

11. *How is heaven described?*

A. Heaven is a place of light and holiness, of freedom from all sorrow and temptation, of blessed society and thankful praise to God. (Rev. 7:9)

Advanced Questions

Q. A. *What do we know as to the period between death and resurrection?*

A. We know that between death and the resurrection there will be conscious existence of the soul, either in torment or in blessedness with Christ. (Luke 16:24; 23:43; Phil. 1:23)

Q. B. *Is there any salvation provided in the future life for persons who died in their sins?*

A. The Bible does not reveal any provision for salvation in the future life for persons who died in their sins, nor dies it authorize any such hope.

Q. C. *Are we authorized to believe in heavenly recognition?*

A. The Bible warrants the hope that we shall know each other in heaven. (1 Thess. 2:19; Matt. 17:3, 4)

Passages for Learning by Heart

It is an excellent thing for the young to commit to memory many portions of Scripture. The following passages are recommended as suitable, and it is hoped that many will learn some of them, and add other selections as thought best.

The Ten Commandments, Exodus 20:1–17.

Psalms 1, 16, 19, 23, 24, 27, 32, 34, 51, 84, 90, 92, 95, 100, 103,115, 116, 130, 139, 145.

Proverbs 3:1-20; 6:6–11; chapter 10; chapter 11, Chapter 20; Ecclesiastes, chapter 12.

Isaiah, chapter 40; chapter 53; chapter 55.

Matthew 5:3–16; chapter 6; chapter 7; chapter 25; 28:18–20.

Mark 14:22–25; 32–42.

Luke 15:11–32; 16:19–31; 18:1–14; 24:13–35.

John 1:1–18; 14:1–15; 20:1–23.

Acts 17:22–31; 20:17–38.

Romans 5:1–11; 8:28–39; chapter 12.

1 Corinthians, chapter 13; chapter 15;

2 Corinthians, chapter 5.

Ephesians 3:14–21; 6:10–20; Colossians 3:1–4; 4:2–6.

1 Thess. 4:13–18; Titus 2:11–14.

Hebrews 4:14–16, 11:1 to 12:3.

1 John 1:5 to 2:6; 3:13–24; chapter 4.

Revelation 1:9–20; 7:9–17; 20:11–15; chapter 21; chapter 22.

CPSIA information can be obtained at www.ICGtesting.com
Printed in the USA
LVOW132302150313

324549LV00001B/100/P